"Joseph Selbie's book on the brain is another welc___ ___ ___ to the growing post-materialist literature on the brain and consciousness. Selbie makes the important point that the normal brain filters out most of what is superconscious in us. You will especially like that he makes a good case that rewiring the brain can help expand the brain's ability. So, what are you waiting for? Learn to rewire the brain."

—Amit Goswami, theoretical quantum physicist
and author of (with Valentina Onisor)
The Quantum Brain and *Quantum Spirituality*

"I loved this groundbreaking book. *Break Through the Limits of the Brain* joyfully guides us to sacred oneness. Joseph Selbie beautifully describes the high states of spiritual awareness and, more importantly, tells us how to personally achieve these exalted states. The book's time-proven practices are extraordinary in their effectiveness."

—Joseph Bharat Cornell, author of
Flow Learning and *Deep Nature Play*,
and founder and president of Sharing Nature Worldwide

"If you have any interest in the brain and consciousness, you'll find this book a gem. It starts with a thorough examination of the latest scientific information on how our brains function. But then it goes beyond the current limitations of scientific materialism to pursue the higher realms of awareness, especially the limitless potential of superconscious. Selbie has a clear, engaging style that allows the information to sink in and expand our understanding. Selbie then goes on to practical techniques of meditation to calm, focus, and expand our minds. All in all, one of the finest books I've ever read on this subject."

—Jyotish Novak, author of *How to Meditate*

"Great hatchet job on Reality! What I used to think of as 'me,' I now understand is just a cascading series of habitual brain synapses. After fifty years of meditation, I have a whole new perspective of what it is and why it works. Hooray! You've given me a clarity I could never access before. A brilliant, original, life-changing, and *entertaining* read. Well done!"

—Asha Nayaswami, author of Lightbearer

"Selbie shows us how to 'rewire' our brains to live at our peak capacity; dancing fluidly between the 'heaven' and 'earth' of our nature. He integrates insights from cutting-edge vanguard science to reveal the emerging science of super-consciousness. He 'grounds' the higher ground, making his most lofty insights concrete and practical. In the peak capacity of superconsciousness, we have access to boundless energy and insight, flowing creativity, and ultimately the bliss of transcendent consciousness."

—Dana Lynne Andersen, artist, author, and founder of
The Academy of Art, Creativity & Consciousness

Praise for *The Physics of God*:

"The book combines science and religion in a way that can change how the reader views reality, the material world, God, and how they see themselves."

—*New Spirit Journal*

"*The Physics of God* is an impressive and thought-provoking work which should be regarded as an important commentary regarding the metaphysical myster-ies of life, physical reality, and human consciousness. Highly recommended!"

—*Spirituality Today*

"Selbie does an excellent job of dispelling the myth that religion and science are incompatible. His unbiased comparison of the findings of science with the testimony of those who have had profound spiritual experience reveal a clear underlying unity. *The Physics of God* is clear, simple, and engaging!"

—Susan Shumsky, award-winning author of
Divine Revelation and *Awaken Your Third Eye*

BREAK *through* *the* LIMITS *of the* BRAIN

Neuroscience, Inspiration, and Practices to Transform Your Life

Joseph Selbie

Foreword by Andrew Newberg, MD

NEW PAGE

This edition first published in 2022 by New Page Books, an imprint of
Red Wheel/Weiser, LLC
With offices at:
65 Parker Street, Suite 7
Newburyport, MA 01950
www.careerpress.com
www.redwheelweiser.com

Cover design by Kathryn Sky-Peck
Cover art by Shutterstock
Interior by Timm Bryson, em em design, LLC
Typeset in Warnock Pro

ISBN: 978-1-63748-004-5
Library of Congress Cataloging-in-Publication Data available upon request.

Printed in the United States of America
IBI

10 9 8 7 6 5 4 3 2 1

My book takes its place in a long line of books that began with the 1946 publication of the spiritual classic Autobiography of a Yogi *by Paramahansa Yogananda, a book that has now sold over twenty million copies and is available in over thirty-five languages. Yogananda lived and taught in America from 1920 until his death in 1952. He was the first advanced teacher from India to explain Eastern spiritual practices and philosophy using Western terms and scientific concepts—concepts drawn from physics, chemistry, medicine, psychology, biology, physiology, neuroscience, and other disciplines. Often said to be the father of yoga and meditation in the West, I believe he is also the father of the currently unfolding reunification of science and religion.*

CONTENTS

PART THREE
HOW TO REWIRE YOUR BRAIN
FOR SUPERCONSCIOUS AWARENESS

FOREWORD

Break Through the Limits of the Brain is filled with fascinating perspectives on neuroscience, spirituality, consciousness, creativity, and, especially, superconscious awareness. Selbie suggests that superconscious awareness is the ultimate expression of human awareness and he points out that the concept of superconscious awareness is embraced by many humanistic and transpersonal psychologists, as well as by contemporary spiritual teachers, who describe it as an always-present reality accessible to everyone. He goes on to suggest that the reason superconscious awareness is not everyone's everyday awareness is that most brains are wired to support only a limited expression of that potential—but that our brains can be *rewired* to support unlimited superconscious expression.

This notion of trying to get the brain out of its own way is an important one and something that is of value to anyone wanting to achieve a state of mindfulness or awareness of the present moment. I have spent almost thirty years conducting studies to explore the biology of spiritual practices such as meditation and the intense spiritual states that come from such practices. It is clear, as I have recounted in my books *How God Changes Your Brain* and *How Enlightenment Changes Your Brain,* that the brains of advanced practitioners of meditation and other intense spiritual practices are wired differently than the brains of those who have not employed such practices for extended periods. The first-person descriptions of the experiences of such advanced practitioners also suggest that not only are their brains wired differently, not only are they able to achieve extraordinary states of brain activation and deactivation, they also have positive, expansive, health-creating, even life-changing experiences while in those extraordinary states.

As a scientist I must remain neutral as to whether these personal experiences are beyond the brain or within the brain, supernatural or material. As a neurotheologian I try to take a neutral stance also. But as one who seeks to understand the relationship between the brain and our religious and spiritual selves, it is always encouraging and rewarding to see other scholars enter the fray. Some have a decidedly materialistic or atheistic perspective, while others have a more spiritual or supernatural perspective. Each of these perspectives has the potential to provide important insights into the relationship between our brain and our spiritual side. That is why *Break Through the Limits of the Brain* is an important work that helps to move the discussion forward.

For those of you who find such perspectives of personal and practical value, exploring them as part of an overall journey through life with the ultimate goal of achieving some form of enlightenment, the pages that follow will be most intriguing.

—Andrew Newberg, MD,
professor and Director of Research at
Marcus Institute of Integrative Health,
Thomas Jefferson University and Hospital

CHAPTER 1

We Are So Much More
than We Know

Stories reach us from around the world and through the centuries of people who have had extraordinary physical, mental, creative, intuitive, emotional, and perceptual experiences far beyond what are commonly considered possible.

Charlotte Hefflemire, nineteen years old and home with her family for Thanksgiving in 2017, heard a loud crash and a shout coming from the family garage. She found her father trapped under his GMC pickup truck, from which flames were rising. Charlotte still can't fully explain what happened next.

> "I lifted it [the truck] the first time, my father said 'OK, you almost got it.' Finally managed to get it on [the jack], it was some crazy strength, [and then] I pulled him out."[1]

In the book *Seeing the Invisible*, Meg Maxwell and Verena Tschudin shared accounts from ordinary people describing extraordinary experiences. This account is one of thousands that have been sent to the Alister Hardy Research Centre. A young woman preparing a meal for her family was suddenly transported.

[T]he kitchen and garden were filled with golden light. I became conscious that at the centre of the Universe, and in my garden, was a great pulsing dynamo that ceaselessly poured out love. This love poured over and through me, and I was part of it and it wholly encompassed me. It was overwhelmingly real, more real than anything I had experienced, although I had been in love, and the feelings after the birth of each of my children had been wonderful. The vision was of a far 'realler' quality.

—An unnamed woman[2]

Ruth Stone, award-winning poet, author, and teacher related the following story to Elizabeth Gilbert, author of *Eat, Pray, Love:*

As [Stone] was growing up in rural Virginia, she would be out working in the fields and she would feel and hear a poem coming at her from over the landscape. It was like a thunderous train of air and it would come barreling down at her over the landscape. And when she felt it coming . . . 'cause it would shake the earth under her feet, she knew she had only one thing to do at that point. That was to, in her words, "run like hell" to the house as she would be chased by this poem.

The whole deal was that she had to get to a piece of paper fast enough so that when it thundered through her, she could collect it and grab it on the page. Other times she wouldn't be fast enough, so she would be running and running, and she wouldn't get to the house, and the poem would barrel through her and she would miss it, and it would "continue on across the landscape looking for another poet."

And then there were these times, there were moments where she would almost miss it. She is running to the house and is looking for the paper and the poem passes through her. She grabs a pencil just as it's going through her and she would reach out with her other hand and she would catch it. She would catch the poem by its tail and she would pull it backwards into her body as she was transcribing on the page. In those instances, the poem would come up on the page perfect and intact, but backwards, from the last word to the first.

—Elizabeth Gilbert[3]

Astronaut Edgar Mitchell, the sixth man to walk on the moon, while on the long return journey to earth, had many profound experiences:

> What I experienced during that three-day trip home was nothing short of an overwhelming sense of universal *connectedness*. I actually felt what has been described as an ecstasy of unity. And there was the sense that our presence as space travelers and the existence of the universe itself, was not accidental but there was an intelligent process at work. I perceived the universe as in some way conscious.
>
> —Edgar Mitchell, Apollo 14 Astronaut[4]

Charles Lindbergh took off from Long Island's Roosevelt Field on the early morning of May 20, 1927, to make the first solo flight across the Atlantic. The flight would require thirty-three and a half hours of unbroken concentration. Lindbergh was already deeply tired from having put weeks of long hours and high energy into getting ready for the flight. The night before takeoff, hoping to get desperately needed sleep, he had instead spent many hours in final preparations, and then was kept up most of the night by a persistent reporter. Already severely fatigued and sleep deprived even before he took off, only a few hours into the flight he described his eyes as feeling like "salted stones."

He struggled desperately against a nearly overwhelming urge to sleep.

To fall asleep was to die. Lindbergh could not allow himself to lift either of his feet from the rudder controls or to take both hands from the stick. To lose control of the plane for even a few minutes could mean crashing into the ocean. Because he was flying by dead reckoning, five minutes of inattention could cause the plane to veer just enough off course to run out of fuel before he found land. For many long hours he fought sleep. He left his cockpit window open to let in a frigid blast of air. Even that wasn't enough. Mid-flight he put every shred of his will and concentration into staying awake. Nearing his utmost limits, his single-minded concentration caused him to break into an awareness unlike anything he had ever experienced.

> There's no limit to my sight—my skull is one great eye, seeing everywhere at once. . . . All sense of substance leaves. There's no longer weight to my body, no longer hardness to the stick. The feeling of flesh is gone. I become independent of physical laws—of food, of shelter, of life. I'm . . . less tangible than air, universal as aether. I'm on the border line of life and a greater realm beyond, as though caught in the field of gravitation between two planets, acted on by forces I can't control, forces too weak to be measured by any means at my command, yet representing powers incomparably stronger than I've ever known. . . . Death no longer seems the final end it used to be, but rather the entrance to a new and free existence which includes all space, all time. Am I now more man or spirit? Will I . . . become a consciousness in space, all-seeing, all-knowing, unhampered by materialistic fetters of the world?
>
> —Charles Lindbergh, *The Spirit of St. Louis*[5]

Richard Maurice Bucke (1837–1902), a Canadian psychiatrist, author of *Cosmic Consciousness*, and friend and admirer of Walt Whitman, had an astonishing experience one evening while out walking. As was the custom of his day he describes his own experience in the third person.

> All at once, without warning of any kind, he found himself wrapped around as it were by a flame-coloured cloud . . . he knew that the light was within himself. Directly afterwards came upon him a sense of exaltation, of immense joyousness accompanied or immediately followed by an intellectual illumination quite impossible to describe . . . he saw and knew that the cosmos is not dead matter but a living Presence, that the soul of man is immortal, that the universe is so ordered that without

any peradventure all things work together for the good of each
and all, that the foundation principle of the world is what we
call love.

—Richard Maurice Bucke[6]

Young Hefflemire's feat of strength and Lindbergh's out-of-body-
awareness point to enormous untapped human potentials. These potentials are usually either ignored or explained away by the scientific
mainstream—sometimes attributed to extreme survival mechanisms
kicking in when the organism is in danger; or to the wonderfully vague
condition known as *hysteria*; or to the effects of an unusually rapid release
of hormones and neurotransmitters, such as adrenaline and dopamine,
which cause hallucinatory experiences that cannot be reproduced consciously and deliberately.

The unnamed woman's overwhelming experience of love, Ruth Stone's
unusual creative experiences, Edgar Mitchell's moment of transcendent
interconnectedness, peace, and openheartedness, and Bucke's inner illumination and perception of a "living Presence" are also dismissed by the
scientific mainstream as irreproducible and unique "mysteries" of the
human brain and nervous system. Most doctors, psychologists, and neuroscientists say that such experiences demonstrate the "amazing" capabilities of the human brain to produce *seemingly* real, but *not actually*
real experiences. Their implication is that the unnamed woman's profound
experience was probably an unusually strong estrogen-induced emotion;
that Ruth Stone's poems didn't come from outside her like a train of air,
that her experience was just her brain's unusual way of coming up with
ideas; that Edgar Mitchell did not experience anything that was beyond
his own brain and body, that his brain had simply provided him a unique
perspective perhaps brought on by lack of sleep, sustained stress, or dis-
orientation caused by weightlessness; that Bucke didn't experience Divine
illumination, that his brain instead had had a seizure that left him with
the blinding light of a migraine headache and that his limbic system had
misfired and given him a more intense than usual experience of his own
emotions.

Belying these unproven explanations are the many people who experience such emotions, abilities, and perceptions without being in the midst of life-threatening danger or extreme circumstances—and who can, at will, repeat their experiences.

"Crazy strength" like Charlotte Hefflemire's can be deliberately harnessed. Joseph Greenstein was one of the last great strongmen, from the nearly forgotten era of the Strongman at the end of the 19th and beginning of the 20th century. His stage name was the Mighty Atom. Joseph Greenstein was only 5'4" tall and weighed only about 140 pounds. Unlike most of his contemporaries, who amazed and astounded by lifting great weights, the Mighty Atom tackled metal. He twisted iron horseshoes into pretzels with his bare hands, bent half-inch rolled steel rods into heart shapes, drove nails through wood with a blow from his open hand, or broke chains that had been wrapped tightly around him by forcefully expanding his chest with a mighty inhalation.

Joseph Greenstein made a lifelong study of the Kabbalah, a Jewish mystical tradition, and among many of his insights he found inspiring connections between the Kabbalah's "inner light" and the Chinese and Japanese notions of life force that we often hear referred to as "chi." It was the quest for mastery of his life force and the demonstration of its power that was Joe Greenstein's personal "spiritual endeavor."

> This spirituality which he sought was pragmatic, for the higher his understanding, the greater the result in his physical performance. For him, the bending of metal became a spiritual endeavor. An indescribable impulse, a wave of energy, would sweep over him, as if it were no longer himself but something much greater. He could feel it being transmitted out of his eyes and converging into the shiny steel, feel the waves of it over his face, coursing through his hands. And at the zenith of this moment, when he had pitted his very being against the center point of the object: ". . . you will give way . . . NOW!" The mind commanded, the body reacted, and the object inevitably succumbed.
>
> —Ed Spielman, *The Spiritual Journey of Joseph L. Greenstein: The Mighty Atom*[7]

Unlike the unnamed woman who had one extraordinary moment of love, but never experienced it again, Paramahansa Yogananda, author of *Autobiography of a Yogi*, experienced such profound love daily.

> Thrill after thrill! Like gentle zephyrs His love comes over the soul. Day and night, week after week, year after year, it goes on increasing—you don't know where the end is.
> —Paramahansa Yogananda, yoga master[8]

Unlike Ruth Stone's highly unusual and unpredictable gifts of poetry, the famous composer Johannes Brahms could deliberately enter a deep state of concentration and receive his musical compositions, "in a semi-trance condition...."

> Straightaway the ideas flow in upon me, directly from God, and not only do I see distinct themes in my mind's eye, but they are clothed in the right forms, harmonies and orchestration. Measure by measure, the finished product is revealed to me.... I have to be in a semi-trance condition to get such results—a condition when the conscious mind is in temporary abeyance.... I have to be careful, however, not to lose consciousness, otherwise the ideas fade away.
> —Johannes Brahms[9]

Unlike Edgar Mitchell's life-changing but never-again-personally-achieved perception of interconnectedness and harmony, the philosopher, yogi, and poet Sri Aurobindo of India states from his own experience that we can "infallibly awaken this presence within us":

> In our ordinary life this truth is hidden from us or only dimly glimpsed at times or imperfectly held and conceived. But if we learn to live within, we infallibly awaken to this presence within us which is our more real self, a presence profound, calm, joyous ... of which the world is not the master."
> —Sri Aurobindo, yoga master[10]

Unlike Lindbergh's one-time experience of life-saving awareness, Paramahansa Yogananda had innumerable body-transcending experiences brought about, not by extreme life-threatening circumstances, but through dedicated meditation, including one in which "ordinary frontal vision was now changed to a vast spherical sight. . . .":

> My body became immovably rooted; breath was drawn out of my lungs as if by some huge magnet. Soul and mind instantly lost their physical bondage, and streamed out like a fluid piercing light from my every pore. The flesh was as though dead, yet in my intense awareness I knew that never before had I been fully alive. My sense of identity was no longer narrowly confined to a body, but embraced the circumambient atoms. People on distant streets seemed to be moving gently over my own remote periphery. The roots of plants and trees appeared through a dim transparency of the soil; I discerned the inward flow of their sap. The whole vicinity lay bare before me. My ordinary frontal vision was now changed to a vast spherical sight, simultaneously all-perceptive.
>
> —Paramahansa Yogananda, yoga master[11]

Unlike Maurice Bucke, who never had again his singular transcendent experience, Britain and Ireland's Poet Laureate, Alfred Lord Tennyson (1809–1892), had similar experiences that he described in his memoirs as having "often come upon me."

> A kind of waking trance (this for lack of a better word) I have frequently had quite up from boyhood, when I have been all alone. This has often come upon me through repeating my own name to myself silently, till all at once as it were out of the intensity of the consciousness of individuality the individuality itself seemed to dissolve and fade away into boundless being—and this not a confused state but the clearest of the clearest, the surest of the surest, utterly beyond words—where Death was an

almost laughable impossibility—the loss of personality (if so it were) seeming no extinction but the only true life.

—Alfred Lord Tennyson,
Poet Laureate of Great Britain and Ireland[12]

In far less dramatic circumstances, and with far less dramatic results, I also had an extraordinary and life-changing experience not readily explainable by science. Mine occurred during my college years when I took a hallucinogenic drug. During the experience, and for days afterward, I felt as I had never before felt. I was completely at ease with myself. All the usual cares of life dropped away. I was spontaneously and generously giving and caring in all my encounters with other people. I quickly accomplished all my usual tasks with relaxed concentration, energy, and success. I was effortlessly happy in a way that had nothing to do with whether good things or bad were happening in my life. I had insights into myself and intuitive clarity about what I would become and do in my life—insights and clarity that have remained true to this day. The entire experience felt *sacred*: I was conscious that an unseen but deeply felt Presence was giving me a gift to awaken me. It was beyond wonderful.

(Lest you draw the wrong conclusion, I do not recommend that anyone try hallucinogenic drugs. There is no guarantee that you would have a transformative experience such as mine. I had other experiences with hallucinogenic drugs during my college days and none were like the one I describe—in fact there were some that were confusing and unpleasant. More importantly, I don't recommend taking such drugs simply because you don't need them. As you will learn in this book there are many safer and more reliable ways to tap into your highest potentials. In particular, I have found that through meditation I can consistently return to the essence of my experience—not every day, and not always as deeply, although sometimes deeper yet, and, best yet, over time my meditation-supported awareness has transformed me and awakened potentials I had never before truly known I had.)

While mainstream science attributes such experiences to mere accidental biochemistry, stories such as the Mighty Atom's or Yogananda's, and scores more I will share ahead, strongly challenge the notion that such extraordinary experiences are only irreproducible and accidental flukes of biology. These individuals have been able, at will, repeatedly to demonstrate such abilities and intentionally attain such high levels of awareness.

Furthermore, when the individuals who have had such experiences are asked about them, they have no doubt whatsoever that their abilities and perceptions arise from a source beyond the brain and body. In fact, a shared theme that runs through the extraordinary experiences of all those who have had them, either by accident or through deliberate preparation, is the sense of tapping into *something greater*, something that transcends normal physical awareness and abilities.

> There are moments of glory that go beyond the human expectation, beyond the physical and emotional ability of the individual. Something unexplainable takes over and breathes life into the known life. Call it a state of grace, or an act of faith . . . or an act of God. It is there, and the impossible becomes possible. . . . The athlete goes beyond herself; she transcends the natural. She touches a piece of heaven and becomes the recipient of power from an unknown source. The power goes beyond that which can be defined as physical or mental. The performance almost becomes a holy place—where a spiritual awakening seems to take place. The individual becomes swept up in the action around her—she almost floats through the performance, drawing on forces she has never previously been aware of.
> —Patsy Neal, Women's Basketball Hall of Famer[13]

This experience of *something greater*, whether experienced mentally, emotionally, or perceptually, is described in the various stories above as both human and sacred, both natural to us and beyond the physical limitations of our perception. But because most of today's enormously influential and commonly shared scientific models rest entirely on the assumption that everything we can do or experience *has* to be a result solely of physical laws, physical reality, and the resulting physical abilities of the body and brain, for many people, this *something greater* is difficult to embrace.

Yet today's mainstream scientific models come with a high and generally unrecognized price. The assumption that we are nothing more than higher animals, governed by physics, biology, familial and societal conditioning, and instinctive drives, imposes a built-in limit to what people believe they can do and perceive. Such an assumption appears to eliminate the possibility that the abilities and perceptions described in the stories told above are anything more than curious anomalies—if true at all—let alone potentially accessible to everyone.

> The story of the human race is the story of men and women selling themselves short.
> —Abraham Maslow, pioneering psychologist[14]

Rebelling against the inbuilt and limiting material assumptions of mainstream science, many people turn to spiritual teachings, especially Eastern experiential teachings, which offer an expansive vision of our highest potentials, and can also explain extraordinary anomalies of human behavior such as the ones shared in the stories above.

At the same time, those drawn to Eastern experiential spirituality's model of the highest human potentials often find it difficult to integrate its conceptual framework with the conceptual framework of science and neuroscience with which they are more familiar. Confronted with the hoary dictum, "atman is Brahman," (the soul is God), most Westerners, and most Easterners for that matter, have no idea how to put that stirring wisdom into action when going to work on Monday morning. Finding such wisdom out of practical reach, and unable to explain it even to themselves using their own understanding of science or neuroscience, they can find themselves in a confused no-man's-land between science and spirituality, drawn to concepts from both, but unable to reconcile them, and so gaining the full benefit of neither.

I have found, however, that the discoveries of science and direct experiential spiritual perceptions are not inherently incompatible—neither conceptually nor practically. Important discoveries in science and, particularly, neuroscience dovetail with the insights of experiential spirituality. In particular, experimental science and experiential spirituality both reveal how our brain can be rewired to awaken our vast human potentials. I hope to convince you that the extraordinary feats and experiences of Lindbergh, Brahms, and the Mighty Atom are not irreproducible and freakish outliers of human experience but rather harbingers of your own high potentials.

You probably have no interest in bending steel bars like the Mighty Atom, but you *are* likely to want to tap into more energy to do the things you want to do. You are unlikely to want to be chased across the landscape by poems, but you *are* likely to want to make your life more creative, whether in the traditional paths of the artist, or in your work and personal life. You may not think you are ready to experience the vast embrace of the universe that astronaut Edgar Mitchell experienced on his return from the moon, but you *are* likely to want to feel a deeper, more heartfelt connection to friends, family, and humanity. You may not (yet) feel any desire to transcend your physical body like Lindbergh, Yogananda, Bucke, and Tennyson but I'm almost certain you *are* attracted to the possibility of experiencing such rich feelings of love and unity.

The key to accessing your highest potentials is to rewire your brain so that you can become more superconsciously aware. The term *superconsciousness* is used by many humanistic and transpersonal psychologists, as well as by contemporary spiritual teachers, to describe an always present reality accessible to everyone. Awareness of the superconscious is not an experience that comes only when in dire need nor one that only the exceptional manage to access. It is central to your being and it is almost certain that you have already experienced the superconscious, even if only momentarily: when you had the perfect idea come to you at just the right moment; when you had accurate intuitive hunches about how things would unfold; when you got a mysterious and welcome "second wind" in the midst of a physical challenge; when you were moved to unexpected compassion; when you had a magic moment of awe in the midst of nature's beauty and bounty; when you had a tantalizing frisson of *something greater* within you.

Superconsciousness is not an odd and unusual expression of human consciousness. It is the other way around: your everyday awareness is only a limited expression of your unlimited superconscious potential. Your innate superconscious awareness gives you access to worlds unseen, to realities beyond the physical. When accessed, your superconscious transforms you, like a river that carries you to a wider sea. It uplifts, improves, enables, inspires, exalts, energizes, and ennobles anyone who taps into it. It is the secret to success, love, health, peak experience, and happiness. It is the bridge between you and God, between your soul and Spirit.

You were born with wings. Why prefer to crawl through life?
—Rumi, Sufi mystic [15]

PART ONE

YOUR SUPERCONSCIOUS POTENTIAL

CHAPTER 2

Neuroscience, Scientific Materialism, and Consciousness

An influential core of scientists dismiss the possibility of there being any truth to all the stories I just shared with you. They do so because they hold to the fundamental belief that everything there is, or ever will be, is solely and completely the result of interactions between matter and energy—and nothing more.

The belief that nothing exists other than energy and matter is known as *scientific materialism*. Scientific materialists believe that nonmaterial realities such as consciousness simply *cannot* exist. The most passionate believers in scientific materialism view even speculation and research into nonmaterial realities as a fundamental assault on true science.

In 1981, biologist Rupert Sheldrake published *A New Science of Life*, in which he explored extensive evidence that there are nonmaterial fields influencing both nonliving and living systems. Sir John Maddox, the editor of the highly influential science journal *Nature*, denounced Sheldrake's work as "a book for burning." He went further and wrote that Sheldrake should be "condemned in exactly the same language that the pope used to condemn Galileo, and for the same reason. It is heresy."[1] For a scientist to use the religious term *heresy* to describe the work of another scientist is richly ironic.

> [M]aterialism [is] a superstition without a rational foundation.
> [It] is simply a religious belief held by dogmatic materialists . . .
> who confuse their religion with their science.
>
> —Sir John Eccles, neuroscientist and Nobel Prize-winner[2]

A working scientist embraces nonmaterial thinking at the peril of their career.

> Consciousness has always been a tricky topic to broach sci-
> entifically. *In most serious scientific circles, merely mentioning
> [nonmaterial] consciousness might result in the rescinding of
> your credentials and immediate exile to the land of quacks and
> occultists* [italics added].
>
> —Sebastian Anthony, science and tech writer[3]

> It's as if there are hooded inquisitors lurking within science who
> are keeping score, and who are continually oiling the rack and
> heating the pincers, just waiting for a scientist to step out of line.
>
> —Larry Dossey, MD, author of *Space, Time, and Medicine*[4]

The two quotes above were no doubt meant to be slightly amusing but the reality they are lightly poking fun at has heavy consequence. Scientific materialists exert an outsized influence especially through their control of peer-reviewed scientific journals. Getting papers published in the most respected peer-reviewed scientific journals, such as the prestigious *Physical Review Letters, Science,* or *Nature Neuroscience,* is almost impossible unless the paper submitted conforms to scientific materialism. A similar influence is exerted over funding for research, the biggest single driver of scientific discovery.

Scientific materialism's outsized influence has meant that psychology and neuroscience, disciplines whose focus is on nonmaterial subjects such as thought, emotion, and consciousness, have had to mold themselves around materialism in order to be considered scientific and thereby enjoy the warm embrace of mainstream science in general, medicine in particular, and funding especially.

Today, the psychological and neuroscientific disciplines that find the warmest embrace—and the most funding for research—are those that can base their practices and research on measurable physical phenomena: increases or decreases in blood flow in areas of the brain as a result of sensory stimuli or the performance of mental tasks (neuroimaging); or a decrease or increase of symptoms in conditions such as depression as the result of drugs (psychopharmacology); or inheritable behaviors that are directly linked to specific genes (behavioral genetics); or any approach that can base its methodologies on prevailing materialist scientific theories such as the idea that all human behaviors are evolved survival mechanisms (evolutionary psychology).

The rise in influence of *cognitive psychology* in the 1930s and 40s was the direct result of psychology's need to embrace scientific materialism—lest it lose both credibility and funding. Cognitive psychology focuses on how the human brain takes in, processes, and acts upon sensory inputs resulting from interactions with the observable physical world. Cognitive psychologists deal in particular with the objectively measurable results of mental processes such as attention, perception, and memory.

The rise of cognitive psychology saw the decline of other psychological disciplines, such as Freudian psychotherapy, which relied on unmeasurable, impossible-to-materially-validate patient self-reporting. With the rise of scientific materialism, what a patient *subjectively* felt and experienced lost credibility; only what could be *objectively* measured was considered credible.

Cognitive psychology also adopted scientific materialism's reductive approach. Reductionism can be defined as the attempt to provide an explanation for how things work in terms of the behavior of ever smaller structures. In biology we are taught that the body is made of cells, and that the cells are in turn made of smaller structures, such as the nucleus, which is in turn made of ever smaller structures, such as DNA, which is in turn made of even smaller structures, such as amino acid molecules. The core belief of reductionism is that if scientists can understand something at the simplest level, such as the atomic level, then they can understand how it works at all levels of increasing complexity, even in such a complex organism as the human body.

Cognitive psychology's reductive models of consciousness posit that the simplest level is made up of *qualia, percepts,* and *stimuli. Qualia* are individual instances of experience. *Percepts* are discrete elements of perception. *Stimuli* are objects perceived by the senses. Thus stimuli cause percepts, which become qualia. Scientific materialists believe that it is only a matter of time before it can be demonstrated that qualia combine and interact with other qualia to create *all* the complexity of human behavior and awareness.

Neuroscience, which we will explore at length, is in many ways the child of cognitive psychology—it is certainly currently the primary tool of cognitive research. It has taken cognitive psychology's findings—which were arrived at through evidence almost completely derived from observations made *outside* the brain—and refined and expanded those findings with evidence derived from observations made *inside* the brain.

To make observations inside the brain neuroscientists use EEG (electroencephalogram) monitoring equipment to measure brain waves or neuroimaging tools such as SPECT and PET (single-photon emission computer tomography and positron emission tomography), which reveal increases and decreases in blood flow in the brain or the uptake of glucose in neurons respectively, both of which indicate neural activation. There are many other tools used to measure activity in the brain as well; the current favorite is fMRI (functional magnetic resonance imaging). Like other tools, fMRI detects increases and decreases to blood flow in the brain, but, unlike other tools, fMRI does so continuously, creating something more like a video than a series of snapshots, allowing neuroscientists to observe brain activity in real time.

You may have seen the computer-generated, three-dimensional images developed from the data produced by PET, SPECT, and fMRI, which often show white, red, orange, yellow, green, blue, and black areas, rather like a temperature map on the evening weather report. The colors indicate the degree of activation in a particular area of the brain: white for the most activated area to black for no activity. The notion that areas of the brain "light up" when activated comes from these colorful three-dimensional computer-generated images of the brain.

While being scanned, subjects are given stimuli that range from physical touch to pictures, to questions, to mental problems to solve. From the resulting lighting up of various areas in the brain we now know, for example, which parts of the brain become active when particular parts of the body are in motion or when our various senses are actively engaged. We know which parts of the brain become active when we are solving problems or being creative. We know which parts of the brain are active in response to particular feelings—everything from sexual arousal to loving kindness.

All of which brings us to where we are today: mainstream psychology and neuroscience are now dominated by the views of scientific materialism and present us with a biomechanical model of brain-body interaction in which we are computer- and robot-like biochemical machines, a model which, I almost don't need to say, relies on no nonmaterial reality such as consciousness, let alone superconsciousness.

While neuroscience has made undoubted and significant advances in our understanding of how the brain and nervous system function, there are fundamental flaws in the biomechanical model.

The Biomechanical Model of Brain-Body Interaction

Before we get to the fundamental flaws in the biomechanical model of brain-body interaction, let's explore it in more detail so that you can understand its strong points as well as its limitations. The model is comprised of a number of basic elements: neurons and neurotransmitters, specialized brain regions, neural circuits and systems, unconscious brain processes, and the brain as a supercomputer.

Neurons and Neurotransmitters

Neurons are the basic building blocks of the brain. It is estimated that there are over one hundred billion neurons in the brain. Each neuron is a single cell. The length of the neuron is usually microscopically short but it can be as long as a meter. Each cell is able to receive an electric charge from another neuron through the tiny gap (synapse) between one neuron and the next. A neuron *automatically* passes the electric charge that it receives from another neuron onto one or more neurons to which it is connected.

Amazingly, each neuron can have up to ten thousand branches, called dendrites, and every dendritic branch ends at the synapse to another neuron, gland, or muscle. It is estimated that the human brain's approximately one hundred billion neurons can therefore branch out to make as many as *five hundred trillion* synaptic connections.

Neurons, in addition to passing on an electric charge, can release chemical neurotransmitters, which take chemical messages to other neurons in the brain, and neuropeptides, which can take chemical messages to nearly every type of cell in the body.

Neural Circuits and Systems

Neural circuits are the workhorses of the brain. A neural circuit can be made up of just a few neurons or contain thousands to millions of neurons. An entire neural circuit is fired by a single *incoming* electrical stimulus from another neuron. When the entire neural circuit fires, it can send *outgoing* electrical stimuli to hundreds, thousands, even millions of other neurons. A single neural circuit can simultaneously activate neurons all over the brain.

Brain Regions

Real-time three-dimensional neuroimaging has given us new levels of detail to the map of brain structures and their interconnections. Neuroscientists have refined the locations and, more importantly, the *functions* of thousands of regions in the brain that were previously known only approximately through surgery and dissection. This more specific and refined understanding of the functions of various brain regions has led to explanations for various cognitive dysfunctions, such as aphasia (an impairment of language) or amnesia (an impairment of memory). It is often found that people suffering from these impairments have damage or congenital defects in very specific areas of the brain.

Unconscious Brain Processing

Materialist neuroscientists believe that the brain *processes* information. They believe that the brain processes information for such activities as coordinating movement with body position, or identifying a particular sound, or coming up with an answer to a question, and for potentially millions of other purposes. Some of these processes come to our conscious attention, such as perceiving a smell, but the vast majority are thought never to rise to our conscious awareness. These *unconscious brain processes* are believed to process input from the senses, input from other neural circuits in the brain, and input from the *autonomic nervous system* that arises from the activities of the body's life systems such as circulation, respiration, digestion, etc.

A highly simplified example of an unconscious brain process might be as follows: a specialized region of the brain that regulates body temperature receives input that there is an elevated temperature in a particular part of the body. This input arrives as an electrical signal propagated through a particular *neural pathway*, which activates a particular *neural circuit* in the processing area, which in turn activates a sequential cascade of potentially thousands of other neural circuits, which runs a specific branching course through yet more connected neural circuits, a course that depends on the presence or absence of other metabolic conditions in the body, and that finally triggers a signal sent back through a different neural pathway that (for our simplified example) activates more sweat glands in the too-warm region of the body.

Such a sequential cascade of neural circuits firing is often compared to a software algorithm. A software algorithm is a set of instructions that lead step-by-step to a final result—for example giving you a search result. It is thought, therefore, that a sequential cascade of neural circuits firing is also an algorithm that leads step-by-step to a final result such as activating sweat glands.

Materialists believe that thousands to millions of algorithm-like hardwired unconscious brain processes are coordinated with and through a brain-wide mesh of other hardwired algorithmic processes. Each algorithm-like process, such as activating a sweat gland, could also be activated by other processes, such as processes that coordinate breath rate, which in turn could be activated by other cascading combinations of processes that coordinate metabolic rates. As the theory goes, all of the unconscious brain processes combine into an enormously complex and intricately accurate input and feedback system that, without us ever being consciously aware of it, successfully maintains our body's twenty-five to fifty trillion body cells in functional coordination.

The Biomechanical Supercomputer Model of Brain-Body Interaction

The materialist vision of how the biomechanical coordination of neurons, neural circuits, specialized brain areas, and unconscious brain processes is achieved is often compared by materialists to how a supercomputer works— in fact it is widely believed that the brain *is* an organic supercomputer.

Today's supercomputers are not simply one superfast computer with one gigantic central processing unit (CPU) but are made up of tens of thousands of computers, each with its own CPU, networked together, and all coordinated by software. Today's fastest and most powerful networked supercomputers have trillions of circuits and can perform over one hundred quadrillion operations per second. This capability is believed to be analogous to the brain's one hundred billion neurons and the potential to fire five hundred trillion branching dendritic interconnections to other neurons.

In a supercomputer, an individual computer or a small cluster of computers can be programmed to perform specific tasks that no other computers or clusters of computers in the supercomputer perform. This arrangement is believed to be analogous to specific brain processes taking place in specific neural circuits or specialized brain regions. In a supercomputer, individual computers or clusters of computers can send processed information to other computers or clusters of computers through physical wires. This transmission of information is believed to be analogous to neural circuits sending neural signals to other neural circuits or specialized brain regions through neural pathways.

In a supercomputer, the processing that takes place in each individual computer, the coordination of processing within clusters of computers, and the communication of data and processed information to other computers happens in accordance with *software* that exists *separately* from the circuits of the computer, i.e., the *hardware*. The supercomputer that today is used to predict worldwide *weather* patterns for the next twenty years can, tomorrow, if different software is used, predict global *economic* patterns for the next twenty years. In contrast, according to the biomechanical model of the brain, the *software* of the brain is embedded in the *hardware* of the brain, i.e., the actual physical connections of neurons to other neurons is both the hardware *and* the software of the brain. For this reason our brains are said to be *hardwired*.

Programmed by Evolution

In the biomechanical supercomputer model of brain-body interaction, the hardwired information processing that happens through every neural circuit or specialized brain region is commonly believed by scientific materialists to have evolved over millions of years. Evolution suggests that millions of tiny improvements occur in a species through millions of accidental mutations occurring over vast eons of time. Many of those beneficial mutations are believed to have occurred in the brain and nervous system. For example, animals that have evolved better heat regulation, or that could identify sounds faster and more accurately, or that could more rapidly coordinate body position and movement—all because of accidental physical mutations to neural circuits—have better odds of survival than other animals within the same species.

The evolutionarily evolved algorithmic equivalent to computer software is therefore believed by materialists to be expressed in *the fixed physical arrangement of our neurons and their synaptic connections to other neurons*. The automatic cascading chain reaction of activated circuits that occurs when any circuit is itself activated by some other neuron—like a line of falling dominoes, which cause other branching lines of dominoes to fall, which cause other branching lines of dominoes to fall, etc.—contains the wisdom of millions of years of evolution.

The brain-as-supercomputer model sounds plausible. It obviously adheres closely to scientific materialism's biomechanical and reductive approach, and it presents a reasonable picture of how physical functions, such as sensory processing, sensory-motor coordination, and regulation of the various autonomic life processes, such as circulation and digestion, might be processed by interlinked neural circuits firing off in mechanical precision in response to inner and outer stimuli.

But, despite its plausibility, there are significant problems with the biomechanical model of brain-body interaction and with the brain-as-supercomputer model. The models are revealed to be either significantly incomplete or fundamentally wrong when three issues are raised: *radical neuroplasticity, intelligence*, and most central of all, *consciousness*.

Radical Neuroplasticity

At variance with the picture of your brain as a fine-tuned Swiss watch—the gears of which are the perfect physical expression of the peak of the evolution of the clockmaker's art—*your brain continuously undergoes physical change.* Not something you would want to see happen to your Rolex!

For most of the 20th century it was believed that the brain was fixed at birth and gradually deteriorated over time as irreplaceable brain cells died. A rather bleak prospect. It is now accepted that the brain can, and nearly continuously does, make new neural connections to other neurons, create new neural circuits, and even—in response to sustained changes of emotional, cognitive, and behavioral stimuli, or in response to congenital defects or damage to the brain—*rewire* entire neural systems.

The classic example that is used to describe brain plasticity is the way the brain rewires when we learn to play a musical instrument. At first one's efforts to play an instrument are challenging and require a high degree of focused concentration to achieve even minimal results, and frequent repetition to improve. It is now known that the concentration and repetition required to learn a new instrument are actually causing the brain to rewire by creating new neuronal connections and circuits linking motor and auditory regions of the brain. Also, the more one practices, the more these new circuits add more neurons and grow more connections to other neural circuits or brain regions. At some point the new learner realizes that certain movements have become easier and that performance does not require as high a level of concentration as when first learning them. The reason is that the brain has rewired to make those movements more automatic, that is, requiring less or even no concentration.

Many people have experienced such a progression as they master a new discipline, whether it be learning a new instrument, sport, field of study, language, or way of behaving. After a while learners recognize that elements of their new discipline have become "second nature." Muscle memory is a term often used to describe such automatic facility for physical tasks—the memory, however, is not in the muscles but in the brain, in the form of neural circuits that coordinate and control the muscles.

Put simply, your brain rewires to support whatever it is you do. Repetition, whether mental, emotional, or physical, creates or improves neural interconnections in the brain. It has been described metaphorically as being like sled after sled going down a snowy slope until a deep track is formed that allows the next sled to go down the hill to the right destination more easily and more reliably.

We see another aspect of neuroplasticity when there has been brain damage. It is now understood that many, perhaps all parts of the brain are *equipotent*. Karl Spencer Lashley (1890–1958), a highly influential researcher and psychologist, defined equipotentiality as, "The apparent capacity of any intact part of a functional brain to carry out . . . the functions which are lost by the destruction of [other parts]."[5] This phenomenon is often seen in recovering stroke victims who regain functional control over parts of their body that lost function in the stroke. It is now understood that undamaged areas of the brain have rewired to take up the functions of the damaged areas.

These and other examples of neuroplasticity make it clear that the brain is *not* as hardwired for specific functions as was once believed. The brain can and will change in response to new conditions and behaviors to a remarkable degree, including adding new functions to existing neural circuits or even rewiring existing neural regions to perform new functions. Far from being fixed from birth, *the brain is the most changeable organ in the body.*

If, as the brain-as-supercomputer biomechanical model requires, the software of the brain is hardwired in precisely organized physical structures, neural configurations, and interconnections to other neurons—what we might call the physical expression of the wisdom of evolution—then how is evolutionary wisdom *retained* if the brain can change those physical structures in response to our behavior?

What happens to the wisdom of evolution when certain evolutionarily evolved neural circuits are rewired or even overwritten altogether? Where is the embedded wisdom-circuitry that manages the rewiring or overwriting? Where is the evolutionary wisdom *stored* that once resided in now-damaged areas of the brain, that would enable such evolutionary wisdom to be *restored* by creating new neural circuits in undamaged parts of the brain? Or put more simply, how can our evolutionary wisdom be destroyed or overwritten without our losing it permanently?

The standard response to these questions is that the brain is *massively redundant*. The notion of massive redundancy in the brain suggests that the same evolutionarily evolved wisdom-circuits exist in multiple places in the brain and that the brain evolved this way because being able to restore brain functionality has high survival value. This theory, and it is a theory, is significantly undercut by two examples.

The science paper "Intrinsic Functional Connectivity of the Brain in Adults with a Single Cerebral Hemisphere" appeared in the journal *Cell Reports* in 2019.[6] The paper reported the results of a study of six people who had had half their brain removed in infancy but were now completely functional adults.

Although there is a degree of functional mirroring in the two halves of our brain, there are also many *lateralized* functions unique to each hemisphere. For example, language, speech, and comprehension of speech are processed primarily in the left hemisphere. Yet these unique lateralized functions of the missing hemisphere were rewired into the remaining hemisphere in the brains of the people who had had one hemisphere removed. How could that happen? Was there an already existing redundant complex neural system for language just sitting in the opposite hemisphere doing nothing? Or, if there were millions of neurons not doing anything but available for rewiring, how does the brain know how to replicate the function of a part of the opposite hemisphere of the brain when that part of the brain is completely gone?

If you are thinking that massive redundancy might still explain how a one-hemisphere brain can rewire to the same functionality as a two-hemisphere brain, there is scientifically gathered evidence that a person can be cognitively fully functional with *far less than half a brain*. A 1980 article in *Science*, provocatively titled, "Is Your Brain Really Necessary?" highlighted discoveries made by John Lorber, professor of pediatrics at the University of Sheffield. Lorber discovered that there were fully functioning adults suffering from extreme hydrocephaly, sometimes called water on the brain, who had *as little as 5 percent* of the brain tissue of an average adult, and that the rest of the brain cavity was filled with cerebrospinal fluid. Among the sixty adult cases of extreme hydrocephaly that Lorber found, *thirty had above-average intelligence, and one had a degree in mathematics and an IQ of 126.*[7]

Lorber's work is referenced in Donald R. Forsdyke's paper "Wittgenstein's Certainty Is Uncertain: Brain Scans of Cured Hydrocephalics Challenge Cherished Assumptions." Forsdyke's paper explores an ongoing issue in neuroscience: the human brain's information content (memory), appears to exceed the capacity of even an *average*-sized brain, as measured according to current theories of how we store memories. The cherished assumption his paper challenged was whether memory is even stored *in* the brain at all. If, as he argues, an adult with only 5 percent of normal brain circuitry has a full range of memory, then memory must be somehow stored "extra-corporeally."[8] Almost in passing Forsdyke comments that a fully functioning adult using only 5 percent of an average brain also makes the notion of massive redundancy untenable since it suggests that at least 95 percent of the brain must be devoted to spare circuitry.

Perhaps you are thinking that our DNA contains the answer to the puzzle of neuroplasticity, that the *real* evolutionary wisdom that is manifested in physical structures in the brain is contained in our genetic code, that the same parts of the genetic code that first created a now-damaged part of the brain can recreate the same neuronal circuitry in undamaged parts of the brain.

Although for most of the 20th century it was believed that our destiny was contained in our DNA, when the complete sequencing of our DNA was achieved in 2003 and the Human Genome Project came to an end, geneticists were confronted with how *little* information was actually contained in our genes.

> When the human genome was sequenced, some scientists were saying, "That's the end. We're going to understand every disease. We're going to understand every behavior." And it turns out, we didn't, because the sequence of the DNA isn't enough to explain behavior. It isn't enough to explain diseases.
> —Denise Chow, "Why Your DNA
> May Not Be Your Destiny"[9]

In a commentary on the surprising results of the Human Genome Project, David Baltimore, one of the world's preeminent geneticists and a Nobel Prize-winner, addressed the issue of human complexity: "But unless the human genome contains a lot of genes that are opaque to our computers, it is clear that we do not gain our undoubted complexity over worms and plants by using more genes."[10]

> Understanding what does give us our complexity—our enormous behavioral repertoire, ability to produce conscious action, remarkable physical coordination, precisely tuned alterations in response to external variations of the environments, learning, memory, need I go on?—remains a challenge for the future.
> —Bruce H. Lipton, *The Biology of Belief*[11]

The hardcoded information that allows our body to rebuild itself, in response to every conceivable type of damage in the body or brain, simply does not exist in either our DNA or the existing biomechanical circuitry of a normal brain.

The reality of radical neuroplasticity and the model of the brain-as-supercomputer do not work well together—if at all. The brain-as-supercomputer model creates a logical paradox rather like Escher's picture of two hands drawing each other. How is it possible for the biomechanical brain to exceed, improve, overwrite, or restore hardwired biomechanical programming? If, as scientific materialists would have it, our biomechanically programmed, hardwired brain gives rise to everything we experience and coordinates everything we do, how can the biomechanical brain itself override pre-existing biomechanical programming? This question points out a major problem for the biomechanical brain-body interaction model and, especially, for the brain-as-supercomputer model.

Intelligence

Intelligence is another major problem for the brain-as-supercomputer model. It is obvious that we are intelligent. It is just as obvious that supercomputers are not. A supercomputer may *appear* to be intelligent—put a search term into Google and it will in moments give you an intelligently sorted set of results—but any of the various ways in which a computer may *appear* to be intelligent are the sole result of *software* written by *intelligent people.*

Yet the brain-as-supercomputer model has no software—only hardware.

A computer is essentially a bunch of circuits used to run software. Those circuits used by intelligently written software of one kind will give you a spreadsheet of all your expenses for the year. Used by another kind of software those circuits will search for and find an email you sent to your boss four years ago or give you a list of all the Italian restaurants within walking distance sorted from highest to lowest rating. Hold your cell phone up toward the night sky and it will show you and identify which constellations you might be able to see. But without software, the electromechanical circuits of a computer *do absolutely nothing at all.*

Nor can a computer running software exceed its programming. Your computer won't ever surprise you and send you an email suggesting the best way to work out a personal problem with your coworker. A computer will never independently compare your credit card statements to your bank balance and suggest to you that you are overspending. A computer will never spontaneously suggest a new kitchen plan and budget to remodel your kitchen based on a history of your web searches into kitchens.

You might be wondering (even clamoring to ask), "Well, what about computer-generated artificial intelligence? Won't it be able to do what you described? Can't artificial intelligence think and learn on its own?" The current answer is a definite NO.

Developing a computer that can think and learn on its own is the domain of artificial general intelligence (AGI): nothing close to independent thought and learning has been developed. When you hear about amazing breakthroughs in artificial intelligence, or AI, you are hearing about Narrow AI, not artificial general intelligence (AGI). Narrow AI focuses on a set of highly defined tasks such as speech recognition, facial recognition, web search, playing chess or go, self-driving cars, and, alas, marketing. When you do a web search on Google and get a matching content ad on Facebook a minute later—you can thank Narrow AI for that.

Narrow AI, however, is effective only at tasks that have clearly definable goals, such as winning at chess by checkmating the opponent, and finite rules, such as the limited number of moves each chess piece can make on a board with a limited number of squares. Narrow AI requires software algorithms written by intelligent people that exactly define the goal, exactly define every single rule for working toward the goal, and then exactly define the order of when and how each rule is used to reach the goal.

The speed of computers makes it possible to run extremely complex software algorithms impressively fast, processing vast amounts of data to arrive at answers millions to trillions of times faster than could an intelligent person. But the intelligence still resides in the people who created the algorithm—not in the computer itself.

Narrow AI doesn't actually have very many applications because there are a limited number of fields that have clearly definable goals and finite rules. One of the main reasons developers of Narrow AI for self-driving cars are finding the challenge difficult is that while the goal of getting from point A to point B may be clear, the rules governing how a car gets from point A to point B are neither finite nor clear. Drivers of other cars disobey traffic rules, pedestrians cross streets without looking, people drive erratically, people exhibit road rage, delivery trucks park in the middle of busy streets, light conditions change from dark to light to highly reflective, it rains, it snows, it gets icy, road surfaces change from smooth to bumpy, gravel to dirt. Negotiating a lane change in tight freeway traffic, something people do frequently, is very difficult to turn into a set of algorithmic rules. The negotiating signals that the other car's driver gives us, such as staring straight ahead rather than acknowledging us, are subtle and vary from driver to driver, and the negotiating signals we give the other driver also vary. There is a growing consensus that safe self-driving cars may only be possible in driving situations where *all* the cars are self-driving, because only then will they *all* obey the same rules.

Unlike Narrow AI, the field of artificial general intelligence (AGI) is try-ing to develop an all-purpose AI that can self-establish different goals for different problems and choose the appropriate rules to solve each problem. As you might guess, very little progress has been made in AGI. Following Narrow AI's approach, it would take the rest of time to provide a supercom-puter with the millions of examples of the thousands of objects required for deep learning, let alone defining the essentially unlimited number of situations that a person routinely encounters while making day-to-day decisions.

> . . . Lee Spector and I have developed a mathematical proof that shows the limits to how creative a computer can be . . . we found that the fastest modern supercomputer couldn't list or explore all the features of an object/thing even if it had started working on the problem way back in the 1950s. . . .
>
> —Tony McCaffrey, chief technology officer of Innovation Accelerator, "There Will Always Be Limits to How Creative a Computer Can Be"[12]

Because duplicating Narrow AI's approach of listing all the minute nu-ances found in every field of human knowledge is realistically impossible, the relatively few research centers that focus on the development of AGI are taking different approaches. The most common approach is to develop a computer simulation that has the same circuitry as the human brain. The thinking is that if one can mimic how the human brain functions, one will discover how it creates intelligence.

This approach to AGI is now focused on mapping all the brain's one hundred billion neurons and their hundreds of trillions of synaptic con-nections. So far no team, such as Google's *DeepMind*, the Swiss *Blue Brain* project that makes use of an IBM supercomputer, or the European consortium's *Human Brain Project* has come close to fully mapping the human brain, let alone creating a functional simulation.

AGI's defenders will often say that artificial general intelligence will be possible only when computer speed and memory storage reach much higher performance levels than even today's supercomputers can manage. This position ignores a fundamental problem as described by Peter Kassan in his *Harvard Business Review* article, "The Futile Quest for Artificial Intelligence": "Sad to say, even if we had *unlimited* computer power and storage, *we wouldn't know what to do with it. The programs aren't* ready to go, because *there aren't any programs.*"[13]

And therein lies the rub for both artificial general intelligence and for the brain-as-supercomputer model. There has been no demonstration, *even on a small scale*, that the firing of silicon-electromechanical or biological-electromechanical circuits gives rise to general intelligence, reasoning capability, good judgment, or creativity. Computer scientists are *not even close* to demonstrating how computerlike biomechanical processes can have given us the creative genius or intuitive leaps for Euclid's invention of geometry, Da Vinci's Mona Lisa, Beethoven's Fifth Symphony, or Einstein's $E=mc^2$.

It is an article of faith, only, that compels scientific materialists to believe intelligence will emerge from matter-energy interaction in supercomputer-like ways.

Consciousness

Consciousness is the most intractable problem for the biomechanical, brain-as-supercomputer model. Just as it's obvious that we are conscious, so is it obvious that computers are not. Why we have an inner world of conscious awareness has become known as the *hard problem* of consciousness—that is to say, the hard problem for the brain-as-supercomputer model.

The hard problem was framed as such by scientific philosopher and cognitive neuroscientist David Chalmers and has become the subject of many debates within psychology and neuroscience. The easy problems, according to Chalmers, such as processing sensory information, appear to be solved by the brain-as-computer theory, but what psychologists call *subjective experience* finds no obvious answer in the biomechanical, ordered-firing-of-neural-circuits model of the brain.

> Why is it that when our cognitive systems engage in visual and auditory information-processing, we have visual or auditory experience: the quality of deep blue, the sensation of middle C? It is widely agreed that experience arises from a physical basis, but we have no good explanation of why and how it so arises.
> —David Chalmers[14]

There is one extreme school of thought in cognitive science that tries to solve the hard problem by saying we have no subjective experience at all. Cognitive scientist and philosopher Daniel Dennett—said to be one of the "Four Horsemen of New Atheism" along with Richard Dawkins, Sam Harris, and the late Christopher Hitchens, all of whom occupy what you might think of as the most extreme materialist wing of science—champions the idea that consciousness, as a separate subjective reality, does not exist. In his book *Consciousness Explained*, Dennett argues that what we experience as being conscious is a combination of automatic awareness of sensory input from our immediate environment and our automatic response to that sensory input arising from thousands upon thousands of unconscious brain processes, almost all of which occur below the threshold of our awareness. He suggests that the small measure of sensory input and brain processes that we *are* aware of constitute what we *mistake* for consciousness.[15]

Most neuroscientists, even those who are firmly in the camp of scientific materialism, consider Dennett's take on consciousness extreme. One of his detractors, cognitive scientist Peter Carruthers, refers to his book as "Consciousness Explained Away."[16] Another, John Rogers Searle, former Emeritus Professor of Philosophy of Mind and Language at the University of California, Berkeley, wrote, "For Dennett there is no difference between us humans and complex zombies who lack any inner feelings, because we are all just complex zombies."[17] Or, as I like to put it, Dennett believes we only think we are driving the car, when all along *the car is driving us.*

Emergent Consciousness

Most neuroscientists today, even those with a materialist bent, would say that Chalmers's hard problem raised by the brain-as-supercomputer model is solved by the phenomenon of *emergent consciousness*. The basic theory of emergent consciousness is that, (perhaps) because of the continual storm of electrochemical interactions taking place in our brain's one hundred billion neurons and trillions of interconnections, our subjective consciousness (somehow) pops into existence, rather like a light bulb lighting up, and it is within this emergent consciousness that (in some way) intelligence, subjective feeling, self-awareness, and self-will have come into existence.

I think of the theory of emergent consciousness as the get-out-of-the-biomechanical-jail-free card or the have-your-cake-and-eat-it-too explanation of brain-body interaction. On the one hand, scientific materialists have their cake when they point to the biomechanical circuitry of the brain and say, "See, there's nothing here but matter and energy interactions." On the other hand, they can eat their cake by saying, "Isn't that emergent consciousness amazing!" It is also a get-out-of-biomechanical-jail-free card because the wide acceptance of the *theory* of emergent consciousness allows materialists to proceed *as if it were established fact*, as if all the logical and causal problems with the brain-as-supercomputer model and consciousness arising from matter have already been resolved.

> The dominant physicalist view that mind and consciousness are products of brain function is served up within contemporary science not as a modest hypothesis or humble conjecture, but as an incontrovertible fact, and anyone who disagrees is likely to be considered an apostate or a traitor to science.
>
> —Larry Dossey, MD, author of
> *Space, Time, and Medicine*[18]

Materialist neuroscientists are so far down the road of acceptance of emergent consciousness that they have been building elaborate theories on *top* of it for decades. One such theory is the currently popular Global Workspace Theory (GWT). The central notion of GWT is that the brain creates a *mental work space* that allows a combination of memories, unconscious brain processes, and executive brain functions to be consciously considered together, resulting in decisions, creative ideas, and solutions that are subjectively experienced as abstract thoughts, language, and sensory constructs such as visual images.

If you study it closely, though, global workspace theory elucidates only how the mental work space *could* facilitate conscious and unconscious brain processes working together—if there *were* a mental work space. It offers no explanation as to how a mental work space could emerge in the first place. It reminds me of my days designing web-based applications. When diagramming a particular sequence of tasks on a white board, we would often not know how a particular task could be programmed, so we would draw a circle on the board and write in it, "Magic Happens Here," and move on to the next task. This could work only temporarily, however, because our application design would come to an abrupt halt if it was determined that no magic *could* happen there.

Scientific materialists are drawing a lot of circles with "Magic Happens Here" written in them without ever having demonstrated *any* of the magic in any of the circles in decades of conjecture.

The notion that electrochemical interactions can (somehow) result in consciousness has become so well accepted that many people believe, like futurist author Ray Kurzweil, that it is only a matter of time—when computer processing becomes fast enough and programming becomes sophisticated enough—before *computers* will becomes conscious. Kurzweil refers to this moment of emergent consciousness as the Singularity. (This notion is well established as a meme in popular culture, such as in the Terminator movies, in which a network of supercomputers becomes conscious. Such a self-aware and conscious supercomputer network apparently always, perhaps after watching lawnmower racing on cable TV, decides it must take over the world and exterminate all humans.)

In fairness there *are* material theories as to how the magic of consciousness could emerge in the brain, but, in equal fairness, they are a long, long way from being even testable.

One, the Conscious Electromagnetic Information (CEMI) theory, suggests that every time a neuron fires it creates a specific disturbance in the electromagnetic field created when the neuron fired, and that the specific disturbance in the electromagnetic field is a magnetic *representation* of the electrical information flowing through the neurons. Synchronized firing of neurons, a phenomenon that is known to occur in the brain, could then lead to synchronized electromagnetic fluctuations in the combined electromagnetic field of the brain, which could in turn activate other neurons in the brain, which create more magnetic fields, and so on. The creators of this theory suggest that the resulting *conscious electromagnetic information field* is our subjective consciousness.

Another collection of theories conjecture that quantum effects could lead to emergent consciousness. One such is known as quantum brain dynamics (QBD), which proposes that the water content that makes up 70 percent of our brain could exist in a quantum field. Another concept put forward by physicist Sir Roger Penrose and psychologist Stuart Hameroff, known as *orchestrated objective reduction* (Orch-OR), proposes that quantum actions could be taking place in microtubules in the brain and thus could create a quantum field. Proponents argue that if there *were* a quantum field in the brain, it could bring into play quantum effects such as entanglement and superposition, which *might* help give rise to what we experience as consciousness.

These material theories offer tempting plausibility, I think, because electromagnetic and quantum fields are invisible phenomena that interact with matter. Because it is easy to imagine that consciousness is also an invisible field, perhaps either an EM field or a quantum field could be the magic field that is consciousness. But realistically these are only conjectures, built on possibilities, resting on unsupported theories that only *begin* to explain how matter-energy activated fields could result in the experience we know as consciousness.

> Science's biggest mystery is the nature of consciousness. It is not that we possess bad or imperfect theories of human awareness; we simply have no such theories at all.
>
> —Nick Herbert, PhD, author of
> *Quantum Reality: Beyond the New Physics*[19]

The scientific study of consciousness is in the embarrassing positon of having no scientific theory of consciousness.
—Donald D. Hoffman, cognitive scientist,
University of California, Irvine[20]

"I think consciousness will remain a mystery," says Princeton physicist Edward Witten. "I tend to think that the workings of the conscious brain will be elucidated to a large extent. But why something that we call consciousness goes with those workings, I think that will remain mysterious."[21]

Panpsychism

Because of the difficulty and lack of success in figuring out how consciousness can emerge from matter-energy interactions in the brain, another conceptual approach, known as panpsychism, is being *very cautiously* embraced by some cognitive scientists. Panpsychism posits that consciousness is an *inherent property of matter*. Panpsychism jumps over the pesky problem of how consciousness *can* emerge from matter-energy interactions by simply asserting that consciousness *already* exists as a fundamental quality of matter, like atomic spin or polarity.

Panpsychism is being embraced, cautiously or otherwise, by some cognitive scientists because by positing that consciousness is an intrinsic part of the tiniest building blocks of all matter, it means that trying to understand how our level of conscious awareness can emerge from matter can be approached in the same reductive fashion as was used to understand how atoms form into molecules, or how iron molecules, when more and more of them are aligned, can create a stronger and stronger magnetic field. Materialists may also be cautiously embracing panpsychism because it regards consciousness as a blind force that does not include any hard-to-explain quotient of intelligence.

Panpsychism, while seeming to solve Chalmers's hard problem of consciousness by eliminating the question of how consciousness can arise from matter, creates yet another problem however: how does the individual consciousness of each atom *combine* to create human intelligence, feeling, and subjective experience? This has become known as the *combination problem*.

One attempt at solving the combination problem is Information Integration Theory (IIT), developed by Giulio Tononi, MD, PhD. Tononi proposes that physical systems become *more and more conscious* as greater and greater amounts of information are integrated together in neural circuits, and neural systems through which information flows in the brain. Or put more simply, the more actively the neurons of your brain send information to other neurons, the more conscious your brain as a whole becomes.

Information Integration Theory still leaves the question of how more circuits firing among more densely connected circuits causes the tiny bits of blind force consciousness in every atom to combine into subjective awareness, intelligence, and feeling. IIT is only positing that *if* the tiny bits of blind force consciousness *could* combine into subjective awareness, intelligence, and feeling then this is how it *might* work.

You could, in fact, say that about all the material theories of intelligence and consciousness. They are all positing that *if* the biomechanical firing of neural circuitry *could* give rise to intelligence and consciousness, then this is how it might work. It is only the deeply held belief system of scientific materialists that *compels* them to try to find a material solution because *there is no evidence* that any of these theories are actually true.

Nonmaterial Consciousness

You might think, given the degree of commitment scientific materialists have toward a purely biomechanical explanation for intelligence and consciousness, that all other possible *nonmaterial* explanations must have been exhaustively explored and found to be wrong.

Nothing could be farther from the truth.

Reams of scientifically gathered evidence, using state-of-the-art science and neuroscience, indicate that consciousness *is* nonmaterial and *does* exist independently from the brain and from matter. The evidence accumulated through these studies has been derived using impeccable scientific methods of experimentation, methods equal to those of any other scientific discipline. The results are not only repeatable—the hallmark of scientific verification—but are *often* repeated. Nonetheless the inconvenient truth of the evidence is ignored by scientific materialists.

During the 1970s and continuing until 1995, the CIA conducted a secret program called Stargate. Stargate was motivated by Cold War fears. In the 1970s, the CIA believed that the Russians were training people to gather secret information psychically from our government and military by means of *remote viewing*. If this remote-viewing ability *could* be developed, the CIA did not want to be at a disadvantage, and thus it started its own program. Eventually, the CIA had twenty-two different labs set up around the United States to test and develop the ability to spy on our enemies without needing to be physically present.

The CIA's Stargate program ran for over twenty years. Eventually, in 1995, the program was abandoned because the intelligence gathered by its remote viewers was not *consistently* reliable enough to make it useful as an intelligence-gathering method. However, in the conclusion of The American Institutes for Research's blue ribbon panel report we find this highly significant passage:

> The foregoing observations provide a compelling argument against continuation of the program within the intelligence community. *Even though a statistically significant effect has been observed in the laboratory* [italics added].[22]

Most people have interpreted the program's closure as proof that such psychic abilities do not exist *at all*, when, in fact, the program established that some remote viewers could properly identify images with an eye-opening degree of accuracy. The problem for the CIA was that that degree of accuracy wasn't close enough to 100 percent to be trustworthy. But the results *were* accurate to a degree that was far, far beyond chance, thus plausibly indicating that the brain can directly receive thoughts from outside the body.

In 1994, taking another approach to experimentally exploring the possibility of nonmaterial consciousness, Jacobo Grinberg-Zylberbaum, PhD, had two subjects meditate together for twenty minutes and then moved them into distantly separated rooms and placed in Faraday cages. The Faraday cages ensured that no electromagnetic waves could reach either subject, thus eliminating the possibility of outside electromagnetic signals influencing the experiment. Both subjects were hooked up to electroencephalographs (EEGs). One subject was then subjected to random bursts of light, which registered as a clear shock response on their EEG readout. Simultaneously, the other subject, *who was not subjected to these random bursts of light,* nonetheless registered a similar shock response *25 percent of the time* on their EEG. Control experiments, in which the subjects had not meditated together, showed no correlation at all.[23] A series of similar studies were conducted by physicist Fred H. Thaheld and had equally significant results.[24]

> We are facing a phenomenon which is neither easy to dismiss as a methodological failure or a technical artifact nor understood as to its nature. No biophysical mechanism is presently known that could be responsible for the observed correlations between EEGs of two separated subjects.
>
> —Jiri Wackerman, neuroscientist[25]

Yet another series of experiments were conducted by Dr. Charles Tart of the University of California, Davis, this time using a galvanic skin response (GSR) device such as is used in lie detectors. Tart's pairs of subjects would meet with each other and "agree" to stay connected. After being placed in separate rooms, one subject would receive small electric shocks, showing a clear response pattern on the GSR device—simultaneously the other subject, who was not receiving any shocks, and who had no idea what kind of stimulus the other would receive, nonetheless registered a similar response pattern on their GSR device.

Psychologists Marilyn Schlitz and William Braud developed a variant experimental strategy using GSR devices. Only one person was hooked up to the device, the *receiver.* A *sender* was placed in another room, completely out of any possible contact with the receiver, and would, at random times, try to influence the receiver to feel either agitated or calm. Various controls were set in place for each of fifteen studies, with a total of 323 sessions and 271 subjects. Even though the receivers had no idea when the influencers were focusing on them, their skin response showed a direct correlation with the influencers' intentions 57 percent of the time.[26]

The various studies described above—and there are many, many more—overwhelmingly indicate that there is something real, a subtle nonmaterial *something*, that makes it possible for people to feel the mental attention of another person, to receive information from another person, or to be mentally or emotionally correlated with another mind and body.

Materialists tend to say, with some degree of impatience, "Well, what is this *something*? Nothing has ever been measured by our devices that can explain these effects!"

True, but a poor argument.

Astrophysicists are currently and determinedly searching—with funding that reaches into the tens, maybe hundreds of millions of dollars—for dark matter or dark energy. Both dark energy and dark matter are called "dark" to specifically highlight the fact that they have *not been measured by any device*. Does the fact that these elusive realities have never been measured mean we should conclude that dark matter and dark energy don't exist? No, because it is clear that there is an effect that needs to be explained. The effect needs to be explained because there is *ample evidence that the universe is expanding at an unexplained and accelerating rate*.

We have the same conundrum in the field of consciousness. There is an effect that needs to be explained. The effect needs to be explained because there is *ample evidence that something is allowing people to receive thoughts, emotions, and even physiological influences from outside their own body and brain*.

Just as it makes sense that tens of millions of dollars are being invested in searching for an explanation to the mysterious accelerating expansion of the universe, so also it would make sense to make a similar investment in searching for an explanation to our mysterious ability to receive information from other people without the usual means of communication. Alas, there is no corresponding investment being made to explain the mystery of consciousness—just the opposite, in fact.

Not content with just defensively blocking funding for research into nonmaterial consciousness, materialists have gone on the offense by discrediting, *in advance*, any results that come out of what is collectively known as *psi* research by labelling it *paranormal or parapsychological*—as if some

aspects of reality that are scientifically observed are real while other aspects of reality that are scientifically observed are unreal.

I imagine that some of you, though sympathetic to the idea that consciousness is a worthy subject of study, nonetheless were thinking as you
were reading about the studies I cited above that they could not possibly
have been conducted in a rigorously scientific manner; had they been, you
might think, they would have been widely accepted. I only wish that were
true. The fact is that these experiments were dismissed or simply ignored
because their results don't fit scientific materialism's view of reality.

This prejudgment of anything psi is exemplified by a comment made
by Professor Richard Wiseman, a psychologist at the University of
Hertfordshire and a leading skeptic regarding the "paranormal":

> I agree that by the standards of any other area of science that
> remote viewing is proven, but . . . because remote viewing is
> such an outlandish claim that will revolutionise the world, we
> need overwhelming evidence before we draw any conclusions.[27]

Professor Wiseman is all but admitting that mainstream scientists
knowingly ignore findings that would be accepted as solid from any other
area of science because they do not fit their matter-centric view—because,
if confirmed, such findings would not so much revolutionize the world as
they would revolutionize science—and the main casualty of that revolution
would be scientific materialism itself.

As pervasive as the materialistic view has become in the popular mind,
and despite scientific materialism's strongly biased hold on the official or-
gans and funding sources of mainstream science, a 2009 Pew study of attitudes among scientists revealed that while 42 percent of scientists aligned
themselves with scientific materialism, a slim *majority* of scientists—51
percent—*believed in God, a higher power, or higher consciousness.*

This largely silent majority of scientists makes it obvious that not all
scientific minds are closed to the notion of nonmaterial consciousness.
In researching my book, *The Physics of God*, I found that many reputable
scientists, particularly physicists, old and new, whose many contributions

have been central to the development of physics, do not accept scientific materialism's view. They instead, largely because of what is known as the intelligent observer effect, believe that consciousness does not emerge from interactions between matter and energy but that matter and energy emerge *from an even more fundamental substrate of all-pervading consciousness.*

> I regard consciousness as fundamental. I regard matter as a derivative of consciousness. We cannot get behind consciousness. Everything that we talk about, everything that we regard as existing, [suggests] consciousness.
> —Max Planck, Nobel Prize-winner in physics[28]

> Instead of positing that everything (including consciousness) is made of matter, this philosophy posits that everything (including matter) exists in and is manipulated from consciousness.
> —Amit Goswami, physicist and
> author of *The Self-Aware Universe*[29]

> I am also betting that scientific discoveries in the new millennium will substantiate that the rich inner world of consciousness we all share is more than just a neurophysiological epiphenomenon. I'm betting that, before too long, we will understand how consciousness, at a fundamental level, creates matter, not vice versa.
> —Dr. Bernard Haisch, astrophysicist and
> author of *The God Theory*[30]

> Will it not turn out, with the further development of science, that the study of the universe and the study of consciousness will be inseparably linked, and that ultimate progress in the one will be impossible without progress in the other?
> —Andrei Linde, Harald Trap Friis Professor
> of Physics at Stanford University[31]

Consciousness cannot be accounted for in physical terms. For consciousness is absolutely fundamental. It cannot be accounted for in terms of anything else.
—Erwin Schrödinger, Nobel Prize-winner in physics[32]

Consciousness Is Fundamental

Given the convictions of numerous highly reputable scientists, such as those quoted above, and, perhaps especially, given the reams of solid experimental evidence for nonmaterial consciousness, some of which I referenced above, it is safe to say that, despite scientific materialism's outsized influence, scientifically informed belief in nonmaterial consciousness is definitely alive and well.

Despite the widespread acceptance of the brain-as-supercomputer model, it does not hold up when presented with radical neuroplasticity and the presence of intelligence and consciousness. While many scientists and neuroscientists believe that consciousness emerges from the bioelectrical activity of millions of neurons simultaneously firing off in the brain, the theories that attempt to explain *how* consciousness can emerge solely from matter-energy interactions in the brain all fall far short of being testable. Panpsychism at least opens the door to the notion that consciousness may simply be a distinct force, just like gravity and electromagnetism, but panpsychism, too, is not testable.

On the other hand, "by the standards of any other area of science," the theory that nonmaterial, all-pervading consciousness exists completely independently of matter and energy is testable and has been successfully tested repeatedly in the remote-viewing experiments of the CIA's Stargate program and in the neuroscientific experiments using EEGs and galvanic skin response equipment conducted by Dr. Jacobo Grinberg-Zylberbaum, Dr. Fred H. Thaheld, Dr. Charles Tart, and Drs. Marilyn Schlitz and William Braud.

I feel very safe in saying that if it weren't for the bias of scientific materialism, nonmaterial consciousness would have long ago been accepted as a distinct reality independent of matter and energy.

Let's move on to exploring the nature of that consciousness and let the materialists wait for the computers to take over the world.

CHAPTER 3

The Superconscious

The experiments highlighted in the previous chapter demonstrating that thoughts in one person's mind can be perceived in another's mind, that the emotional states of one person can be felt by another, that even a person's physiological states, such as a startle reflex, can be simultaneously experienced by another, all suggest that we are connected with each other in ways that cannot be explained by scientific materialism's view that our body and brain are a closed system, that we are material, mental, emotional, and biological islands.

Instead, what these experiments imply is that *our* consciousness is connected to *everyone's* consciousness. Fundamental consciousness is *all-pervading, that is to say, it is everywhere, underlying everything, within every atom of creation, within every cell of our bodies, within every thought and emotion we experience.*

Many notable physicists go further than stating that consciousness is all-pervading. They present another, even more paradigm-changing aspect to the nature of consciousness. They believe that all-pervading consciousness is not a blind force like gravity; they believe that consciousness is also inherently *intelligent.*

> You will hardly find one among the profounder sort of scientific minds without a peculiar religious feeling of his own. But it is different from the religion of the naive man. His religious

feeling takes the form of a rapturous amazement at the harmony of natural law, which reveals an intelligence of such superiority that, compared with it, all the systematic thinking and acting of human beings is an utterly insignificant reflection.

—Albert Einstein, Nobel Prize-winner[1]

I have concluded that we are in a world made by rules created by an intelligence. To me it is clear that we exist in a plan which is governed by rules that were created, shaped by a universal intelligence and not by chance.

—Michio Kaku, string theorist[2]

As a man who has devoted his whole life to the most clear headed science, to the study of matter, I can tell you as a result of my research about atoms this much: There is no matter as such. All matter originates and exists only by virtue of a force which brings the particle of an atom to vibration and holds this most minute solar system of the atom together. We must assume behind this force the existence of a conscious and intelligent mind. This mind is the matrix of all matter.

—Max Planck, Nobel Prize-winner[3]

The stream of knowledge is heading toward a non-mechanical reality; the universe begins to look more like a great thought than like a great machine. Mind no longer appears to be an accidental intruder into the realm of matter, we ought rather hail it as the creator and governor of the realm of matter. Get over it, and accept the inarguable conclusion. The universe is immaterial—mental and spiritual.

—Sir James Jeans, physicist[4]

Einstein, Kaku, Planck, and Jeans are but a few prominent examples of physicists and scientists who believe that not just consciousness, but *intelligent* consciousness, is the foundation of all reality. The vision of such scientists creates a scientific bridge from the materialist's narrow biomechanical view of consciousness to a vastly more expanded conception: all of creation, including our own consciousness, arises from and is an expression of one underlying and intelligent *super*consciousness. In their vision not only does our own individual, intelligent consciousness *arise* from all-pervading intelligent superconsciousness; it gives us innate access to *superconscious awareness, superconscious feeling, and superconscious thought.*

Superconscious awareness is not simply *more* of the awareness with which we are familiar. It is a qualitatively different kind of awareness that transcends our usual sensory experience. People who have experienced superconscious awareness, such as those who have had peak experiences like the ones I shared in chapter 1, often say that never before have they felt so alive, so joy filled, so love filled, so safe, or so free as they did during their superconscious experience. Superconscious experiences are also often accompanied by a vastly expanded sense of self, of oneness, timelessness, of divinity and sacredness.

> I still saw the birds and everything around me but instead of standing looking at them, I'm them and they were me. I was also the sea and the sound of the sea and the grass and sky. Everything and I were the same, all one. I was filled, swamped, with happiness and Peace. . . .
> —Unnamed person in *Seeing the Invisible*[5]

> I have the impression, after a descent, of dropping all restraints— my heart is open and free, my head is clear . . . all the beauty of the world is within the mad rhythm of my blood.
> —Patrick Vallençant, extreme skier[6]

> Then . . . everywhere surrounding me was this bright, sparkling light, like sun on frosty snow, like a million diamonds, and there was no cornfield, no trees, no sky. The feeling was indescribable, but I have never experienced anything in the years that followed

that can compare with that glorious moment; it was blissful, uplifting, I felt open-mouthed in wonder.

—Unnamed person in *Seeing the Invisible*[7]

It was like I reached a place where clarity and intuition and effort and focus all came together to bring me to a higher level of consciousness. . . .

—Sam Drevo, extreme kayaker[8]

The Superconscious in Psychology

Although psychology in general, as we explored in the last chapter, is heavily influenced by scientific materialism, there is, as we find in physics, an influential core of psychologists who embrace the reality of an all-pervading superconsciousness and its implication of vast, largely untapped human potential.

One psychologist in particular, Abraham Maslow (1908–1970), through the many decades of his very influential career, did much to move psychology from a focus on only subconscious and conscious states of awareness to include greatly expanded superconscious states. His impact on psychology first began in the 1940s when he rebelled at what had become psychology's almost exclusive focus on exploring the material conditions, causes, and cures of the mentally *ill*—which included extreme and abnormal mental conditions, such as schizophrenia and sociopathy. He wryly observed that "the study of crippled, stunted, immature, and unhealthy specimens can yield only a cripple psychology and a cripple philosophy."[9]

To counterbalance what he saw as a "cripple psychology," Maslow began to study individuals who were mentally *healthy*. In addition to the mentally healthy he also studied the exceptional, such as Albert Einstein and Eleanor Roosevelt; those who had realized and creatively expressed their own unique capabilities; those who had become *self-actualized*, as he eventually defined it. His various studies led him to conclude that self-actualization was the apex of a natural progression of human development. He observed that self-actualization—realizing one's full and unique potential—was as much a human need as physical and emotional security or satisfying relationships.

> A musician must make music, an artist must paint, a poet must write, if he is to be ultimately at peace with himself. What a man can be, he must be. This tendency might be phrased as the desire to become more and more what one is, to become every-thing that one is capable of becoming.
>
> —Abraham Maslow[10]

Maslow's new approach to psychology, developed along with other collaborating psychologists, especially Carl Rogers (1902–1987), even-tually became known as *humanistic psychology*. Humanistic psychol-ogy has inspired thousands of self-help books aimed at helping people to self-actualize. In the 1960s it inspired what became known as the *human potential movement*, in which the importance of creative expression and personal fulfillment came to the fore in the popular mind. Pursuing self-actualization became for many an alternative to both mainstream psychol-ogy and organized religion.

Surprisingly, given the widespread acceptance and impact of humanistic psychology, by the 1960s Maslow had come to the conclusion that human-istic psychology was incomplete, that it could not explain all aspects of human experience—that self-actualization was not the pinnacle of human development. Maslow arrived at this conclusion because he had become deeply interested in peak experiences, such as the ones I shared in chapter 1 and above, which he observed are "rare, exciting, oceanic, deeply mov-ing, exhilarating, elevating experiences that generate an advanced form of perceiving reality, and are even mystic and magical in their effect upon the experimenter."[11]

Maslow's new insights led him, together with many other psychologists, including Ken Wilber, Stanislav Grof, and Roberto Assagioli, to help pi-oneer the school of *transpersonal psychology*. Transpersonal psychology studied our innate ability to *trans*cend "everyday" *personal* conscious awareness to experience the "mystic and magical."

In his book, *Toward a Psychology of Being*, Maslow identified common characteristics of the state of awareness of those who have had peak experiences and transpersonal awareness. These characteristics describe not only someone performing beyond their normal abilities, but, more significantly, having profoundly positive—often life-changing—perceptual or emotional experiences:

- loss of judgment to time and space
- the feeling of being one whole and harmonious self, free of dissociation or inner conflict
- the feeling of using all capacities and capabilities at their highest potential, or being "fully functioning"
- functioning effortlessly and easily without strain or struggle
- feeling completely responsible for perceptions and behavior
- using self-determination to become stronger, more single-minded, and fully volitional
- being without inhibition, fear, doubt, and self-criticism
- spontaneity, expressiveness, and naturally flowing behavior that is not constrained by conformity
- a free mind that is flexible and open to creative thoughts and ideas
- complete mindfulness of the present moment without influence of past or expected future experiences
- a physical feeling of warmth, along with a sensation of pleasant vibrations emanating from the heart area outward into the limbs.[12]

Peak experiences are often considered to be part of a broader phenomenon known as *flow*. The leading light regarding flow is Dr. Mihaly Csíkszentmihályi, Distinguished Professor of Psychology and Management at Claremont Graduate University and author of *Flow: The Psychology of Optimal Experience*. Dr. Csíkszentmihályi describes flow as "being completely involved in an activity for its own sake. The ego falls away. Time flies. Every action, movement, and thought follows inevitably from the previous one, like playing jazz. Your whole being is involved, and you're using your skills to the utmost."[13] The flow experience is known to occur not just in sports but in creative activities or at any time one is deeply immersed in any physical, emotional, or mental activity.

The characteristics of both peak experience and flow as described above are expressed in the somewhat dry and impersonal tone of observing psychologists. The actual experience is rather more moving. As I quoted in the introduction, Patsy Neal, women's basketball hall of famer, says one who has a peak experience in sports "touches a piece of heaven and becomes the recipient of power from an unknown source. The power goes beyond that which can be defined as physical or mental."[14] That unknown source is superconsciousness.

The concept of superconsciousness became central to transpersonal psychology.

Roberto Assagioli, in his book *Psychosynthesis*, writes about identifying procedures aimed at "the awakening, the releasing and the employment of the potent *superconscious* spiritual energies, which have a transforming and regenerating influence on the personality."[15]

Stanislav Grof divided awareness into two types: hylotropic and holotropic. Hylotropic awareness roughly equates to normal, everyday experience. Holotropic awareness, on the other hand, comes from activation of "deep . . . *superconscious* levels of the human psyche."[16]

Ken Wilbur, an early influence on transpersonal psychology, later went on to found a new psychological approach which he calls *integral psychology*, in which he champions a comprehensive approach to human development. He writes that ". . . the study of psychology ought ideally to be the study of . . . subconscious to self-conscious to *superconscious*. . . ."[17]

As superconsciousness is innate to all of us it can naturally express itself in everyone's experiences from intuitive hunches to peak experiences, but the fullest expression of superconscious experience is found among the saints, sages, mystics, and near-death experiencers. Their experiences are of a profounder sort.

Knowledge

One becomes wholly Mind, the One Mind of God, in which exists all-knowledge, all-power, and all-presence.

—Walter Russell (1871–1963),
sculptor, musician, author,
philosopher, and mystic[18]

It was instant and total knowing. I could think on several levels at once and communicate them simultaneously. You can't know something without knowing everything around it, what causes it, what sustains it. Knowledge dovetails in the spirit world, each piece fitting with other pieces. Every fact connected to it is seen instantly, in totality.

—RaNelle Wallace, near-death experiencer[19]

Joy

Then I simply remember I became more blissful, more rapturous, more ecstatic. I was just filling and filling with this light and love that was in the light. The dynamics of this light are not static at all. They are so dynamic and so much going on in there of love and joy and knowledge.

—Jayne Smith, near-death experiencer[20]

My head is bursting
with the joy of the unknown.
My heart is expanding a thousand fold.

—Rumi, Sufi mystic[21]

Love

Every part of my being was satisfied with an unconditional love beyond description. All questions were answered. An inner peace without striving or achieving was created and understood.

—Laurelynn Martin, near-death experiencer[22]

There is such tremendous LOVE, PEACE and JOY there that you can think of no other place you would rather be.

—Christian Andréason, near-death experiencer[23]

[In a vision I saw an angel,] in his hand a long spear of gold, and at the iron's point there seemed to be a little fire. He appeared to me to be thrusting it at times into my heart . . . and to leave me all on fire with a great love of God.

—St. Teresa of Avila[24]

Light

If therefore thine eye be single, thy whole body shall be full of light.

—Matthew 6:22

Like a nuclear explosion, the light pierced me. Every particle of me was shot through with blinding, brilliant light, and I had a feeling of transparency. My eyes still saw. I floated in this light, bathed in it, and the love that surrounded me and filled me was sweeter and finer than anything I had ever felt.

—RaNelle Wallace, near-death experiencer[25]

While these particular experiences may seem beyond us, think of them as pinnacles of possibility; pinnacles that we can climb using the wisdom of the saints; pinnacles that, even if we only climb partway, will still bestow experience far more positive, moving, and profound than our ordinary conscious awareness. *Any* amount of superconscious experience can be life-changing because such experience literally changes our brain—more on this later—and because the experience is so vivid, powerful, and wonderful that it will often make people want to reorient the entire focus of their lives.

The Science of Superconscious Awareness

There is a science to attaining superconscious awareness that we can use whether our intention is mystic experience or simply seeking more joy in our life. The science of attaining superconscious awareness is made up of practices that have been used over and over again by people of all ages and genders, in all walks of life, in all cultures and eras.

This rational application of the laws of unfolding consciousness acts exactly on the same principles that you see applied around you every day in other departments of science.

—Annie Besant, clairvoyant,
Theosophical Society president[26]

We must take up the study of the super-conscious state just as any other science.

—Swami Vivekananda, yoga master[27]

Repeatable results are what give credibility to scientific discovery. If one scientist gets the same result as another scientist by using the same experimental methodology, then the results of both scientists become more credible. If *hundreds* of scientists get the same results using the same methodology then the credibility rises to certainty. Consider, for a moment, that *thousands* of saints, sages, and mystics have for millennia achieved superconsciousness results using the same methodology.

Mystics have all employed the same timeless methods—learning to achieve one-pointed focus and perfect stillness—and, as a result, have consistently experienced superconscious states of awareness; they have as well perceived subtle realms and realities only discernable in out-of-body transcendent awareness.

When . . . [one] enters [the state], wherein his eyes, breath, and heart are quieted, another world comes into view.

—Paramahansa Yogananda, yoga master[28]

One-Pointed Focus

In the many examples and quotes I've shared of people who have had superconscious experience, whether peak, flow, mystic, or near-death experience, you will find the common theme of one-pointed focus.

One-pointed focus can be brought about by extreme need, as with Charlotte Hefflemire lifting the truck off her father, Lindbergh knowing that to fall asleep was to die, or any of numerous examples of athletes who put themselves in extreme danger.

[Y]ou feel free of all mind-body constraints, suddenly so free of them you don't perceive yourself as being free, but vigilant, a seeing eye, without judgment, history or emotion. It's that shudder out of time, the central moment in so many sports, that one often feels, and perhaps becomes addicted to, while doing something dangerous.

—Diane Ackerman, aviator[29]

Such one-pointed focus can come about simply by being mentally and, especially, emotionally immersed in a flow, such as happens to many people intent on creating or performing.

You are in an ecstatic state to such a point that you feel as though you almost don't exist. I have nothing to do with what is happening. I just sit there watching it in a state of awe and wonderment. And [the music] just flows out of itself.

—Dr. Mihaly Csíkszentmihályi
quoting a composer, author of
Flow: The Psychology of Optimal Experience[30]

You're not thinking about the past, you're thinking about now, right now. And that seems to initiate the joy.

—Ed Lucero, extreme kayaker[31]

One-pointed focus can come about because of the deliberate intention to accomplish or create something, such as the Mighty Atom's intense concentration before bending a horseshoe like a pretzel, or Brahms's depth of trancelike concentration that brought him entire symphonies, "clothed in the right forms, harmonies and orchestration."

The great composers, sculptors, painters, inventors and planners of all time were in such an ecstatic condition during their intensive creating hours that the million petty trivialities which short circuit the energy and waste the time of most men, never found an opportunity for even entering their consciousness.

—Walter Russell, sculptor, musician,
author, philosopher, and mystic[32]

One-pointed focus can come about through techniques and practices that are specifically designed to focus your mind. You find the principle of interior focus in various meditation techniques from various experiential spiritual traditions.

> I myself had my experience of Nirvana . . . it came first simply by . . . blotting out . . . all mental, emotional and other inner activities.
>
> —Sri Aurobindo, yoga master[33]

Stillness

Stillness also leads to superconscious experience. Unlike peak and flow experiences that happen when we are physically active or involved in the physical world, the determined practice of stillness—eyes closed, body relaxed, breath and heart rate slowed—can take us into deep superconscious awareness.

In a close study of the lives of saints, sages, and mystics you will find that they all had disciplined themselves to be able to remain profoundly still for hours, days—even weeks. Gautama Buddha is said to have sat beneath the Bodhi tree in determined meditation for forty-nine days. Jesus is said to have spent forty days in the desert in fasting and intense prayer. Accounts abound of Himalayan yogis, Zen masters, and Christian monks and nuns remaining locked in stillness for lengthy periods.

> Sit quietly, and listen for a voice that will say, "Be more silent." Die and be quiet.
>
> —Rumi, Sufi mystic[34]

> Be still and know that I am God.
>
> —Psalms 46:10

> Stillness is the altar of Spirit.
>
> —Paramahansa Yogananda, yoga master[35]

> Attain complete emptiness, Hold fast to stillness.
>
> —Lao Tzu, Tao Te Ching[36]

Stillness is the door that leads ultimately to the profound and transcendent experiences of the saints, sages, mystics, and near-death experiencers. In the case of the saints, sages, and mystics, complete stillness is achieved through discipline. In the case of near-death experiencers, complete stillness is achieved by accident.

Relaxed One-Pointed Focus and Stillness Combined

Practitioners of the science of superconscious awareness soon discover that one cannot achieve perfect physical stillness without achieving one-pointed focus, and vice versa. The two are inextricably linked.

> Not till your thoughts cease all their branching here and there, not till you abandon all thoughts of seeking for something, not till your mind is motionless as wood or stone, will you be on the right road to the Gate.
>
> —Huang Po, Zen master[37]

> Still the bubbling mind; herein lies freedom and bliss eternal.
>
> —Swami Sivananda, yoga master[38]

> To the mind that is still, the whole universe surrenders.
>
> —Lao Tzu, Tao Te Ching

> As long as a restless thought or a bodily motion remains, you cannot hear the Inner Voice, or see with the Inner Eye. In an inwardly and outwardly still body temple. . . . Real intuition and real vision will be awakened.
>
> —Paramahansa Yogananda, yoga master[39]

Used together, one-pointed focus and stillness—two of the core practices of meditation—can soon give even the beginner tastes of superconscious experience. With practice, we can tap into superconsciousness at will. After repeated experiences of superconsciousness achieved in one-pointed focus and stillness we can learn how to bring superconscious awareness into our everyday life. With determination, during periods of deep stillness and one-pointed focus, we can transcend awareness of the physical world altogether.

The Neuroscience of Superconscious Awareness
Stillness

Why the need for stillness? Spiritual teachers from all traditions say the purpose of such profound stillness is to withdraw our awareness from the continuous flood of information coming through our senses into the brain, because it is the sensory flood that drowns out our ability to perceive other, more subtle, but always present, realities, and that keeps us, therefore, in a conscious rather than superconscious state.

Neuroscientific studies confirm that deep states of stillness result in a pronounced shift in awareness away from the sensory input that usually accompanies our wakeful, conscious state. In the late 1990s, leading neuroscientists Andrew Newberg and his colleague Eugene d'Aquili (now deceased) studied the brains of Buddhist monks during meditation and of Christian nuns during intense prayer sessions.[40] They discovered that during their subjects' meditation or intense prayer sessions there was significantly decreased activity in *all* regions of the brain that process sensory information (Figure 1).

In other studies, Newberg and d'Aquili also saw, as a result of such deep stillness, a significantly decreased level of activity in the *orientation association area* (OAA), located near the top of the brain. In our normal waking state, nerves constantly send information to the OAA, from which we get a continuously updated mind's-eye view of our body's current position, orientation, sensations of temperature, points of contact with other objects, etc. In deep stillness, such nerves, normally stimulated by movement, stop sending new information to the OAA. When the nerves stop sending new information to the OAA because of the conscious practice of disciplined stillness, test subjects say that they became increasingly less aware of their bodies until many felt entirely bodiless.

When in stillness, and the flood of sensory information abates, we become less aware of our bodies. We are not left, however, with nothing of which to be aware. On the contrary, our awareness expands into

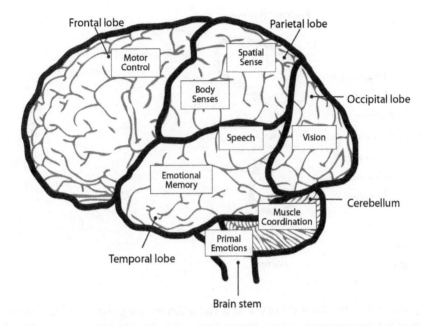

Frontal lobe

Parietal lobe

Motor Control

Spatial Sense

Body Senses

Occipital lobe

Speech

Vision

Emotional Memory

Cerebellum

Muscle Coordination

Primal Emotions

Temporal lobe

Brain stem

Figure 1: The cerebellum, the occipital, parietal, and temporal lobes, parts of the frontal lobe, and the brain stem become less and less active during meditation. These areas of the brain are associated with input from the senses and the body and are involved in motor control, spatial sense, speech, and object recognition.

superconscious feeling, into superconscious clarity and intuition, into superconscious awareness itself. We, in our essence, are without physical bodies or boundaries.

One-Pointed Focus

One-pointed focus during meditation brings mental stillness, and mental stillness allows you to turn your attention inward toward superconsciousness. While the areas of the brain that process sensory input and coordinate movement become *less and less* active during meditation, the areas associated with attention, creativity, and the finer emotions, such as love and compassion, become *more and more* active. These areas are located in the frontal lobe of the brain, including, especially, the prefrontal cortex,

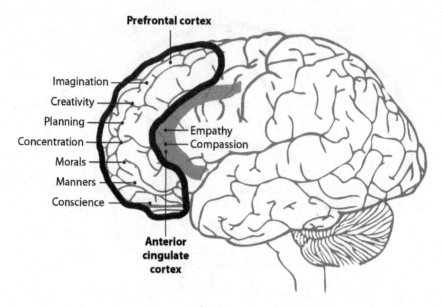

Figure 2: The prefrontal cortex and the anterior cingulate cortex become activated during meditation. These areas of the brain are associated with attention, creativity, and the finer emotions, such as love and compassion.

which lights up on the fMRI computer screen when we become more one-pointed in our focus.

The frontal lobe, especially the prefrontal cortex, is also associated with our higher abilities: visualization, creativity, appreciation of art and music, problem solving, planning, conscience, manners, and morals. Activation of our higher abilities lights up the prefrontal cortex. The converse is also true: when we activate the prefrontal cortex through meditation, our higher abilities are awakened as well. It is also significant that the frontal lobe includes the specific areas of the limbic system—the anterior cingulate cortex—that are activated by feelings of compassion and empathy (Figure 2).

More recent studies conducted by Newberg have revealed an even more pronounced state when deep stillness and profound one-pointed focus occur—withdrawal not only from body and sensory input but also from the brain altogether. In his 2017 book, *How Enlightenment Changes Your Brain*, he shares several studies he conducted where even the usual meditation-induced increased activity in the prefrontal cortex diminished to the point that the entire brain became inactive. From one study, in which subjects used certain *pranayama* (breathing) techniques to achieve deep physical stillness and mental focus, Newberg concludes:

> In our study, we initially saw increases in the frontal regions, but they were followed by significant decreases as the intensity of the meditation practice increased. This is consistent with our theory of what occurs in the brain when a person experiences a profound spiritual or mystical state.
>
> —Andrew Newberg, MD, author of
> *How God Changes Your Brain*[41]

The Neuroscience of Superconsciousness Bypasses the Brain

What we learn from Newberg's studies, and what is confirmed by the saints and sages, is that our brain filters out or blocks our innate superconscious awareness. What comes through the brain filter is, at its most, conscious awareness and, at its least, subconscious awareness. When we die, the saints, sages, and near-death experiencers tell us that we will immediately and automatically begin to be superconsciously aware of heavenly realms, heavenly feelings, and heavenly knowledge, because at death we become completely free of the neural limitations of our physical brain.

> The part of my brain that was responsible for creating the world I lived and moved in and for taking the raw data that came in through my senses and fashioning it into a meaningful universe: that part of my brain was down, and out. And yet despite all of this, I had been alive, and aware, truly aware, in a universe characterized above all by love, consciousness, and reality. There was, for me, simply no arguing this fact. I knew it so completely that I ached.
>
> —Eben Alexander, neurosurgeon, near-death
> experiencer, and author of *Proof of Heaven:*
> *A Neurosurgeon's Journey into the Afterlife*[42]

I was more clear then, than now, when I'm stuck back in the brain again.

>—Dr. Bruce Greyson, author of *The Handbook*
>*of Near-Death Experiences*, paraphrasing numerous
>people who have had near-death experiences[43]

I often say that we are conscious in spite of our brain, not because of it.[44] It's not increased activity in any brain region that leads to such extraordinary phenomenal experiences. It's actually the brain turning off.[45]

>—Eben Alexander, neurosurgeon, near-death
>experiencer, and author of *Proof of Heaven:*
>*A Neurosurgeon's Journey into the Afterlife*

One often hears references to "altered states of consciousness." Implied in the expression is a suggestion that higher states of awareness are anomalies. Actually, there is only one state of consciousness: superconsciousness. The conscious and subconscious minds are our "altered states," representing as they do the downward filtering of superconsciousness through the brain. [T]he brain and nervous system limit consciousness like a reducing valve limits the flow of water. At death, this reducing-valve function ceases and consciousness is then free to expand. *Superconsciousness takes human awareness outside the brain* [italics mine].

>—Swami Kriyananda, yoga master[46]

We Can Rewire Our Brains for Superconscious Awareness

We do not need to die to experience superconscious awareness, as you might think after reading the quotations above. The science of superconscious awareness, which can be practiced by everyone, is, in large measure, the science of rewiring our brain to enable us to bypass our brain's filters. We can rewire the brain to enable us to intentionally bypass the usual flood of sensory information that keeps us preoccupied with the body and the world around us. We can rewire our brain to support subtler perception, intuitive thinking, and higher feeling.

In Part 3 I will offer numerous practices that will help you rewire your brain for greater and greater superconscious awareness. Of those I will offer, the most effective is meditation. Many neuroscientific studies of meditation are corroborating that regular meditation makes significant physiological changes in the brain.

> It is fascinating to see the brain's plasticity and that, by practic-
> ing meditation, we can play an active role in changing the brain
> and can increase our well-being and quality of life.
> —Dr. Britta Hölzel, first author of the groundbreaking
> Harvard study on meditation and brain change[47]

Meditation has been proven to make lasting structural changes in your brain that support our quality of life: increasing attention;[48] enabling positive emotion and empathy;[49] reducing fear and anxiety;[50] improving learning and memory;[51] overcoming childhood maltreatment;[52] altering behavior and mood.[53]

I could go on—and on—but I don't want to drown you in the hundreds of such studies available to us today.

Superconscious Awareness Is a Natural Expansion of Your Conscious Awareness

Superconscious awareness is not all or nothing. We grow gradually *more* superconsciously aware as we rewire our brain. Superconsciousness is the *natural expansion* of our own and more familiar conscious awareness, just as conscious awareness is the natural expansion of subconscious awareness.

> Because these three states—the unconscious, conscious and
> superconscious states—belong to one and the same mind . . .
> there are not three minds in one man, but one state of it devel-
> ops into the others.
> —Swami Vivekananda, yoga master[54]

We can, and often do, experience *degrees* of superconscious awareness: points on a continuum between being fully conscious and being fully superconscious.

Our all-knowing superconscious can be experienced first as subtle, often unrecognized, intuitive flashes, such as hunches; our love-filled superconscious can be experienced first as moments of compassion and kindness; our joy-filled superconscious can be experienced first as quiet surges of happiness that have nothing to do with anything that is happening in our world.

If you regularly practice the science of superconscious awareness, particularly meditation, you will begin to experience superconscious awareness more often—and with the increased awareness you will find that you are awakening your own highest potentials.

Clarity and deep feeling: Greater superconscious awareness is accompanied by heightened mental acuity, as well as by deep and often sacred feeling, experiences that are more empowering and fulfilling than the thoughts and feelings we experience in either subconscious or conscious awareness. Superconscious feeling is always positive. The thoughts we have in superconscious awareness are insightful, creative, and expansive.

High Energy: Greater superconscious awareness and higher energy go hand in hand. Mystics often do not feel the need for sleep and can go days without it. Strong men like the Mighty Atom are able to draw tremendous strength and energy through their bodies when their minds and feelings are in uplifted superconscious states. Creative concentration that draws superconscious awareness can bring inspiration and energy that sustain mind, feeling, and body far beyond what the body's chemical reserves of energy should provide.

Flow: Superconscious experience is something that catches us up and carries us along and that we do not and cannot fully control. Because both the subconscious and the superconscious are beyond our usual conscious control, you will sometimes see superconscious awareness defined by psychologists as the "higher subconscious." Subconscious awareness, however, is nothing like superconscious awareness. For example, entering into subconscious sleep is like slowly wading into a warm and slowly moving current that pulls you, almost unawares, beneath the surface of conscious awareness into a fragmented and less aware experience. Entering into superconscious awareness, on the other hand, is like diving into an invigorating and powerful river, in which you are carried out of narrow canyons of conscious feeling, thought, and awareness into vast mental and emotional seas of experience.

We Are Innately Superconscious

From foundations in physics, psychology's breakthrough studies of the phenomena of peak and flow experiences, neuroscientific support for the science of meditation and superconscious awareness, moving recountings by near-death experiencers, and from the testimony of the saints, sages, and mystics, we see revealed the natural and increasingly expansive continuum of experience that is superconsciousness. The continuum of superconscious experience ranges from a hunch that proves true, to peak and flow experiences that are "rare, exciting, oceanic, deeply moving, exhilarating, and elevating," to life-changing feelings of love, peace, and joy, visions of light, and transcendent awareness of heavenly realms.

We are so much more than we know.

CHAPTER 4

The Superconscious,
Self, and God

We are, indeed, much more than we know. Paraphrasing the recently deceased Ram Dass, we aren't human beings having superconscious experiences, we are superconscious beings having human experiences. Or as Anthon St. Maarten somewhat playfully puts it: "You are a Deity in jeans and a t-shirt, and within you dwells the infinite wisdom of the ages and the sacred creative force of All that is, will be and ever was."[1]

In the experiential spiritual traditions of the world—the prime hallmark of which is some form of meditation or deep prayer practice—you will find two core teachings:

- We are capable of superconscious awareness because we are innately superconscious. We are able to reason and discriminate because we are innately intelligent. We can transcend the physical body because we are innately formless and immortal. We are capable of astonishing creativity because we are innately powerful and free-willed. We can experience profound love and joy because we are created from them.

- We have been, are, and always will be One with God, Who created us "in His image." We can fully be aware of our true potential—the full expression of our high qualities and abilities—only when we realize that Oneness. We can fully realize our Oneness only through dynamically expressing our true potential.

The relationship between soul and God was described by Paramahansa Yogananda in this way: "The Creative Spiritual Consciousness abides within the soul of man and he may do with it whatever he wishes, for he has been created in the image of God with unlimited powers. He is the master of his own destiny, if he will but accept and use that God-given power. The only limitation on man is imposed by himself, through his thoughts. The statement in Proverbs, 'As the man thinketh in his heart, so is he,' is a truth which has revolutionized and transformed the lives of thousands."[2]

> My presence fills the room. And now I feel my presence in every room in the hospital. Even the tiniest space in the hospital is filled with this presence that is me. I sense myself beyond the hospital, above the city, even encompassing Earth. I am melting into the universe.
>
> —Josiane Antonette, near-death experiencer[3]

> That light is the very essence, the heart and soul, the all-consuming consummation of ecstatic ecstasy. It is a million suns of compressed love dissolving everything unto itself, annihilating thought and cell, vaporizing humanness and history, into the one great brilliance of all that is and all that ever was and all that ever will be. You know it's God. No one has to tell you. You know.
>
> —P. M. H. Atwater, near-death researcher and experiencer[4]

In Western esoteric descriptions, the attributes of our purest essence as described above—superconscious, intelligent, formless, eternal, powerful, free-willed, and capable of transcendent feeling—are ascribed to the Soul. In Eastern descriptions they are ascribed to the Self.

Though both terms, *Soul* and *Self,* are used interchangeably, I prefer to use *Self* rather than *Soul* because when most people think of their Soul they are likely thinking of it as something passive and that plays no significant part in their life. They might think of their Soul as if it were a stock certificate in a safe deposit box that will at some point have great value or as if it were an especially well-behaved alter-ego that only emerges on special occasions.

The term *Self*, on the other hand, suggests greater immediacy. The Self is *you*. You are your *Self*. There is not and cannot be any separation between you and Self. All that we can do—be consciously aware, reason and discriminate, accomplish tasks we set out to do, and respond emotionally—arise *directly* from the eternal abilities of our Self.

More importantly, all the things we can do *now* are only the lower octaves of our true potentials. We can raise ourselves through meditation and other practices into higher octaves: conscious awareness can become superconsciousness; reason and discrimination can grow into intuitive wisdom; the ability to accomplish tasks can expand into creative power; emotional response can develop into profound feelings of love, peace, and joy.

> We are the most beautiful creations. The human soul, the human matrix that we all make together is absolutely fantastic, elegant, exotic, everything.
>
> —Mellen-Thomas Benedict, near-death experiencer[5]

> The Self in you is the same as the Self Universal. Whatever powers are manifested throughout the world, those powers exist in germ, in latency, in you. . . .
>
> —Annie Besant, clairvoyant,
> Theosophical Society president[6]

> When we raise ourselves through meditation to what unites us with the spirit, we quicken something within us that is eternal and unlimited by birth and death. Once we have experienced this eternal part in us, we can no longer doubt its existence.
>
> —Rudolf Steiner, mystic and founder of Anthroposophy[7]

> And the glory which thou gavest me I have given them; that they may be one, even as we are one.
>
> —St. John (17:22), recording the words of Jesus

I began to see during my near-death experience that everything that is, is the Self, literally, your Self, my Self. Everything is the great Self.

—Mellen-Thomas Benedict, near-death experiencer[8]

This Self is not born, nor does it perish. Self-existent, it continues its existence forever. It is birthless, eternal, changeless, and ever the same.

—Krishna speaking to Arjuna, Bhagavad Gita 2:20[9]

[T]he Self is Everything-ness, the All in which everything is known and obvious in its perfect expression of its own essence. One is total and complete, beyond all identities, gender, or even humanness itself. One need never again fear suffering and death.

—David R. Hawkins, author of *Power vs. Force*[10]

Jesus answered them, Is it not written in your law, I said, Ye are gods?

—John 10:34

In our efforts to become more superconsciously aware, we may begin to experience God's conscious response to us in superconscious *feeling*.

Ever-new Joy is God. He is inexhaustible; as you continue your meditations during the years, He will beguile you with an infinite ingenuity. [Those] who have found the way to God never dream of exchanging Him for any other happiness. . . .

—Sri Yukteswar, yoga master[11]

Along with the consciousness of the cosmos . . . is added a state of moral exaltation, an indescribable feeling of elevation, elation, and joyousness, and a quickening of the moral sense, which is fully as striking and more important both to the individual and to the race than is the enhanced intellectual power. With these

come, what may be called a sense of immortality, a consciousness of eternal life, not a conviction that he shall have this, but
the consciousness that he has it already.

　　　　　　　　　　　—Richard Maurice Bucke, psychologist and
　　　　　　　　　　　　　friend and admirer of Walt Whitman[12]

This new experience bestows new enlightenment which places
the experiencer on a new plane of existence. There is an indescribable feeling of elation and indescribable joy and Bliss. He
experiences a sense of universality, a Consciousness of Eternal
Life. It is not a mere conviction. He actually feels it.

　　　　　　　　　　　　　　　—Swami Sivananda, yoga master[13]

　　The ever-new Joy of God ramifies into endless experiences of profound
love, peace, calmness, and many other felt experiences described through
the ages by the saints, sages, and mystics. A purely intellectual defini-
tion or conception of God can be inspiring, guiding, and motivating but
is only truly meaningful when God comes alive in our direct experience.
Ultimately God must be *felt* to be real to us.

The Western Paradox of God and the Self

The full experience of our superconscious Self brings us the full experience of superconscious God: the full experience of superconscious God
brings us the full experience of our superconscious Self. This is a mental
paradox to most westerners. With few exceptions Western thinking follows
the laws of Western logic: something is *either* one thing *or* another—*either/
or*—not both. The theological doctrines of Western religions—Christianity
especially—have been shaped over the centuries by this either/or Western
logic and, to avoid a Western logical paradox, treat the soul as being ever
separate from God, a high but eternally lesser creation. The highest aspira-
tion orthodox Christianity offers us is eternal life in a heaven full of abundance and love—but forever separate from God.

　　This logic satisfies the mind of a theologian but not the heart of a mystic.
And, indeed, the teachings of Christian mystics suggest much more.

Oh, wonder of wonders, when I think of the union the soul has with God! He makes the enraptured soul to flee out of herself, for she is no more satisfied with anything that can be named. The spring of Divine Love flows out of the soul and draws her out of herself into the unnamed Being, into her first source, which is God alone.

—Meister Eckhart, Christian mystic[14]

Eastern religions, on the other hand, were not shaped by Western logic. The teachings of India include the logic-defying dictum: "atman is Brahman"—the atman (Self) is Brahman (God). Many experiential traditions embrace the seeming contradiction that all beings are One in God:

The one who sees, and the one who hears, is not this eye or ear, but the one who is this consciousness. This One appears in every mind. This One is common to all sentient beings, and is God.

—Sokei-an , Zen master[15]

I always thought that I was me—but no, I was You and never knew it.

—Rumi, Sufi mystic [16]

Our Superconscious Potential

It is in superconscious awareness that we experience both the true potentials of our Self and the transcendent reality of God. In the full realization of the superconscious, we realize that we, too, are the ever-existing, ever-conscious, ever-new Joy that is God. Our Self *is* one with God; a unique expression of God with all His attributes.

We are so much more than we know.

PART TWO

ONE FOOT IN HEAVEN, ONE FOOT ON EARTH

CHAPTER 5

We Have Two Bodies

We always have one foot in the physical world and one foot in the heavens. What we experience, in every moment, is a mixture of the familiar physical world and hidden-to-our-senses subtle realities.

The experiential spiritual teachings of the world—from yoga to Sufism, from mystical Christianity to Zen Buddhism, from the Kabbalah to modern mysticism—tell us that *most* of what we routinely experience, right now and in every moment, does not actually exist in the physical world. Life force, emotions, thoughts and memories, personality and character, subtly coexist with and interpenetrate the physical body. These subtle aspects of ourselves are just as real, just as present, just as immediate, as body and brain—they just aren't physical.

If this concept is new to you, you may be surprised by how much this seemingly "out there" idea is actually supported by science:

> We must liberate man from the cosmos created by the genius of physicists and astronomers, that cosmos in which, since the Renaissance, he has been imprisoned. We now know that we . . . extend outside the physical continuum. . . . In time, as well as in space, the individual stretches out beyond the frontiers of his body. . . . He also belongs to another world.
>
> —Dr. Alexis Carrel, Nobel Prize-winner in medicine[1]

[We are] rather like a beautiful, exotic flower, flickering in and out of many dimensions simultaneously. That would constitute our quantum self, created from the entanglements of past experiences, the memory of all we have suffered and celebrated, the totality of our anxieties and fears, our hopes and dreams.

—Mae-Wan Ho,
geneticist and quantum biologist[2]

[T]he only acceptable point of view appears to be the one that recognizes both sides of reality—the quantitative and the qualitative, the physical and the psychical—as compatible with each other, and can embrace them simultaneously.

—Wolfgang Pauli, Nobel Prize-winner[3]

Nonlocality

Scientific support for the existence of subtle, nonmaterial aspects of reality comes to us largely from the fields of quantum physics and string theory and is expressed in one of their most central concepts—*nonlocality*.

Nonlocality is an awkward sounding word but it joins other more familiar words used to describe aspects of reality that are unlike the physical world: infinite (non-finite), boundless (non-bounded), immeasurable (non-measureable), etc. Just as a reality that is infinite is called infinity, a reality in which things behave nonlocally can be called *nonlocality*.

M-theory, the most accepted discipline within string theory, posits that nonlocality is a vast two-dimensional realm made up solely of super high-frequency energy, divided into layer-like zones they call *branes*. The energy in each ascending brane-layer vibrates at an increasingly higher frequency range than the brane below. M-theorists refer to this vast multi-braned realm of pure energy as the *bulk*—as in the "bulk of reality"—because it is theorized to be so vast that essentially *unlimited* numbers of physical universes, similar to our own physical universe, can exist within it like bubbles in a shoreless ocean.

M-theory, to say the least, is mind-openingly expansive.

The physical universe has *local* laws and nonlocality has *nonlocal* laws. An example of a local physical law: a magnetic field rapidly weakens the farther it is from its magnetic source, which means that the strength of a magnetic field is *affected by distance*. An example of a contrasting nonlocal law: either of two nonlocal entangled particles can communicate with the other instantaneously, no matter how far apart they are physically, which means that entanglement is *not affected by distance*.

The reason nonlocal events are not affected by distance is that in two-dimensional nonlocality *there is no space* and therefore *there is no distance*. As counterintuitive as this concept may seem—because two-dimensional nonlocality is actually *one undivided whole*—there is no distance between any part of the whole and any other part of the whole.

There is not only no distance in nonlocality, there is no distance *between* nonlocality and any point in the physical universe because non-locality *interpenetrates our physical universe everywhere*. Although nonlocality sounds like it must be somewhere else, it's not—it's *all* right here—interpenetratingly present.

Hard to grasp, I know.

Our senses tell us there are three dimensions; a two-dimensional space-less reality just confounds what our senses tell us. Even though, however, our physical senses do not perceive the nonlocal interpenetrating pure-energy reality, nonetheless we are unknowingly and continuously using subtler means to perceive nonlocal reality.

The Holographic Principle

M-theory further posits that our three-dimensional universe is a *holographic projection* that is being projected from a *hologram* that exists in two-dimensional nonlocality. M-theorists believe that the *information* that creates our three-dimensional physical universe is not present in the physical universe, but exists instead in nonlocality as two-dimensional holographic blueprints or templates.

If we put M-theory's holographic universe concept together with the concept that the fundamental consciousness out of which everything is made is *inherently intelligent,* as we explored in chapter 3, then we can make the mental leap that the holographic information that exists in non-locality is an expression of that inherent intelligence: an intelligently organized holographic energy template exists in nonlocality and continuously projects our universe. This concept matches the testimony of saints, sages, and near-death experiencers:

> In a word, absolutely everything in nature, from the smallest to the greatest, is a correspondence. The reason correspondences occur is that the natural world, including everything in it, arises and is sustained from the spiritual world.
> —Emanuel Swedenborg, Christian mystic[4]

> Everything was created of spirit matter before it was created physically—solar systems, suns, moons, stars, planets, life upon the planets, mountains, rivers, seas, etc. This Earth is only a shadow of the beauty and glory of its spirit creation.
> —Betty J. Eadie, near-death experiencer[5]

The Heavens

There are close parallels between M-theory's structure of nonlocality—a vast realm of high-frequency pure energy, a realm composed of multiple brane-layers of increasingly higher frequency energy—and the structure that we find in all religions of a vast, luminous heavenly realm, composed of multiple layers of increasingly greater wisdom and awareness.

In the Christian tradition we find many biblical references to an ascending order of heavens:

> I know a man in Christ who fourteen years ago was caught up to the third heaven. Whether it was in the body or out of the body I do not know.
> —2 Cor. 12:2-4

But who is able to build a temple for him, since the heavens, even the highest heavens, cannot contain him?

—2 Chron. 2:6

In Judaism there is a long tradition of mysticism contained in the teachings of the Kabbalah. The Kabbalah describes ten subtle angelic realms existing within ten emanations of Light to form a continuous chain of higher realms. Each emanation of light is described as being progressively more refined, higher, and more subtle than the one before.

One of the highest holy days of the Muslim calendar, *Lailat al Mi'raj*, celebrates Mohammed's journey through seven heavens, as described in the *Hadith*. Mohammed was taken, while his body slept, through seven increasingly more exalted levels of heaven, each with its own qualities and purpose.

Buddhist teachings, including Zen and Tibetan Buddhism, similarly include a hierarchy of heavens. Some traditions have ten heavens through which souls move between incarnations as they work out their karma. Hinduism's heavenly descriptions contain a hierarchy of seven heavens or *lokas*, each more subtle than the preceding, culminating in *Satya Loka*, the highest heaven.

The reality of the heavens has been experientially confirmed by saints, sages, and near-death experiencers:

> There are many different Heavens and Realms of Heaven. They are stacked one atop the other like pancakes and scattered all throughout God's super Universe. Everything is regulated by vibration, current and frequency. . . .
>
> —Christian Andréason, near-death experiencer[6]

> The higher realms are a world of inexpressible beauty. They are realms of endless possibilities for creativity and full realization of self; and they are where the love of God is like the air we breathe.
>
> —Nora Spurgin,
> near-death researcher and experiencer[7]

[Heaven] is filled with some sort of beautiful light . . . people . . . flowers . . . angels. . . . All is filled with some indescribable joy. Heaven . . . has a brilliant light which does not leave it.

—Vicka Ivanković-Mijatovic, one of
the six children who experienced the
Visions of Mary in Medjugorje, Bosnia Herzegovina[8]

The [heavenly] astral kingdom is a realm of rainbow-hued light. Astral land, seas, skies, gardens, beings, the manifestation of day and night—all are made of variegated vibrations of light. Oceans heave with opalescent azure, green, silver, gold, red, yellow, and aquamarine. Diamond-bright waves dance in a perpetual rhythm of beauty.

—Paramahansa Yogananda, yoga master[9]

Our Physical Bodies, Too, Are Holographic Projections

M-theory's holographic principle suggests that not only is the physical universe a holographic projection, so, too, are each of our *physical bodies*—and that all the necessary information to create and sustain our bodies, what we might call our *personal hologram*, exists nonlocally.

The blueprints of everything in the physical universe have been astrally conceived—all the forms and forces in nature, *including the complex human body* [italics added], have been first produced in that realm where God's causal ideations are made visible in forms of heavenly light and vibratory energy.

—Paramahansa Yogananda, yoga master[10]

You may recognize another parallel between scientific theory and experiential spiritual teachings: M-theory's concept of a personal hologram made of pure energy is mirrored by the concept in many experiential spiritual traditions of a luminous energy body variously called our astral, light, subtle, or spirit body. Your personal hologram and your energy body are one and the same—the former implied by M-theory, the latter testified to by saints and sages.

Your interpenetrating energy body is your one foot in heaven.

The Energy Body and the Physical Body Are Entangled, Interpenetrating, and (Nearly) Identical

The astral body is an exact counterpart of the last physical form. Astral beings retain the same appearance which they possessed in youth in their previous earthly sojourn. . . .

—Sri Yukteswar, yoga master[11]

An organic whole is an *entangled* whole, where part and whole, [nonlocal] and local are so thoroughly implicated as to be indistinguishable, and where each part is as much in control as it is sensitive and responsive.

—Mae-Wan Ho, geneticist and quantum biologist[12]

Almost all people who arrive [in heaven] from this world are as astonished as they can be to find that they are alive and that they are just as human as ever.

—Emanuel Swedenborg, Christian mystic[13]

The Energy Body Interpenetrates the Physical Body

As an "exact counterpart" of the physical body our energy body mirrors the physical body not just in outer shape but also in inner structure. This casts a very different and highly significant light on the *cause* of certain kinds of neural activity in the physical brain.

For decades now, using neuroimaging techniques such as fMRI, neuroscientists have been able to demonstrate consistently that specific areas in our physical brain electrochemically activate, or fire, in concert with specific *physical* actions such as muscle movement and sensory perception. It has also been consistently demonstrated that specific areas of the physical brain electrochemically activate in concert with specific *nonphysical* actions such as thought, memory, and emotion.

Consistent brain activation in concert with nonphysical actions has led materialists to assume that our thoughts, memories, and emotions must therefore *originate* in the physical brain. Materialists explain thought, memory, and emotion as the result of computerlike brain processing. Computerlike brain processing, however, as I have commented earlier, is currently no more than a circle in a neuroscientist's diagram in which is written, "magic happens here," or as neuroscientists might prefer, "processing happens here." Scientists, however, have yet to demonstrate how any of that magical processing actually happens.

Put aside the materialists' speculative assumption that computerlike brain processing will be validated some day in the future, and what we are left with is *ample* neuroscientific proof for the correlation of brain activation with specific nonphysical actions of thought, memory, and emotion, but *no* neuroscientific proof for any unconscious computerlike processing that could *create* those thoughts, memories, and emotions. While this lack of proof is a big problem for materialists, it is *exactly* what we would expect to see if our nonmaterial thoughts, memories, and emotions originate nonlocally in our energy brain.

The entangled interpenetration of our local physical brain and our nonlocal energy brain results in a seamless holism between the local and the nonlocal brain. In this seamless local/nonlocal holism each brain has unique functions: the local brain is involved in physical functions, such as the sensory process and voluntary and involuntary control of the body; the nonlocal brain is involved in nonphysical functions of thought, memory, and emotion. Despite the separation of functions, however, an activation in one brain can and often does stimulate an activation in the other brain.

Our Cells Are Intelligently Maintained by Our Nonlocal Hologram

Another implication of our simultaneous local and nonlocal existence is that our local physical body, the holographic projection, is being continuously created, sustained, and coordinated by our intelligently guided nonlocal energy body, the hologram itself. This notion fills a giant hole in the fields of genetics, biology, and medicine, a hole that was left when the role of DNA had to be extensively reconsidered as a result of the Human Genome Project. Repeating a quote you have already read:

> When the human genome was sequenced, some scientists were saying, "That's the end. We're going to understand every disease. We're going to understand every behavior." And it turns out, we didn't, because the sequence of the DNA isn't enough to explain behavior. It isn't enough to explain diseases.
>
> —Denise Chow, "Why Your DNA
> May Not Be Your Destiny"[14]

Although we explored this concept briefly in chapter 2, it is worthwhile now to take a deeper look at the implications of DNA's far smaller than expected role in our physical functioning.

The average adult body has approximately fifty trillion cells. Each cell generates approximately fifty thousand biochemical events *per second*. This means that there are twenty-five quadrillion biochemical events taking place in your body *each and every second*. If the brain alone were responsible for coordinating all those biochemical events, each of our approximately one hundred billion neurons would have to be responsible for millions to billions of biochemical events per second. It would be like trying to run the entire New York Stock Exchange with a single personal computer.

Our nervous system's limited neural capacity allows it to provide macro-control but not micro-control over our life processes. The brain can send signals through the nerves or release neuropeptides into the bloodstream that *influence* macro life processes such as switching on or off digestive processes and increasing or decreasing circulation, but that limited number of nerve signals or neuropeptides cannot possibly micro-control the thousands of life processes that occur every second inside trillions of cells.

The brain and nervous system's limited macro-only level of control over life processes was not previously considered to be an issue because it had been long believed that the astonishing complexity of micro-processes occurring within cells was coordinated by biological programming hardwired into each cell's DNA. It was also long thought that this hard-wired programming in our DNA could handle every possible response the cell would ever need for its internal functioning and for its external contributions to the functions of the body, such as the production of hormones, digestive enzymes, or neuropeptides.

Now we know, from the Human Genome Project, that there is, in fact, no hardwired micro-level life processes programming embedded in our DNA. Instead, it appears that our DNA double helixes are simply very long strands of connected protein templates; nowhere in our DNA to be found are coded instructions for *when* our cells should make any of those proteins. DNA protein templates are like individual blueprints for constructing all the millions of individual parts needed to make a skyscraper, but our DNA does not contain instructions for how to put the parts together to build the skyscraper, when to make which parts, or what to do when the skyscraper doesn't function properly.

The relatively new discipline of epigenetics has thrown geneticists yet another big curve. It was long believed that our DNA, which contains both active and inactive protein templates, was fixed at birth: if a protein template was inactive at birth, it would remain inactive all our life. Today we know that protein templates for specific proteins are routinely deactivated and activated in response to environmental, physical, mental, or emotional conditions. Identical twins, born with the same sets of activated and deactivated protein templates, can end their lives with two very different sets of activated and deactivated protein templates depending on how they have lived and thought and on the emotions they have experienced.

We come then to the currently most perplexing question in all of genetics: If there are no hardwired biological instructions embedded in our DNA to tell our cells which proteins to produce at any given moment, how do our cells produce the correct proteins for every need at the hundreds-of-thousands-per-hour pace at which a typical cell makes proteins? And how does our cell know which DNA protein templates to activate and which ones to deactivate?

Obviously bazillions of precisely the right proteins *are* continuously produced by the body's cells, with a nearly flawless synchronization in perfect and dynamic response to whatever we are demanding of our body at the moment, from running to meditating, from eating to sleeping. Such coordination is far beyond what a single brain could ever manage, nor has our DNA the programming to do so. The existence of such coordination instead suggests the influence of intelligence of a very high order.

> A subtle spiritual mechanism is hidden just behind the bodily structure.
>
> —Sri Yukteswar, yoga master[15]

The subtle spiritual mechanism that is hidden behind the bodily structure is our innately intelligent energy body, or, if you prefer, our nonlocal personal hologram.

As we go through our day, our physical brain causes the neurons of our voluntary and involuntary nervous systems to initiate and coordinate macro life processes that enable us to eat, walk, talk, exercise manual dexterity, etc. Simultaneously, our hidden and intelligent energy body exerts a vastly more minute control over the micro life processes within our trillions of cells. This micro life process control and coordination enable the body to digest food; distribute oxygen and glucose to every cell; eliminate toxins, dead cells, and indigestible food; combat harmful viruses and bacteria; grow new cells; and heal damaged tissues.

The body's amazing coordination and synchronization of micro life processes to support macro life processes is not a wonder of *nature*—it is a wonder of *Intelligence*—the innate intelligence of our energy body.

Life after Death

When we die, our awareness automatically becomes centered in our energy body, which makes us become aware of the heavens—just as many saints, sages, and near-death experiencers have described. We do not really die; we simply no longer have a physical body. We, in our superconscious essence, live on in our look-alike energy body.

> Never before had I considered that there might be such things as coexistent realities. Never had I imagined that there might

be concurrent realms. I realized that in life, death is merely the other side of a threshold over which I could not "normally" see. So, too, in death, life and the land of the "living" were on the other side of a very thin veil.

—Lynnclaire Dennis, near-death experiencer[16]

Using radio as an analogy, [death] is comparable to having lived all your life at a certain radio frequency when all of a sudden someone or something comes along and flips the dial. You shift frequencies in dying. You switch over to life on another wavelength. You don't die when you die. You shift your consciousness and speed of vibration. That's all death is . . . a shift.

—P. M. H. Atwater, near-death
· researcher and experiencer[17]

What we consider the here and now, this world, it is actually just the material level that is comprehensible [to the senses]. The beyond is an infinite reality that is much bigger. Which this world is rooted in. In this way, our lives in this plane of existence are encompassed, surrounded, by the afterworld already. . . . The body dies but the spiritual quantum field continues. In this way, I am immortal.

—Dr. Hans-Peter Dürr, former head of the
Max Planck Institute for Physics, Munich[18]

A Subtle Dance

Our energy body gives us one foot in heaven and our physical body gives us one foot on earth, and what we experience, in every waking moment, is a mixture of awareness of the sensorily familiar physical realm and the hidden-to-our-senses heavenly realm. Our dual existence involves a seamless and highly dynamic holistic relationship, a kind of subtle dance, between our local physical body and our nonlocal energy body: information passes back and forth instantaneously; each body initiates different processes; the innately intelligent energy body shapes the physical body.

Just as one dancer often takes the lead in partner dances, so our energy body and our physical body lead at any given time. When we are engaged in sensory experiences such as eating or listening to music, or are physically active, as in walking, dancing, playing sports, or having sex, our physical body has the lead in the dance. When we are engaged in thinking, recalling memories, feeling an emotion, or meditating, the energy body has the lead.

The body that takes the lead at any given time dominates our awareness. When the physical body has the lead, we are more aware of the physical world. When the energy body takes the lead, we are more aware of subtle nonphysical realities.

CHAPTER 6

One Foot in Heaven

All of what are known as *subjective experiences*—perception, thought, memory, emotion, and life force—actually originate in the energy body.

The physical body is experienced *objectively* and the energy body is experienced *subjectively*. The local objective world is perceived though the senses; the nonlocal subjective world is perceived by subtler means. Nonlocal subjective experience is just as real and just as valid as local objective experience; it simply can't be measured by local physical instruments.

Nonlocal subjective experience comprises many elements: it is the minds-eye view we create when we recall memories, daydream, dream, or visualize; the nonmaterial zone in which we consider our thoughts, make decisions, plan, or create; the intelligent life force that manifests and energizes our physical body; the movements of our life force that we experience as emotion. Even our all-surrounding perception of the world, created from objective bioelectrical information coming into the physical brain from the physical senses, is actually subjective.

Perception

We tend to assume that our perception of the world around us is the purely objective product of our senses, analogous to the output we see on the screen of a video camera while videoing. The reality is that although our perception of the world around us is based on objective sensory signals coming into our local *brain,* our actual five-sense all-surrounding mind's-eye view of our physical world is a subjective creation put together for us and experienced in our intelligent nonlocal *mind* (which I have previously referred to as the energy brain).

There are several reasons to believe that the mind's-eye view is a subjective representation of physical reality rather than an objective one. First, the senses do not and cannot continuously send to the brain complete objective sensory signals of everything in our field of awareness. The eye, for example, rapidly scans small areas of the visual field and sends to the brain only partial updates of the entire field of view. Yet our mind's-eye view of the visible physical world continuously appears to us to be a seamless whole—courtesy of our intelligent nonlocal mind knitting together partial sensory updates, recent sensory updates, and even memory into this apparent whole. The instant we enter a familiar room, we have in our mind's eye a complete visual representation of the entire room, even though our eye hasn't had nearly enough time to scan every corner.

Second, the subjective mind's-eye view does not always conform to objective sensory reality. There are many studies that show that the intelligent mind *interprets* objective sensory signals based on prior perceptual experience. The mind will interpret certain flat shapes, for example, as being three dimensional. The intelligent mind actually *adds* shadows to the subjective mind's-eye view—where those shadows *would be* if the shape *were* truly three dimensional—when there were actually no shadows at all.

Objective sensory information can also be *left out* of our subjective mind's-eye view. A somewhat comical but very revealing online experiment was conducted called the Gorilla Experiment. In this experiment I was asked to watch a video and very carefully count the number of times a basketball was bounced back and forth between six people. The pace at which the ball bounced was pretty brisk so it took focus and concentration to count. When the short video was over I was asked to type in how many bounces I counted. After my answer was submitted I got another question: *Did you see the gorilla?* What? I was sure there was no gorilla. But when I played the exact same video again, this time not focusing on counting the number of bounces, I could plainly see that a person in a gorilla suit walked slowly through the middle of the six people who were bouncing the basketball back and forth to each other! I, and the many others who engaged in the counting of bouncing basketballs, would have sworn there was no gorilla. Why? Because in my subjective mind's-eye view, made up only of what I was concentrating on, there *was no gorilla*.

A third confirmation that the mind's-eye view is not objective is that it is frequently not even a representation of physical reality. Dreams appear in the mind's-eye view that are not based on any immediate sensory input. Our dreams can even create sensory impressions that we've never experienced or that do not exist in physical reality.

Finally, we can deliberately create subjective sensory experiences such as visual scenes, sensations of touch, music, or aromas in our all-senses mind's-eye view. Although this ability is commonly called *visualization*, a more accurate term for it is *creative imagining*: because when using the ability we can create not only a subjective visual experience but subjective experiences of all sensory types. While not everyone has strongly developed their innate creative imagining ability, an experienced cook can taste and smell a dish that he is only imagining how to make, a practiced composer can hear a piece of music she is mentally composing, a devoted artist can see his future painting, a master carpenter can touch the grain of the imagined wood he is working, an accomplished dancer can feel the movements of her body as she mentally choreographs a sequence of steps.

The intelligent mind behind the subjective mind's-eye view can seamlessly add or remove objects and shadows, can summon entire fantasy worlds in our dreams, and through creative imagination can conjure up everything from symphonies to supersonic jets.

Emotion

Emotion colors everything we experience. We react with some degree of emotion, from slight to strong, to nearly everything we experience in our local world—we like some things and we dislike others; we find some experiences pleasant and others unpleasant; we prefer or take pleasure in some sensory experiences and not in others.

The *origin* of emotion, however, eludes objective neuroscientific explanation. The source of emotion cannot be pinpointed through neural imaging.

Most people would naturally tend to assume that we feel pleasure in the taste of an apple because the atoms of the apple came into contact with the physical taste buds on our tongue. It might seem equally obvious that this pleasure is the immediate and sole result of a physical process and that nothing nonlocal need come into it at all.

But pleasure in the taste of an apple is actually a *subjective* experience. If two people bite into the same apple, they can have entirely different subjective experiences. The taste buds on their tongues work the same way. The electrochemical signals that go from their taste buds into their brain perform in the same way. But, when the raw electrochemical sensory information from their tongues crosses the entangled local-nonlocal boundary into their nonlocal mind, where their intelligent discrimination identifies the substance being chewed as an apple, one may experience pleasure while the other experiences disgust.

According to various spiritual teachings, it is impossible for us to *feel either pleasure or disgust* in the taste of the apple, or to experience any other emotion arising from interactions with our physical world, without nonlocal subjective experience.

> [Emotions] are felt *inside* first in the mind or the heart, and are then transmitted through the nervous system to the physical body.
>
> —Paramahansa Yogananda, yoga master[1]

The notion that emotion is experienced nonlocally has been given significant support by the recently emerging neuroscientific theory of constructed emotion.

For most of the 20th century it was widely accepted that we can experience only a small set of basic emotions, such as fear, disgust, happiness, and joy, and that these combine in differing proportions to form all the emotional states that we are capable of experiencing. You can think of this as being similar to the three basic colors of the tiny dots that make up an image on a TV screen that can combine in differing proportions to produce all the colors we are capable of seeing. It was also widely accepted that the basic emotions originate in fixed locations in the brain, particularly in the brain stem.

In the last few decades, however, fMRI and other neuroimaging techniques have not provided support for either the existence of basic emotions or fixed locations. Dr. Lisa Barrett, highly influential and distinguished professor of psychology at Northeastern University and Director of the Interdisciplinary Affective Science Laboratory, puts it this way: "accumulating empirical evidence . . . is inconsistent with the view that there are kinds of emotion with boundaries that are carved in nature."[2]

Instead of fixed locations for basic emotions, what Barrett and others have discovered is that we experience very specific emotions in response to very specific situations—situations that are unique to each individual. An example might be an employee feeling happy about praise from his boss for solving a vexing programming problem.

If these specific situations stimulate an emotion often enough, they will cause the brain to construct neural circuits to automatically stimulate the emotion when the situation occurs—thus the theory of constructed emotion. Such emotion-producing neural circuits often make no connection with the fixed locations, such as in the brain stem, long thought to be the origins of emotion.

If shown a picture of a mother and child, fMRI test subject A's activated neural circuits may include connections to areas that subject A's brain associates with playing musical instruments and cooking because A's well-loved mother was a wonderful pianist and cook. If shown the same picture of mother and child, fMRI test subject B's activated neural circuits may include connections to areas that subject B's brain associates with skiing and gymnastics because B's well-loved mother was a skier and a gymnast. Although both A and B might tell the neuroscientist conducting the experiment that they felt love when shown the same picture of the mother and child, the areas of the brains that lit up may be completely different.

Dr. Barrett's most significant conclusion, as far as nonlocality is concerned, is that not only are our emotions constructed rather than evolutionarily hardwired but also all our emotions arise from what she calls core affect.[3] Affect is psychology-speak for emotion, and according to Barrett (and many others), core affect is the raw potential to produce any type of emotion. Most significantly, Dr. Barrett believes that core affect does not originate from any specific location in the brain.

While the idea of a locationless core affect solves Dr. Barrett's problem of why there are no fixed areas "carved by nature" as the source of particular emotions, she offers no explanation of how core affect originates from the local physical brain or body. Instead, Dr. Barrett seems to be implying that core affect is somewhat like electricity. If you flip a physical switch that connects a circuit of wires to a light bulb, the light bulb will light because electricity is energizing the circuit. If a situation flips one of our neural switches that connects a circuit of nerves to a constructed emotion, we will feel an emotion because core affect is energizing the circuit. We know that the electricity that lights the light bulb does not come from the circuit itself but from an outside source. This parallel suggests that core affect does not come from the brain itself but from an outside source. According to many experiential spiritual traditions, the experience we perceive as emotion is actually the experience of subtle energy moving in the nonlocal energy body.

The concept of emotion as nonlocal energy explains many otherwise hard-to-explain phenomena: how, for example, we can feel, and be affected by, the emotions of others. You have probably had the experience of being in a crowd that leapt to its feet to give a standing ovation for an extraordinary performance. In that moment you shared the experience of an electric, upwardly moving thrill going through you. If you had been watching the same performance by yourself at home on a screen, even if on the screen you had seen the audience leap to its feet, it is unlikely that you would have leapt to your own feet and applauded at the end. It is the experience of the combined upward flow of subtle energy generated by the entire crowd that would have all but compelled you to rise to your feet.

You've probably also experienced that spending time with someone who is experiencing a powerful emotional state can result in you feeling what they are feeling. Being with someone depressed may leave you feeling dragged down and moody while being with someone bursting with enthusiasm may leave you energized and positive. We can interact with these movements of subtle energy in another person because their subtle energy, like our own, exists in a nonlocal realm, a realm in which space does not exist—which means that there is no "distance" between your emotions and another person's emotions.

The notion of a separate organism is clearly an abstraction, as is also its boundary. Underlying all this is unbroken wholeness even though our civilization has developed in such a way as to strongly emphasize the separation into parts.

—David Bohm and Basil J. Hiley,
authors of *The Undivided Universe*[4]

You may be thinking that audial or visual cues given to us by other people, such as in the examples I cited above, could simply cause our own neural circuitry to fire in response and stimulate the same emotion as in the person giving us the cues. This notion has been explored in the somewhat controversial concept of *mirror neurons.* The basic idea of mirror neurons is that the same area of the brain lights up whether we are performing an activity or watching someone else perform the activity. While this concept may explain some of the experience of sharing the same emotions with others, it cannot explain why we do not even have to be directly aware of other people to be affected by their emotions.

Evidence that our emotions may influence someone remotely has surfaced in a recent analysis of social networks. In 2008, political scientist James H. Fowler of the University of California, San Diego, and medical doctor and social scientist Nicholas A. Christakis of Harvard Medical School published "Dynamic Spread of Happiness in a Large Social Network" in the *British Medical Journal.*[5]

Your happiness depends not just on your choices and actions, but also on the choices and actions of people you don't even know who are one, two and three degrees removed from you. . . . Emotions have a collective existence—they are not just an individual phenomenon."[6]

A *Washington Post* journalist summed up Fowler's and Christakis's findings: "[E]motion can ripple through clusters of people who may not even know each other."[7]

This field may be a bomb with a delayed fuse that is getting ready to explode in the very heart of materialistic medicine.
—Larry Dossey, MD, author of *Space, Time, and Medicine*[8]

Emotion, or core affect, is, in essence, the movement of nonlocal subtle energy. The movement of subtle energy and feeling an emotion happen simultaneously: emotional experience *is* the movement of subtle energy. Even many of the words we use to describe emotions suggest movement and energy: stirring, moving, uplifting, powerful, electric, etc.

Subtle energy rising rapidly in the energy body is experienced as excitement or exhilaration, a feeling of being "up" or "on top of the world." Subtle energy contracting in the energy body's navel center is experienced as fear or anger. Subtle energy moving downward in the energy body is experienced as sadness, as being "down" or "in the dumps," and, if long lasting, as depression. Subtle energy steadily expanding in the subtle energy body's heart center is experienced as the emotion of personal satisfaction or love. Subtle energy moving upward and expanding in the energy body's brain center is experienced as inspiration or spiritual upliftment.

Thought

Many prominent people, not just those we would consider to be spiritual, speak of directly *receiving* thoughts, as opposed to the more common assumption that we *create* thoughts in our local brains.

People say I have created things. I have never created anything. I get impressions from the universe at large and work them out, but I am only a plate on a record or a receiving apparatus—what you will. Thoughts are really impressions that we get from outside.
—Thomas Edison, inventor[9]

I don't know exactly where ideas come from, but when I'm working well ideas just appear. I've heard other people say similar things—so it's one of the ways I know there's help and guidance out there. It's just a matter of our figuring out how to receive the ideas or information that are waiting to be heard.

—Jim Henson, creator of the Muppets[10]

All thoughts vibrate eternally in the cosmos. Thoughts are universally and not individually rooted; a truth cannot be created, but only perceived.

—Paramahansa Yogananda, yoga master[11]

The brain does not generate thought . . . any more than the wire generates electric current.

—Paul Brunton, author of *A Search in Secret India*[12]

Intense and prolonged concentration on a particular matter will draw new thoughts into your mind—not just thoughts with which you are already familiar. Prolonged concentration is the beginning of creativity and the essence of genius. The "trancelike" state that Brahms entered into in which he saw "distinct themes in my mind's eye . . . clothed in the right forms, harmonies and orchestration" is an extraordinary example of how deeply we can concentrate and how bountiful are the results.

Because thoughts are universally, not individually rooted, each of us has access to solutions to problems, to new creative concepts, and to profound understanding of any subject. We need only remain focused on a subject long and deeply enough to receive them.

Memory

There is significant neuroscientific evidence to support the idea that not just our perception, emotions, and thoughts, but our memories, too, exist nonlocally.

As mentioned in a previous chapter, Queen's University professor Dr. Forsdyke published a paper entitled "Wittgenstein's Certainty Is Uncertain: Brain Scans of Cured Hydrocephalics Challenge Cherished Assumptions."

In it he referred to Lorber's work with extreme hydrocephalics who were cognitively indistinguishable from other people with complete brains. The "cherished assumption" mentioned in the title is that our memories are stored in the local physical brain. Forsdyke's paper convincingly challenges this assumption. If, as he argued, an adult with only 5 percent of typical brain circuitry has a full range of memory, then memory may well be stored "extra-corporeally."[13]

Like the discoveries that overturned the model that emotions exist only in fixed locations in the brain, various other studies have also overturned the model that memories exist in specific locations in the brain.[14,15] It is now commonly accepted that the *same memory* can be recalled when *different* parts of the brain are activated.[16] People who have had extensive brain damage caused by strokes, for example, can still recall memories previously assumed to have been stored in a now-damaged area of the brain.

These and other findings that indicate memory is not stored in specific locations in the brain led Stanford Professor Karl Pribram to the conclusion that memory functions in much the same way as a hologram functions.[17] Any part of a hologram contains all the information to create the complete three-dimensional holographic projection. Thus Pribram's theory of *holonomic memory* suggests that any area of the brain can have a nonlocal connection to any memory.

Life Force

Without knowing precisely how we know, we are all aware of the presence of life force within us. We know how much "energy" we have at any given moment. An abundance of life force puts a bounce in our step and a smile on our face. It tingles through our body when we feel delight and knots our stomach when we're stressed. It warms our hearts when we feel love and tenses the body when we feel fear. It gives us an upward "rush" when we feel excited or inspired and drags us downward when we are fatigued or depressed.

Clairvoyants see subtle life force—a multi-hued, lucent *aura* shining from within and surrounding the physical body.

> I can tell you that anything that happens in the physical body
> will happen in the pattern of the energy fields first.
> —Barbara Brennan, healer, author of *Hands of Light*[18]

> Clairvoyants can see flashes of colour, constantly changing, in
> the aura that surrounds every person: each thought, each feeling,
> thus translating itself in the astral world, visible to the astral sight.
> —Annie Besant, clairvoyant,
> Theosophical Society president[19]

In India's spiritual tradition, our life force is known as *prana*; in China, *chi* (also spelled *qi*). The ancient Egyptians referred to it as *ka*; the Greeks, *pneuma*. In Judaism, the life force is known as *ruach*; in Christianity, *spiritus*. At the heart of every experiential religious tradition in the world are techniques that enable one to become more aware of one's subtle life force—techniques such as meditation, tai chi, yoga postures, and breathing techniques, to name just a few.

The "crazy strength" that allowed teenager Charlotte Hefflemire to lift the front end of a pickup truck, the Mighty Atom's ability to bend a horseshoe as if it were made of rubber—stories such as these demonstrate that we have something more than biochemical energy to draw on. With practice, or in response to dire need, we can draw on unlimited reserves of life force directly from its nonlocal source.

> The electric energy which motivates us is not within our bodies
> at all. It is a part of the universal supply which flows through us
> from the Universal Source with an intensity set by our desires
> and our will.
> —Walter Russell (1871–1963), sculptor,
> musician, author, philosopher, and mystic[20]

More of Our Experience Is Nonlocal and Subjective than Is Local and Objective

The hidden library where our memories are stored is nonlocal. Thoughts are nonlocal. The mental work space in which we consider our thoughts, remember, plan, and create is nonlocal. The subtle energy that puts a bounce in our step is nonlocal. The emotional experience that colors every aspect of our life is nonlocal. Even our mind's-eye view of the physical world that integrates and interprets our local physical body's sensory signals is nonlocal.

> It is an almost absurd prejudice to suppose that existence can only be physical. As a matter of fact, the only form of existence of which we have immediate knowledge is psychic. We might as well say, on the contrary, that physical existence is mere inference, since we know of matter only in so far as we perceive psychic images mediated by the senses.
>
> —Carl Jung, psychologist[21]

The energy body is like the part of the proverbial iceberg that lies beneath the surface. What we see of the iceberg that lies above the surface, our local physical body, is dwarfed by the nonlocal energy body that lies beneath the surface. The various influences of our energy body—perception, thought, memory, emotion, and life force—shape our lives far more than do the influences of the physical body.

There is nothing we do or experience in our local physical world, using our local physical senses and bodies, that does not require nonlocal aspects of ourselves to be meaningfully perceived or experienced. Pleasure or pain, happiness or sadness, satisfaction or dissatisfaction with events *happening* locally are actually *experienced* nonlocally. Even if we are thinking about situations that *exist* locally, our actual thoughts, reasoning, and discrimination are nonlocal. We can't even *move* our local physical body without nonlocal will and life force being involved.

Increasing Awareness of the Energy Body Increases Superconscious Awareness

The energy body is not only essential to the functioning of our physical body and our experience of life; it also plays a key role in our ability to become more superconsciously aware. You might call the following a basic law of awareness: The more we are directly aware of the subtle energy body, the less we are directly aware of the physical body. The less we are aware of the physical body, the less our awareness is limited by the neural filters in our brain; the less our awareness is limited by the neural filters in the brain, the more superconsciously aware we become.

This basic law of awareness is why the techniques at the heart of all experience-based spiritual traditions—such as yoga postures and meditation—are practiced. Greater awareness of the energy body results in profound feelings of peace, harmony, expansion, calmness, well-being, joy, and an awed superconscious awareness of greater sacred realities beyond the physical. When we attune ourselves deeply to our one foot that is in heaven, and, as a result, our one foot on earth recedes or disappears from our awareness, we naturally and automatically have heavenly experiences.

CHAPTER 7

One Foot on Earth

Our one foot on earth does not, alas, make it easy for us to become aware of our one foot in heaven. Although the one foot in heaven is always there, our physical brain with its billions of neural circuits keeps us almost overwhelmingly focused on our one foot on earth.

Most of us, by late childhood, have unintentionally rendered ourselves *neurally blind* to everything except what the senses reveal—the physical body and the physical world around us. From earliest childhood onward we are encouraged to learn to operate *exclusively* within the physical world and as we do so the brain wires more and more neural circuits to support that exclusive purpose.

Our well-established physical world-supporting neural wiring is so thoroughly and continuously engrossing that it is quite easy to become convinced that there simply can be no other reality of which we *could* be aware. Our day-to-day experience of the world makes it very difficult for us to embrace the testimony of saints, sages, and near-death experiencers that other worlds, other realities, and other levels of awareness exist and are accessible to us—or that we could possibly be anything more than the physical body.

We would, however, perceive reality entirely differently if the billions of neurons we have devoted to functioning in the physical world did not fire automatically in response to stimuli. Were we to die, so that the local physical brain was no longer functioning, we would, the saints, sages, and, especially, near-death experiencers tell us, *immediately and automatically* begin to be aware of heavenly realms, heavenly feeling, and heavenly knowl-edge, because we would be free of the automatically firing neural circuits that have been compelling us to be aware only of the physical world:

> [T]he brain and nervous system limits consciousness like a re-ducing valve limits the flow of water. At death, this reducing-valve function ceases and consciousness is then free to expand. Superconsciousness takes human awareness outside the brain.
> —Swami Kriyananda, yoga master[1]

Thankfully, we do not need to die to experience superconscious awareness because we can *rewire the brain to bypass the brain.* We can rewire the brain to support habitual superconscious awareness that "takes human awareness outside the brain."[2] In order to rewire the brain to bypass the brain we need first to understand how and why the brain wires its neural circuitry.

Neural Habit Circuits

At birth, human children have surprisingly few preformed neural circuits to support their voluntary actions. From birth they have to learn to do al-most every voluntary action. Think of a one-year-old child trying to place one block on top of another. Invisible to us are the new dendritic connec-tions being made in the child's brain—millions of which can be made in a *single day*—as the child maneuvers the block. The dendritic connections made between the various neurons responsible for moving body, arms, hands, and fingers will eventually form into interconnecting neural cir-cuits that will support thousands of physical movements.

We would find it nearly impossible to function in the physical world without the neural habit circuits that we develop in childhood. The brain-wiring process lasts for many years—children have much to learn: how to use their bodies, how to coordinate their movement with sensory input; and how to understand and use both written and spoken language. The end result of many years of such learning is the formation of millions of what I call *neural habit circuits,* circuits that support habitual movements such as walking, talking, eating, and manual tasks.

The process of forming new neural habit circuits is the same for adults as for children. The first time you try to do something you've never done before, such as trying to catch a baseball with a mitt, it requires full concentration. Repeated concentrated practice catching a baseball will cause the formation of neural circuits that support the required movements.

Once supporting neural habit circuits have formed to support any habitual physical activity, it requires far less concentration to perform that activity. Catching a baseball in a mitt becomes "second nature." The brain has created a complex neural habit circuit ready to fire when a baseball is perceived to be coming toward us. Neurons in the circuit send electrochemical signals through the nervous system that cause scores of muscles in our hand and arm to relax or contract in the proper way, and in the proper sequence, to allow us to catch the ball in the mitt.

Neural habit circuits, however, do not turn us into robots! We still need to exercise sufficient awareness and concentration to respond to ever-changing situations. In the example above, the catcher must be aware and concentrated in order to adjust body position to the speed and trajectory of an incoming baseball. What does become nearly robot-like is the opening of the baseball mitt, the way we hold the mitt to receive the ball, and the closing of the mitt once the ball has arrived.

Neural habit circuits that support physical movements get us through the day with the least amount of conscious attention on those movements. Imagine if we had to fully concentrate on every movement we made throughout our day. We'd be mentally exhausted. By the end of the day probably the most we would have accomplished would be bathing and dressing ourselves. Such is the experience of stroke victims who have suffered damage to the thousands or millions of neural habit circuits that enable movement. For stroke victims, regaining habitual movement requires long hours of concentration on repeated movements to create new neural habit circuits—just as when they were children.

Habitual Behavior

Once we have made our way through childhood, the new neural habit circuits we create will be not so much to support more and different ways to move the body as to support habitual behaviors, emotional responses, and patterns of thinking.

The most studied example of behavior that is supported by neural circuits is the sleep-wake cycle. If we go to sleep at regular times and wake at regular times, neural circuits will form to support that habitual behavior. When we approach our usual time to go to sleep, neural habit circuits will fire to prepare the body for sleep. Less blood will be sent to the regions of the brain that are associated with our higher subjective functions—concentration, will, planning. Other neural habit circuits will fire that begin a process of detoxification throughout the body that cause us, among other things, to yawn to get rid of excess carbon dioxide. When we actually fall asleep, all nonessential functions of the body are switched off: neural habit circuits will fire to switch off our ability to receive sensory signals in the higher brain and to deactivate our ability to move our muscles voluntarily. Other neural habit circuits fire to speed up the process of resupplying glucose to our neurons. All these processes are coordinated by yet more neural habit circuits in sixty- to ninety-minute cycles that include periodic rapid-eye-movement dream episodes.

It is difficult to stay up during our normal sleep cycle not simply because we are tired, but because our neural sleep-habit circuits continue to fire throughout our normal sleep cycle regardless of whether we want to stay awake. Some of those neural habit circuits are causing less blood to be sent to the areas of the forebrain associated with our higher mental functions. Thus we feel continuously "fuzzy brained."

While most of the neural habit circuits that support our sleep-wake cycle come inbuilt, most of the neural habit circuits that support our habitual behaviors are built by us. If you habitually exercise first thing in the morning, just before you begin, your neural habit circuits will prepare the body for physical activity by increasing heart rate and breathing rate and by increasing blood flow to the large muscles and cerebellum, the part of the brain that coordinates movement. If, on the other hand, you habitually meditate first thing in the morning, just before you begin, your neural habit circuits will prepare the body for sitting still by slowing the heart rate and breathing rate, by slowing blood flow to the large muscles, and by increasing blood flow to the forebrain.

Habitual Emotional Response

In addition to supporting habitual movements and behaviors, your brain will also build neural habit circuits to support your habitual emotional reactions. We touched on this a bit in the last chapter on the subject of constructed emotions. When we consistently experience a particular emotion in response to a repeated stimulus, situation, or condition, our brain "constructs" a neural circuit to stimulate that emotion which fires whenever that same stimulus, situation, or condition occurs.

Over time we create innumerable neural habit circuits which stimulate habitual emotional responses. Over the course of a lifetime, we will construct neural habit circuits that stimulate or support our emotional reactions to individuals, places, things, situations, colors, smells, sounds, weather, foods, friends, colleagues, siblings, loved ones, children, parents, bosses, sports teams, athletes, music, musicians, politics, politicians, cars, houses, countries, cities, activities, books, movies, actors, artists, religion, philosophy, and *much* more. Whew! Consider that if we form a *specific neural habit circuit for each individual piece of music for which we have a like or dislike,* the number of neural habit circuits that support our emotional reactions to *all* aspects of everything *else* we experience can easily number in the millions.

Habitual Trains of Thought or Memories

When we consistently entertain a train of thought in response to the same stimulus, situation, or condition, our brain forms a neural circuit to stimulate that train of thought, which fires whenever that stimulus, situation, or condition occurs.

A neural habit circuit that stimulates nonlocal thoughts acts much like a station preset button on a radio that, when pressed, brings in a preselected radio station. A preset-like neural habit circuit, when fired, will tune us to a preselected *thought station.* Once tuned to a particular thought station, thoughts associated with a particular subject, emotion, or mood enter our awareness in a stream. You might see this in yourself in areas of particular interest to you. If you are a psychologist, and you come across a new trend in treatment for depression, a neural habit circuit will tune you into your habitual thought station about treating depression.

We all have a tendency—or certainly we have witnessed, perhaps with amusement, such a tendency in others—to automatically articulate the same arguments in response to the same subject. When combined with strong emotion our automatic articulation of arguments may come out as a rant. Without emotion, but with strong conviction, we might come off as a bore. I've often heard people say about others that, when they brought up a particular subject, it was as if they had *pressed a button* and out came a long and obviously often-shared train of thought.

Complex Interconnected Neural Habit Circuits

Neural habit circuits that are triggered by or that initiate sensation, movement, behavior, emotion, thought, and memory can form into one complex interconnected neural circuit. When a complex interconnected neural habit circuit fires, it can automatically activate physical movements and behaviors and/or stimulate nonlocal emotions, thoughts, and memories.

For example: Imagine that you are an avid coffee aficionado and you unintentionally walk by a coffee shop. Since you love coffee and drink it often, your coffee-drinking neural habit circuit will be well developed and will send signals all over the brain that activate other areas of the brain and central nervous system, which in turn activate many physiological processes such as salivating, increasing the heart rate, increasing the breath rate, releasing of glucose, increasing muscular tension, and contracting and relaxing the muscles of the face to form a smile.

The firing of your coffee circuit will also stimulate nonlocal emotional pleasure, trains of thought, and memories associated with coffee—the taste, the feel of the cup in your hand, goodies you've eaten while drinking, friendly caffeine-enhanced conversations, the question of how coffee is prepared in this coffee shop, a long history of how coffee is prepared around the world, and your treasured opinion as to the best way to prepare coffee—to all of which thoughts you may react with even greater emotional pleasure.

Your greater pleasure can cause a reinforcing activation of your brain's coffee-drinking circuit, which may cause it to release dopamine. Dopamine is a neurotransmitter and a hormone that, among other things, can enhance physical pleasure. This feedback cycle may continue—especially if you've already gone into the coffee shop and are now drinking a cup of coffee you thoroughly like—until all the pleasure-enhancing dopamine receptors in your neural coffee-drinking circuit are saturated.

Neural Habit Circuits Have a Lasting Physical Reality

Once created, neural habit circuits take on a life of their own. Neural habit circuits are *actual physical structures in the brain.* Even if a neural habit circuit was created to stimulate nonphysical nonlocal experiences—thoughts, emotions or memories—the neural habit circuit itself is local and *physical*. Once created, neural habit circuits remain in the brain for a long time and will *slowly* degrade over time only if the habits they support are no longer practiced.

Neural Habit Circuits Are Compelling

The activation of neural habit circuits makes their associated thoughts, emotions, and behaviors *almost irresistibly automatic.* Even with the best resolution to avoid a negative habit, if any of a number of stimuli causes the negative neural habit circuit to fire, we can easily find ourselves helplessly falling into the behavior, or emotion, or thinking pattern we want to avoid.

We can, with concentrated attention, deliberately make new choices of behavior. We can make food choices different from our habitual ones. We can rearrange our habitual schedule. We can behave differently in our relationships. However, unless we are consciously *willing* otherwise, the path of least resistance created by the automatic firing and activation of already established neural habit circuits will take us into the well-worn groove of behavior that the firing of our neural habit circuits automatically initiates.

In his book *Thinking Fast and Slow*, Daniel Kahneman explains how our automatically firing neural habit circuits—fast thinking, as he calls it—dominate behavior and bypass reason. Automatically firing neural habit circuits are the main reason we are prone to make poor decisions. Unless we deliberately pause to reason and consider—to exercise slow thinking—we are basically on autopilot and autopilot may not take us where we want to go.

A Continuous Fireworks Show

The most important thing to understand and appreciate about our neural habit circuits is that *any* trigger of any *type* that is a part of a neural habit circuit—sensation, movement, memory, behavior, thought, or emotion—will automatically cause the entire neural circuit to fire. Let me repeat that: any trigger, from sensation to emotion, will automatically cause the entire neural circuit to fire.

Our hypothetical well-established neural coffee-habit circuit will fire at the slightest smell, or lightest thought, or vaguest memory of coffee. Which, like lighting any firecracker in a woven chain of firecrackers, will set off all the other firecrackers. If we merely *see* our favorite coffee cup, our emotional associations to coffee will be stimulated. Our physiological reactions to coffee will be initiated. Our behavior associated with coffee will begin. Thoughts and memories associated with coffee will arise in the mind. And—for good or ill—we will *want* to drink a cup of coffee.

Because each complex interconnected neural habit circuit often interconnects with other complex interconnected neural habit circuits, the firing of one circuit means the firing of many others—rather than a single woven string of firecrackers, we have a continuous fireworks display. The continuous noise of a fireworks display can be compared to the continuous sensory stimuli we experience when awake. The big explosions of light and color can be compared to experiencing a stimulated thought, memory, or emotion. In our wakeful minds it is pretty much always the fourth of July—and, like children at a fireworks show, we are captivated.

As long as the attention is held captive by the fireworks show in the brain, we remain unaware of the more subtle energy body. The chain-reaction firing of complex neural circuits that keeps us exclusively aware of the sense-revealed physical world around us is what, in Kriyananda's words, "limits consciousness like a reducing valve."[3] This neural-circuitry reducing valve keeps us so sense-conscious that it is very difficult to be superconsciously aware of other realities.

You Can Rewire Your Brain

The good news is that your destiny is not written in your neural circuits. Do not make the life-limiting mistake of believing that the way you are now is genetically inevitable, that your brain is fixed, or that emotional trauma or childhood conditioning have left you helpless to change unwanted automatic behaviors.

The brain is perpetually plastic. We *can* rewire it. *We* created our existing neural habit circuits; *we* can create new neural habit circuits. We can form new neural circuits that support a new diet, a new exercise regime, new skills, or that improve our relationships with others. Most life-changingly, we can rewire our brain to enable us to bypass the continuous fireworks storm of neural circuits that keep us preoccupied with the physical world, to become instead more superconsciously aware of the subtle energy world.

We have *unintentionally* created most of the neural habit circuits that exist in the brain. We have more or less gone along with the influences of outer conditions presented by our parents, education, friends, spouse, jobs, and opportunities and over *years, even decades,* have built our existing habit circuits; circuits which now have a tenacious hold on how we behave and what we experience.

We can, however, *intentionally* rewire the brain much more quickly and effectively than we did unintentionally. If we set a new mental and emotional intention, and maintain sustained attention on that new behavior for *weeks to months,* we can create a new neural habit circuit that will make that new behavior increasingly compelling.

Meditation Is the Key to Rewiring Our Brain for Superconscious Awareness

Meditation is the key to rewiring the brain for superconscious awareness because meditation connects us directly to the superconscious. We don't have to have fully rewired the brain before we can experience some degree of superconscious awareness in meditation. Repeatedly connecting to the superconscious in meditation gradually and naturally rewires the brain so that attaining superconscious awareness becomes progressively easier. The deeper the connection to the superconscious the more effective and rapid the rewiring process.

People who have had near-death experiences, who have experienced profound emotional release and surpassing heart-opening feelings, often share, even years after their experience, that their lives were instantly and *permanently* changed by their experience. Long after the experience ended they still felt *different.* They were emotionally transformed and simultaneously neuronally rewired. Even neural habit circuits that support deeply rooted, habitual emotions, such as fearfulness, buried anger, emotional wounds, or lifetime anxieties, have been, in rare instances, as the result of deep and powerful superconscious experience, *instantly* rewired into new and positive neural habit circuits.

> In a survey of thousands of people who reported having experienced personal encounters with God, Johns Hopkins researchers report that . . . a majority of respondents attributed lasting positive changes in their psychological health—e.g., life satisfaction, purpose, and meaning—even decades after their initial experience.[4]

> Even though awakening experiences typically only last from a few moments to a few hours, they frequently have a life-changing effect. Many people described an awakening experience as the most significant moment of their lives, reporting a major change in their perspective on life, and in their values.
> —Dr. Steve Taylor, psychologist[5]

> [A]lmost every belief I had embraced only hours before—that I was a physical being, that love was outside of me, that God was some patriarchal monarch sitting on a marble throne somewhere in the sky, that death was something to fear, that I was doomed by my past, that religion and spirituality were the same, that spirituality and science were different—was no longer true

to my experience. Virtually every picture of reality I had used to define my existence—not to be confused with my life—had been cremated. The ashes of the woman I thought I was were scattered on the wind.

—Lynnclaire Dennis, near-death experiencer[6]

I was lying in a field under a tree thinking rather deeply of love and the joy it brings. Suddenly . . . all materialism disappeared completely, and I felt like a torch burning in the darkness. I seemed to be filled with the rays of the sun. This experience lasted for about three minutes. It is interesting to note that my behavior pattern has changed since this experience.

—Unnamed woman from *Seeing the Invisible*[7]

I was changed by it, refined, rarified, made pure. I basked in its sweetness, and the traumas of the past were far behind me, forgotten and transformed by peace.

—RaNelle Wallace, near-death experiencer[8]

While few of us may have such profound and instantly life-changing experiences, whatever superconscious experience we do have, including, especially, superconscious contact in meditation, will increase the speed and depth of change to our neural habit circuits. Superconscious experience can be thought of as producing a strong magnetic field that changes the patterns of our iron filing-like brain circuits into new patterns. The more intense the superconscious experience, the stronger the magnetic field. The stronger the magnetic field, the more the brain is changed.

An Enlightenment experience radically rearranges many neuronal connections in a relatively short time. The result is a tremendous benefit to our brain and body as we discover new positive ways of thinking, feeling, and experiencing the world around us.

—Andrew Newberg, MD, author of
How God Changes Your Brain[9]

Meditation is the single most effective practice for enabling us to immerse ourselves in such a superconscious magnetic field. Meditation taps us into the superconscious power that changes us and into the Joy that fulfills us.

Superconscious Awareness, Too, Can Be Made a Habit

The difference between most of us and the saints and sages is that through their deep and repeated contact with the superconscious, neural habit circuits have formed in their brains that make superconscious awareness a stronger habit than conscious awareness.

They have developed neural habit circuits that support withdrawal from physical awareness. When they withdraw in meditation their awareness becomes purely superconscious, unlimited by the firing of neurons.

The saints and sages have also mastered the ability to be able to function in the physical world while remaining superconscious. Their superconscious awareness makes them highly productive, creative, energetic, brilliant, wise, and compassionate. Even more significantly, even when fully engaged with people and projects, their dominant awareness is of superconscious peace, love, and joy.

They have the best of all realms: one foot on earth—healthy, capable, and energetic; one foot in heaven—an open door to the superconscious; and beyond heaven and earth—oneness with the ever-new joy that is God.

CHAPTER 8

A Day in the Dance

Every day and in every moment we are caught up in an inner dance: one foot on earth dancing with one foot in heaven, matter dancing with energy, local dancing with nonlocal, brain dancing with mind, senses dancing with life force, consciousness dancing with superconsciousness, Self dancing with God.

I thought it might be helpful to present the dance as an experiential story. I describe the dance as a day in the life of an imaginary someone—in whom I hope you will be able to see yourself—if not closely, at least in broad strokes. This imaginary someone—and I will pretend that it is you—has quite a dance today.

You are dreaming. Your nonlocal mind's eye is showing you a shifting view of a reality stitched together from fragments of memories and new nonlocal mind-created scenes. You are unaware of your sleeping body and could not move it if you were, as neural habit circuits have switched off your voluntary control. In your dream you are experiencing a mildly unsettling emotion of frustration. You are trying to accomplish something over and over—it's not clear what—without success.

Your automatic and time-sequenced neural sleep-habit circuits begin to release you from sleep. For a minute or two you are in between subconscious and conscious awareness. In your half-awake state you muse on your dream. You remember that the day before, while at work, you had been frustrated by a co-worker and now you understand the emotional theme of your dream. Your mind's-eye view of your dreamscape begins to fade but your unsettling feeling of frustration lingers.

In a few more moments your neural sleep-habit circuits completely release you. The neural switch is thrown that allows sensory signals once again to make it to your higher brain. You open your eyes and your nonlocal mind creates its mind's-eye view of your physical reality. Your *conscious* mind's-eye view crowds out any lingering *subconscious* dream images. At the same time, the neural switch is thrown that once again gives you control over your voluntary muscles. You stretch and move, becoming increasingly aware of your body, of which, only moments before, you were completely unaware.

Neural habit circuits to support movement fire automatically. You sit up, stand, stretch, grab a robe, and go off to the bathroom. As you move through your morning routine only half-aware, more and more neural habit circuits fire automatically and in sequence—your hand moves to brush your teeth, your arms move to brush your hair. You are aware that you are doing familiar things but you are not focusing on them. Other neural habit circuits begin to fire that bring into your awareness thoughts and feelings about your day ahead.

It's Saturday. No work today. You decide to meditate longer than normal today. You have been meditating first thing in the morning for over a year and are experiencing increasingly good results. At the thought of meditating, neural habit circuits fire, stimulating your life force to move in a gentle upward surge in your subtle energy body and, as a result, giving you a positive feeling about the prospect of meditating. Another series of neural habit circuits begin to fire in automatic sequence. You sit in your customary position. Your body settles and releases physical tension. Your breathing slows. Your heart rate slows.

Because you are becoming still, the orientation association area at the top of the brain is receiving fewer and fewer nerve signals regarding the orientation of your body. The immediacy of your physical body gradually fades from your awareness. Eyes closed and body increasingly still, your mind's-eye view, no longer receiving as many sensory signals as when the body is active, gradually reveals another world. At first you "see" only darkness but gradually the darkness becomes tinged with more and more light.

Competing with the vaguely seen light, memories or thoughts moving through your mind bring up associated images in your mind's eye—fuzzy to begin with, the longer you focus on your memories or thoughts, the clearer the associated images become.

The less aware of the physical world you become, the more aware you become of your inner world of sensation, emotion, and thought. Today, succeeding in remaining more still than usual, watching your memories and thoughts come and go, you sink into a deeper state than you normally achieve. As your thoughts naturally slow down, you become more clear, focused, and alert. A release of tension spreads through your being. A wonderful feeling of peace builds in the subtle heart center. With an upward joyful thrill, you appreciate that you are superconsciously aware of subtle realities beyond body and brain.

Restless movements and fading concentration eventually end what has been one of your best meditations. You open your eyes, gently move and stretch, your nonlocal mind's eye now once again revealing an integrated interpretation of all sensory signals.

Your stomach growls. Supportive behavioral neural habit circuits have previously fired and have already released digestive enzymes into your stomach in anticipation of a meal. You get up and begin to think of what to have for breakfast. The continued firing of your morning neural habit circuits brings a memory mélange of tastes and smells into your mind. Your habitual breakfast, which you always like, swims into your mind, setting off your salivary glands and stimulating a feeling of pleasure.

Today though, already practically tasting your usual breakfast, but still elevated by your unusually deep meditation, you think, as you have been thinking for some time now, that your favorite Saturday morning breakfast is too rich, too sweet, and leaves you enervated before it's even lunchtime. Your well-established neural habit circuits are all but compelling you to have your usual breakfast. You have not built up any neural habit circuits that support any new ideas for breakfast, but your still partially awakened superconscious state helps you win out over your morning habit circuitry. You prepare a more healthful breakfast.

Feeling inspired and energized by your dip into superconscious experience and by your healthy breakfast choice, you decide to work on your painting. For years you have painted on and off. Today though you paint at a new level. New creative ideas come into your mind without conscious intention. Your technique is surer. Your vision for the final form of the painting is clearer. The limits of the physical body are forgotten. Though still aware of your surroundings and body, you are centered in your non-local energy body. You are aware of life force moving within you. You feel a well of calm and peaceful energy in the heart center. You scarcely notice that two hours go by in an effortless *flow*.

Lunch time arrives. An old neural habit circuit fires that awakens memories of how pleasing it feels to relax after hard work. Other interconnected neural habit circuits fire and suggest that relaxing is always best with a little indulgence. Intuitive warning bells are ringing but your old neural habit circuits prevail and you decide to prepare a lunch of rich food followed by your favorite ice cream.

Lunch over, your life force is now over-tasked with the digestion and assimilation of the large dose of fats and sugars you put into your body. Less energy is being sent to the brain. You begin to think of having a nap. You are drifting in low-energy conscious-subconscious awareness. You ease into a soft chair and check your mobile for messages. You inhale in shock. Your frustration-producing co-worker has sent an email to your entire team with comments that make you seem to be the main cause of a big problem. A jolt of life force goes to the pit of your stomach. Your stomach muscles tighten unpleasantly. Your heart starts racing. Your breath rate increases. Your muscles tense, just as they would if you were being physically attacked.

Lulled into a state of low energy by your too-rich meal and caught off-guard by the unexpected email, old and unwanted neural habit circuits automatically fire, stimulating the emotions of anger, hurt, and outrage before you can center yourself. Then, like a chain reaction, other interconnected negative neural habit circuits fire, calling up subconscious memories of other times this co-worker treated you unfairly. Yet more associated neural habit circuits fire and memories of *other* people who have treated you unfairly in *other* circumstances flood your mind. Over the course of ten minutes, you feel progressively more angry, tense, and miserable.

Potentially offsetting positive neural habit circuits are not firing simply because you are not *choosing* to initiate any positive thoughts, feelings, or actions. You are too caught up in the negative. One part of you knows that this will eventually pass like a bout of fever, but that knowing is not strong enough to motivate you to initiate other positive habit circuits to stop the runaway cascade of negative interconnected neural habit circuits. Instead, you obsessively keep going over and over the situation, mentally writing harsh and emotional email responses.

Another part of you, the intelligent wisdom of your Self, keeps you from actually writing or sending an email response. Memories surface of past situations in which sending an email while upset and uncentered proved disastrous. Today the wiser part of you prevails. You convince yourself to do something to move your awareness away from your emotional pain.

This does not prove to be easy. Your negative neural habit circuits keep firing, strengthened by dopamine and reinforced by your body's natural opiate release, which, ironically, gives you a perverse pleasure in being miserable. You try watching a movie, but the still-firing negative neural habit circuits keep you from getting the distraction you hope for. You miss long sections of movie dialog and action as you continue to assess and reassess your negative thoughts and feelings. Your life force continues to focus uncomfortably at the pit of your stomach and you remain in fight-or-flight mode.

The wisdom of Self comes to your rescue once again. You realize that you need to do something more energetic. Watching a movie is too passive to redirect your now strongly flowing life force away from your negative feelings. You need to do something that is involved enough to coax your life force into a different flow. A tennis player, you call around to people you've played with and manage to find a partner. In an hour you are playing with such concentration that everything else is forgotten. Without noticing it, your body's fight-or-flight mode has switched back to the rest-and-digest mode. Your muscles have relaxed; more energy has returned to the higher brain regions; you can think more clearly; the feeling of being under attack has passed. Your match ends. You thank your friend and head back home.

You occupy yourself with household chores until it is time to eat dinner. While you go through the motions of your routine chores, your neural habit circuits automatically producing most of your movements, your life force moves downward, which you experience as being drained and depressed. You recognize that your strong reaction to your co-worker is another instance in a long history of feeling like a victim of other's actions. For many years you have seen this tendency in yourself. Although you have tried to overcome this tendency you are unhappily aware that, though you react less strongly than you have in the past, you still react. You are also remembering that there is an unwelcome emotional aftermath to these episodes that you are once again experiencing. You feel both emotionally down and fragile.

Thinking that there *must* be a more successful way to deal with such past tendencies, suddenly, out of the blue, your intuition reminds you of a talk being given that evening by a well-known spiritual teacher. In your thoughtful and introspective mood, you decide to go.

After a light dinner you arrive at the talk. Still feeling fragile, you avoid speaking with the other attendees. You take a chair and sit quietly until the talk begins. You feel an unusually strong sense of positive anticipation. Your intuition is telling you this talk is important. The speaker is engaging and down to earth, and speaks to the crowd as to old friends. The speaker shares a number of stories that are self-deprecatingly funny, stories that you can relate to from your own life experience. You and the audience laugh appreciatively. The audience's positive emotions stimulate your life force to flow upward. The fragility that you've been feeling begins to lessen. Your mood lifts; you relax and become open to the moment.

Toward the end of a fascinating talk, the speaker persuasively offers you a way to think about God that is new to you. You have long thought that God must exist—but at a great emotional and mental distance from you. The speaker's obvious sincerity and personal experience open your mind, for the first time in your life, to the possibility that *you* could directly commune with God. At that moment of insight, you feel a shift in your heart and uplifting, inspiring waves of energy begin rising through the center of your subtle body into your mind. The speaker ends the talk and you leave quietly, not wanting to break the magic of your experience.

As you drive home, waves of subtle energy continue to rise through your core; you have the curious perceptual experience that you remain unmoving in the center of your being while your surroundings are com-ing toward you. Arriving home, you decide to meditate again even though you normally meditate only in the mornings. After your body settles, the waves of subtle energy that have been rising from your core intensify. You become more still than you have ever experienced before. Your thoughts slow. Shyly, you open your heart and mind to receive some sign of God's presence.

You are taken by surprise by the immediate and profound response. You feel your heart center expand. Life force surges throughout your body; every cell is tingling. You feel Joy pouring into your being. Each time you consciously open yourself to receive, wave after wave of love and joy flood into heart, mind, and body. You are more alert than you have ever been. Your mind's-eye view is filled with varying intensities and colors of light. You feel a profound release of tension around your heart center. You feel safe as never before.

There is no question in your mind that you are experiencing God. You know. You are in an inner dialog of feeling with a conscious Being. You feel grateful beyond measure and are filled with a Joy you have never before known. The experience feels sacred and, at the same time, perfectly natu-ral. You understand with the heart that you are experiencing your Self in God.

You don't know how long the experience has lasted but it is eventually interrupted by little body aches and pains from holding your meditation pose much longer than usual. Slightly easing your position helps you re-gain your inward focus but the body interrupts your concentration more and more often. Finally, reluctantly accepting that you are no longer able to maintain physical stillness and inner absorption, you open your eyes, stand up, and slowly move to a comfortable chair.

Your usual conscious awareness partially returns. While your mind's-eye view is of the physical world around you, you are simultaneously still superconsciously aware of the subtle energy body. This affects your percep-tion. Everything you see is suffused with a glow of energy, as though you were seeing faintly the energies that create the physical world. Most of your awareness remains inward. You feel yourself in a bubble of contentment and well-being.

Still moved to your core, you begin to reflect on your experience. You realize that while your morning meditation was joyful, during this meditation Joy Itself had burst within you with depth and power. Your communion with God supercharged your superconscious experience far beyond what you had ever been able to achieve before. You also reflect that, although you have had a thrilling peak experience, you have experienced only a small portion of God's ever-new Joy and of your own superconscious potential.

You remain comfortably happy to sit without specific purpose immersed in the feeling of contentment and well-being. You have bypassed your brain and are aware of realities beyond the physical. You feel none of your usual habitual urges to read, listen to music, check your computer, watch a video, or eat. Although it is now quite late, you feel no fatigue, no need to sleep.

Unbidden, your co-worker's email rises to the surface of your mind. No automatic neural habit circuit fires. In your elevated superconscious state the issue behind the email hardly seems to matter. You are able to be dispassionate about yourself. Your co-worker is either right or wrong about you. Either way, if the fault is yours or not yours, you appreciate that you need not destroy your peace of mind by reacting emotionally. In this moment, with superconscious joy washing through you, it doesn't matter what your co-worker or anyone else thinks of you.

Feeling profoundly clear-minded and safe emotionally allows you also to be dispassionate about your co-worker. You realize that the frustration your co-worker is feeling is not really about what you did or didn't do. You can now compassionately appreciate that your co-worker is stressed. You remember that there are problems at home; that there is even fear of losing the job. You now see your co-worker not as an attacker but as someone who could use some support. You see that you can ease your co-worker's stress by simply and genuinely apologizing for anything you may have done and suggest a fresh start on Monday.

With that thought, you realize with an immense sense of relief that even if you *are* a victim of unfairness you don't need to *feel* like a victim. This dispassionate insight is a major inner victory in a long emotional battle. Further, this victory gives you confidence that you will not always go into emotional tailspins when inevitably you are treated unfairly.

You have realized that the key to happiness lies in your inner reaction to the events of your life. Even though outer events are largely beyond your control, your inner reaction to those events *can* be within your control. Although you've heard this principle described many times before, you are now experiencing the liberating truth of it. You realize that you are the master of your happiness.

You also realize, with calm dispassion, that tonight's experience of God is life-changing but not completely life-transforming. Tonight you are on the top of a mountain. Tomorrow, after a sleep-journey in subconsciousness, you may awake to find yourself well below the summit of superconsciousness. You know there is work to be done. You will need to deepen your stillness and concentration in meditation. Most important you are strengthened by the knowledge that you can climb the mountain again— that you can tap into superconscious experience; that you can commune with God.

Deep in the night, with waves of Joy still rising from your core, sleep eventually calls and you head to bed.

This dance is the joy of existence. I am filled with you.
—Rumi, Sufi mystic [1]

All of these experiences are unlikely to happen to you in one day. You may never have as dramatic a life-changing peak experience as I have described. But what *will* happen, if you learn to become more still and inwardly absorbed in meditation, is that you will have superconscious experiences of God, whether dramatic or building over time. You will also discover your own superconscious potentials—aspects of your eternal Self—effortless relaxation, limitless energy, dynamic concentration, intuitive creativity, and transformative superconscious experience of God. And what will happen simultaneously, though hidden from you, is that your brain will rewire to support those emerging potentials and to support ever greater superconscious awareness.

PART THREE

HOW TO REWIRE YOUR BRAIN FOR SUPERCONSCIOUS AWARENESS

CHAPTER 9

Rewire Your Brain for Superconscious Awareness

No matter how we use the brain, or rewire the brain, the brain won't *create* superconsciousness by itself. The superconscious simply exists. What we need to learn is to *access* the superconscious, to tap into the magic storehouse of our amazing superconscious abilities and, in the process, rewire the brain so that our normal state becomes superconscious awareness.

Accessing the superconscious is the purpose of the universal practices of experiential spirituality—meditation, deep relaxation, life force control, concentration, creativity, and direct superconscious perception. (You can learn how to use these practices when we explore them in upcoming chapters.)

Regular experience of the superconscious will rewire the brain to automatically stimulate superconscious awareness. In a previous chapter I used the analogy that we have created thousands of neural circuits that act like "presets" on a radio. When stimulated, these neural circuit presets give us access to nonlocal "thought stations," each of which allows us to receive a particular train of thought. Once the station is accessed, thoughts flow effortlessly into our awareness. We have also created neural circuit presets that give us access to memory and emotion stations, each of which allows us to receive a particular association of memories or flow of emotion. Once these stations are accessed, memories and emotions flow effortlessly into our awareness.

Our innate ability to access the nonlocal realities of thought, memory, and emotion, and the brain's innate ability to form neural circuits to automatically trigger such access, extends to accessing the superconscious as well. Using the universal practices that give us access to the superconscious will cause more and more superconscious neural circuit presets to form and so make superconscious awareness progressively more accessible. Once accessed, the all-joyous, life-transforming superconscious will flow into our awareness just as effortlessly as do thoughts, memories, and emotions.

Superconscious Awareness Is Transforming

As previously explored, when we access the superconscious we are effortlessly transformed from the inside out by the magnetic power of superconscious experience to change our brain's neural circuits.

> In deep meditation, the superconscious uses the relaxed energy of the mind, concentrated in the brain, to go deep into the brain grooves where habits are secreted, and cauterize habits.
> —Paramahansa Yogananda, yoga master[1]

Entering the flow of superconscious as often as possible will not only effortlessly change old, and now unwanted, neurally supported habits, it will also effortlessly create new neural circuits that support new life-enhancing qualities and abilities: increased life force, peace of mind, greater kindness and compassion, awakened intuition, dynamic health, and an all-satisfying feeling of happiness.

Some Neural Habit Circuits Limit
Our Access to the Superconscious

Our primary focus should always be on developing greater access to superconscious awareness because it gives us far more transformational bang for the buck of effort than does any other method. At the same time, we have to deal directly with existing habits that limit our access to the superconscious.

We may, for example, have often-triggered neural circuits that cause us to experience emotional stress. Emotional stress blocks access to the superconscious—thus blocking access to the very experience that can magnetically change the brain circuits that cause stress.

Certain negative habits are therefore worth a specific effort to overcome. The most effective way to overcome such a habit is to rechannel the life force that is going into that negative neural habit circuit into an opposite positive neural habit circuit through which the life force can flow. The art to this rechanneling we will explore in detail in the upcoming chapter on relaxation.

On the other hand, don't be preoccupied with negative habits. Not every unwanted habit we have needs to be taken on directly—superconscious awareness will ultimately eliminate all of our negative habits. You need make only enough change in your habits to allow yourself regular access to the superconscious. Be careful not to be overwhelmed by the avalanche of self-help advice in every bookstore, nor to scatter your efforts in multiple efforts at self-improvement. Be strategic. Don't let lesser efforts at self-transformation distract you from using the universal practices of experiential spirituality to tap into transformative superconscious power.

Be Methodical and Efficient When Establishing New Habits that Rewire Your Brain

The following process is highly effective at rewiring our brain to support any new habit—whether you use it to establish new habits that support accessing the superconscious, such as meditation, or to establish a new positive habit to offset an old negative habit that is preventing you from accessing the superconscious.

As we explored previously, most of our neural habit circuits have formed without our deliberate intention. Such unintentional neural habit circuit formation is often slow because our unintentional actions that cause the circuit to form are often haphazard, inconsistent, and intermittent. Intentional neural habit circuit formation, on the other hand, can be much more rapid because we can be deliberately focused, consistent, and steady in the process of forming a new neural habit circuit. We can, in fact, become quite proficient at rewiring the brain. A hallmark of highly successful people in any field—from business to art to spirituality—is the ability to form new neural habits circuits quickly and efficiently.

The Process
Get the Most from Your Efforts

Gain the most benefit you can from your neural-habit-circuit-forming efforts. Think carefully about what new neural habit circuit you want to wire. The first habits you should establish, if you haven't already, are habits that support superconscious experience, especially meditation, because superconscious experience will not only transform you from within, it will also supercharge your ability to form new neural habit circuits to support any other goal you choose. The more attuned you are to your innate superconscious awareness, the more dynamic you become; the more dynamic you are, the more rapidly and successfully you can form new neural habit circuits.

Focus on Wiring One Major Neural Habit Circuit at a Time

Don't try to establish more than one major new neural habit circuit at a time. A major habit is simply one that will require significant time, attention, and willpower to establish. We form and change minor habits almost without thinking—where we store information on our computer, the order in which we perform our morning routine, how long we steep our tea, the kind of toothpaste we use. Forming minor habits requires very little willpower; forming major neural habit circuits requires significantly more willpower, attention, and effort.

When embarking on rewiring your brain, don't make the classic New Year's-resolutions mistake—making long lists of major new habits to transform one's entire life. Surveys have shown that most people do not achieve *any* of their New Year's resolutions because, in their enthusiasm, they take on too many changes at once. In the beginning, they take on their new resolutions with strong will and high energy. But, after a few weeks, the constant willpower required to maintain so many resolutions wears on them. The initial joy in self-change is replaced by tension. They begin to feel less, not more, happy. Tension and discouragement eventually undermine their resolution. Their old neural habit circuits reassert themselves because they no longer *want* to exert the willpower to resist them. Any progress they made toward creating new supportive neural habit circuits is lost. Their partially formed new neural habit circuits begin to degrade. Their resolutions are forgotten until next year.

Be mindful of the power of existing habits. Existing, automatically firing, hard-wired neural habit circuits remain active even though you have made a decision to change. Your existing neural circuits fire just as easily and will be made to fire by the same incoming sensory, mental, or emotional stimuli as before you made your decision to change. Be mindful that every day the *vast majority* of your life force is automatically directed into behaviors by *existing* neural habit circuits. Don't try to rechannel too much of your life force at one time.

A note of warning about what is ahead in the remaining chapters: I suggest rewiring your brain to support many new habits that will make you more superconsciously aware. I make *many* more suggestions than you can immediately turn into habitual behavior. Even if you are as enthusiastic about integrating those suggestions into your life as I hope you will be, don't let your enthusiasm make you try to establish more than one major new habit at a time.

Be Positive

Another major mistake people make in efforts at self-improvement is trying to *stop* doing something negative, such as overeating, rather than to *start* doing something positive, such as eating healthier foods. It is wiser to systematically wire a new and positive neural habit circuit in order to *rechannel* your life force in a new direction than to try to suppress life force that is already being routed in an old and unwanted direction. When employing this strategy, make sure to focus your attention on your positive new habit, not on the negative old one.

Before choosing any new habit to establish make sure that you feel *especially* good about the new behavior you want to establish. Your new habit should be rewarding in and of itself, not just the remedy for an old negative habit. Whatever you choose, you should look forward to it, rather than feeling it is something you *should* do—but don't really *want* to do. The more positive, rewarding, and forward-looking you can make your efforts at wiring new neural habit circuits, the more successful you will be.

Be Realistic

Even if you winnow your choices to one new neural habit circuit, you need to be realistic about whether you have the willpower to do it. If, for example, you choose to establish a habit of meditation, when you have none today, don't set out to meditate three times a day for an hour at a time.

Know your limits and exceed them only by a little. Better to succeed at establishing the habit of meditating for ten minutes before going to bed than to fail at meditating for one hour three times a day. Better a small victory that builds your confidence, than a large failure that erodes your determination.

Be Methodical

Once you've made your choice of the most beneficial, positive, and realistic new neural habit circuit to wire, it is time to methodically plan as many ways as you can to make your effort successful. In order to give you concrete ideas of methodical planning, I'm going to use the example of establishing a meditation practice. If you already have wired a strong supporting neural habit circuit for meditation, mentally substitute any other positive habit you might want to establish instead.

Be Clear

Part of being methodical is to be as clear, specific, and exact as you can about your planned new habit. If you want to establish a new habit of meditation, what meditation technique are you going to use? If you haven't learned that particular technique, how are you going to learn it, and when? What time during your day are you going to meditate? Are there other habitual activities that you have been doing at that same time? If yes, what are you going to do with the old activity? Do it another time? Stop doing it? If you are going to meditate in the mornings, what time will you meditate and for how long? What does that mean for your rising time in the morning? Do you need to awaken a quarter, half, or a full hour earlier? Where are you going to meditate? What space can you use to meditate that will be quiet and allow you to leave your meditation things set up? How will you sit? Cross-legged? On a kneeling bench? On a chair?

Thoroughly answering these and similar questions pertinent to a specific habit you want to establish will bring into play the power of visualization. Visualization has been shown to build or strengthen neural circuits before you actually take any action. More on this in an upcoming chapter.

Don't Leap into It

After working out the details of your plan for establishing a new habit, give yourself enough time to consider and emotionally accept your plan—one person might need a day; another, a week; yet another, a month. When you get home in the evening and you are tired, how does your plan feel? When you are doing your usual morning routine that you are planning to change, how do you feel about changing it? Are there other people who will be affected by your choice to meditate? Do you think they will be impacted by your new behavior? What will you need to do to make it work for them? How do you feel about that?

After taking enough time to thoroughly consider your plan, modify it if you need to. Be creative in your modifications. If, after much consideration, waking at midnight to meditate for a half an hour and then returning to sleep feels like the only possible way you are really going to start meditating, then do so. Admittedly, it is highly unlikely that you or anyone else would make the choice to awake at midnight to meditate, but the point is to choose what you most believe will *work*.

Finally, set a specific date that you are going to begin establishing your habit of meditation. If you have a choice, don't choose to begin establishing your meditation habit during a period when you are going to travel a lot, have guests for extended periods, or have particularly challenging demands on your time. If avoiding these situations means waiting indefinitely before you start then rethink your plan and be as creative as possible in adapting your plan to work with travel, interruptions, or intensity of work.

Allow for Occasional Failure

If establishing a regular habit of meditation is going to be a challenge to your will, chances are you will falter a few times over the course of the weeks to months before new neural habit circuits have wired enough to support your practice. If you have been unrealistic about never faltering and then you do falter, you may feel that you are failing, or even worse, that *you* are a failure; your confidence will be shaken and your will weakened. By accepting in advance that you may falter you will be better able emotionally to take it in stride. Don't let a single lapse ambush your efforts with a strong attack of self-doubt.

Plan ahead for failure. Think about what you will do when you do falter. Perhaps allow yourself a certain number of get-out-of-jail-free days, days during which you give yourself permission to *not* meditate because you "just don't feel like it." Perhaps allow yourself to miss a certain number of meditations over the course of a month. Give yourself some kind of "out" if you have unexpected disruptions to your regular schedule.

Think these allowances through carefully. Even commit them to writing. Once you begin to establish your new habit, however, stick to these allowances—and no more. If you make too many allowances, the neural habit circuit will take much longer to wire and may not be as strongly supportive of your new habit as it could be.

Nor should these allowances be permanent. In time you should be able to meditate regularly even if you don't particularly "feel like it," even with the distractions of travel and visitors, or even if there are challenging situations in your life.

Support Your Goal

The advice in this section, more than perhaps in any of the sections above, takes advantage of today's deeper understanding of how neural habit circuits wire and how they support our behaviors.

One thing in particular that makes our most established neural habit circuits so powerfully supportive of behavior is that their complex interconnected circuits fire in response to many different types of stimuli—sensory perception, voluntary movement, autonomic physiological processes, thoughts, emotions, and memories. Any *one* of those stimuli will cause your entire neural habit circuit to fire.

What this means for you, in the context of deliberately wiring new neural habit circuits to support positive behaviors, is that the more activities and experiences you can *associate* with your goal, the more powerfully supportive your new neural habit circuit will become. The more things that positively remind you of your desired new habit—each of which will cause your neural habit circuit to fire—the stronger the support you get from your new neural habit circuit.

What does this mean in real terms? Here are some suggestions for our example of establishing a habit of meditation.

Create a place to meditate that is attractive and inspiring. You should *enjoy* your meditation space for any of a variety of reasons: it's beautiful; it feels peaceful; it contains pictures or objects that are inspiring to you; it reminds you of other spaces you've seen that inspire you. Once you've taken the time to make your meditation space as attractive to you as you can, just *seeing* your meditation space will become a positive stimulus that will make your entire meditation-supporting neural circuit fire, thus stimulating positive emotions and thoughts that make you want to meditate.

Make your meditation position as comfortable as possible. Once you have found the meditation position most comfortable for you, just *thinking* about how relaxed you have been in your meditations, or at any time when *sitting* in a similar way, will make your entire meditation-supporting neural circuit fire, thus stimulating positive emotions and thoughts that make you want to meditate.

Other suggestions for similar positive stimuli to make your entire meditation-supporting neural circuit fire, to stimulate positive emotions and thoughts that make you want to meditate:

- Activate favorite scents—such as incense, potpourri, natural oils—just before you begin to meditate. Activate the scent at other times during your day as well. Soon just smelling that scent will cause your fledgling neural habit circuit to fire and awaken your desire to meditate.

- Play music that moves or uplifts you—such as chanting, singing, or orchestral music—for a few minutes before you begin your meditation. Play the music at other times during your day as well. Again, hearing that music will strengthen your fledgling neural habit circuit by causing it to fire, making you want to meditate.

- Read a short passage of anything that moves or uplifts you before you meditate. Read such passages at other times during your day as well. You will find that even a *memory* of that short passage will strengthen your fledgling neural habit circuit by causing it to fire.

- Choose an affirmative sentence or two that sum up the positive reasons you want to meditate. Repeat with concentration a few times at the end of your meditation. Repeat the affirmative sentences at other times during the day as well. *Repeating the affirmative sentences*, or *considering the thoughts* in your affirmation, will strengthen your fledgling neural habit circuit by causing it to fire. (More on affirmations coming up.)

In all these ways—and I'm sure you can think of others—you will be building the strength of your new neural meditation-habit circuit. You are interconnecting particular positive and desirable *thoughts, smells, memories, body positions, sounds, emotions, and physical contact* with meditating. If your neural meditation-habit circuit fires because of any of these stimuli, the whole circuit will fire.

Set Your Intention

Make a pact with yourself. Emphasize to yourself the importance of whatever you are setting out to make into a habit. Make sure that your heart is fully in it. Visualize yourself being successful. Imagine how you will feel when you have succeeded. Awaken whatever feelings will make you the most determined to succeed. If your goal is establishing a meditation habit, imagine experiencing the expansive, peaceful, joyful feeling of the superconscious.

If you are feeling enthusiastic about whatever new neural habit circuit you are setting out to wire it may seem unnecessary to set your intention. But setting your intention with especial care can make all the difference when your will falters—when you aren't having the wonderful experience you'd hoped for, or when your life's demands are making establishing your new habit difficult, or when your existing neural habit circuits are stronger than you expected.

Expect to Put Out More Effort in the Beginning

When we start our process of wiring a new habit we do not yet have any neural wiring supporting our efforts, and initial success relies solely on our will and commitment. Think of riding a bicycle up to a plateau. Getting to the plateau is all uphill and will require determination, but once you make it to the plateau it will be far easier to maintain a steady pace. Similarly, getting started with a new habit is an uphill effort, but once your new neural habit circuit is established it will be far easier to maintain your new behavior.

Be Patient

It takes time to establish and benefit from a new habit. We may not reap significant benefits from our efforts for months. If we are establishing a new habit of meditation, inner superconscious experience may come slowly. Be patient. Even if your new habit takes a long while to give you its benefits—it *will* do so—and, once you have established your new habit, you will have wired *actual and lasting physiological changes in your brain* that will make your new habit easier to maintain indefinitely. Resist the temptation to give up on your new habit, or to move your focus to establishing another habit before the first one is fully established.

Summary

1. Get the Most from Your Efforts—Choose to establish a major new habit, and thus wire a new neural circuit to support it, that will give you the most benefit for the time, energy, and willpower it will require to establish it. New habits, such as meditation, that lead to super-conscious experience have the added benefit of supercharging your efforts and automatically strengthening other positive neural habit circuits.

2. Be Positive—Make sure that the new habit you set out to establish is something you truly *want* to do, not just something you think you *should* do.

3. Be Realistic—Better to be cautious and successfully wire a new neural habit circuit that supports a modest new habit than to be over-enthusiastic and fail at wiring a new neural habit circuit to support something more expansive. Build your confidence with modest successes until you are ready to take on more expansive goals.

4. Be Methodical
   a) Be Clear—Determine the particulars of your new habit. Visualize your goal. Be specific. Know exactly what and, more

importantly, how you are going to establish your new habit before you set out to do it.

b) Don't Leap into It—After setting your goal and before you embark, give yourself time to see how you feel about it, to measure it against the realities of your life, to consider its impact on other people in your life. The time spent considering your goal may reveal needed adjustments. Alter your goal, if necessary. Doing so will build your confidence in your ability to rewire your brain—to establish your chosen habit.

c) Allow for Failure—You may well fail to perform the actions of your new habit many times before you have fully established it. It is healthy to allow yourself *some* leeway. Don't let overly rigid expectations of yourself plunge you into thoughts of being a failure if you lapse a few times before you succeed.

5. Support Your Efforts—Take advantage of modern discoveries of how the brain works. Deliberately associate as many other positive things with your new habit as you can. Be creative in thinking of ways that you can associate your new habit you are trying to establish with other positive actions, thoughts, feelings, and memories. *These associations will make your goal much easier to achieve.*

6. Set Your Intention—Before you begin establishing your new habit and wiring a new neural habit circuit, make yourself as determined as you possibly can be to succeed. Set your heart's intention.

7. Expect to Put Out More Effort in the Beginning—When you begin your effort to establish a new habit, you do not yet have a neural habit circuit supporting your efforts. After some time your neural habit circuit will start to form and make it easier to establish your habit, but in the beginning you will need to be especially determined.

8. Be Patient—It will take time before your new habit is established and you are receiving the benefits. Even if your new habit takes a long while to give you its benefits—it *will* do so—and, once you have established your new habit, you will have wired *actual and enduring physiological change in your brain,* change that will make your new habit easier to perform and more successful.

CHAPTER 10

How to Meditate and Why

Meditation is the methodical application of the two key practices of the science of superconscious awareness: stillness and one-pointed concentration. One-pointed concentration at the point between the eyebrows, a technique at the heart of many meditation practices, intensely activates the prefrontal cortex of the brain, and physical stillness causes the rest of the brain to deactivate. The combination of the two minimizes physical awareness and maximizes superconscious awareness. The key practices of stillness and one-pointed concentration are in time supported by the formation of new neural habit circuits that make them successively easier and superconscious awareness successively deeper.

Meditation makes us more aware of our nonlocal energy body—our one foot in heaven—and this awareness makes us feel heavenly. Meditation gives us greater access to nonlocal realities: uplifting and harmonizing emotions, intuition and creativity, and an abundance of health-giving life force.

Meditation makes us aware of our Self in God. The Self is independent of both the physical and energy bodies. But greater awareness of our nonlocal energy body gives us greater awareness of the Self. Greater awareness of the Self simultaneously brings greater awareness of the ever-new joy that is God.

Lest you think that realizing the Self in God is far more than you want to commit to, be aware that you don't need to make such a commitment for meditation to be rewarding. Meditation will make you feel better no matter why you are practicing it. A wise man once said, "If people only *knew* how good they would feel if they meditated, *everyone* would meditate."

How to Meditate

I am going to teach you the *Hong-Sau* technique of meditation, which has been practiced in India for millennia. Why this particular technique rather than any other? It's not that I have personally tried every other meditation technique and decided this is the best one to offer you. Rather, my reason is simply that I have used this technique successfully for decades and I can therefore unhesitatingly recommend it. If you already have another technique that you practice, or have an interest in practicing, by all means do so.

How to Sit for Best Results

Find a sitting positon that allows you to sit as comfortably as you can with the spine erect and the body relaxed. You can sit in a chair, on a kneeling bench or kneeling pillow, or cross-legged with or without a pillow. All of these positions are equally effective. Deep meditators with many years of experience often use a chair for their meditations.

If you are sitting in a chair, sit with your feet flat on the floor and your thighs parallel to the floor. You can put a pillow under your feet if your legs are too short or a pillow on the seat of your chair if your legs are too long. Do not lean against the back of the chair. The idea is to sit with an upright, unsupported spine, with the body relaxed. If you are not used to this position, or if the condition of your back makes it difficult, you can put a pillow between your back and the back of the chair. If you use a pillow behind your back, the feeling you want to have is that the pillow is supporting your upright position, not that you are leaning your weight against it. Adjust the pillow until you achieve this feeling.

Your choice of sitting position should allow you to relax the shoulders and keep the chin parallel to the floor with eyes facing directly forward. As an aid to keeping your spine erect rest your hands with the palms facing up at the juncture between thighs and torso.

If you prefer to sit on the floor, kneeling benches can help make your legs feel comfortable and help keep the spine straight. Finding the right size and height is important. Padding on the bench seat often helps. Adding small pillows under the knees or ankles may also facilitate your comfort. Those who are more comfortable sitting cross-legged on a pillow can try the crescent-shaped or round meditation pillows designed to help with this position, but any pillow you have that makes you comfortable will do just fine.

If you sit on the floor without a meditation pillow, make sure your spine is still straight, your shoulders relaxed, and your chin parallel to the floor with eyes facing directly forward. Your knees should remain close to the floor. If your knees do not remain close to the floor your spine will bend. Your position should allow you to place your hands comfortably, palms facing upward, at the juncture between thighs and torso.

Where to Meditate

If possible, set aside an area where you will not be disturbed and that you use exclusively for meditation. A small room, or a corner of your bedroom—even a closet can suffice, as long as it is well ventilated. The place where you meditate should be a little on the cool side with a source of fresh air if possible, so that you are alert and awake.

Brief Preparation before Practicing the *Hong-Sau* Technique

Once you are sitting comfortably, I recommend doing two brief breathing exercises to relax and harmonize body and breath before you begin the *Hong-Sau* technique.

Tense and Relax

Inhale sharply through the nose, with one short and one long inhalation, while simultaneously tensing the whole body. Hold breath and tension for a few seconds, then exhale forcibly through the mouth, with one short and one long exhalation, simultaneously releasing the tension in your muscles. Repeat three to six times.

Balance Your Breathing

After you complete the tense-and-relax breathing exercise, inhale slowly, counting to eight, hold the breath for eight counts, then exhale slowly for eight counts. Without pausing, inhale again, hold, and exhale, once more to the count of eight. Repeat this exercise three to six times. You can vary the count according to your lung capacity, but always with inhalation, holding, and exhalation equal in length. Finish your practice by inhaling deeply, then exhaling completely.

Hong-Sau Technique of Concentration

You are now ready to begin the *Hong-Sau* technique. Close your eyes (if you haven't already). Wait for your next breath to come in of its own accord. When it does, mentally say *hong* (rhymes with *song*). Don't hold the breath. Exhale naturally. As you exhale, mentally say *sau* (rhymes with *law*). *Hong sau* is an ancient Sanskrit mantra. It means "I am He" or "I am Spirit."

Make no attempt to control the breath. Simply observe the breath as it flows naturally in and out. In the beginning you may be aware of your breath primarily in your chest and abdomen as your lungs expand and contract. As the breath grows calmer, focus your attention on the cool sensation in your nostrils when you inhale and the warm sensation in your nostrils when you exhale. Gradually become aware of the cool and warm sensations higher and higher in the nasal passages, until your awareness of the cool and warm sensations of the breath is focused at the point between the eyebrows.

Now also bring your closed eyes to a focus at the point between the eyebrows. Do not cross or strain your eyes. Your eyes should be relaxed, as if looking slightly up at some distant point. Without muscular tension, let your focus at the point between the eyebrows deepen, while continuing simply to observe the cool and warm sensations of the breath at the point between the eyebrows. If you find that your mind has wandered, gently bring it back to an awareness of the breath, to your mental repetition of *hong* and *sau*, and to your eyes' focus at the point between the eyebrows.

Once you reach the point where your awareness of the breath is centered at the point between the eyebrows, try to become as focused at that point as you can without inadvertently tensing the facial muscles or holding the breath in or out. Try to feel as if your entire being is focused at this point. When you can do so, you will find a wonderful world opening to you. I will describe below some of the amazing things that can happen.

Sit in the Stillness

Finish your practice of *Hong Sau* by deeply inhaling and exhaling and then forget the breath. Concentrate deeply at the point between the eyebrows.

Keep your mind focused and your energy internalized. Absorb yourself in the peace generated by your practice. Continue for at least five minutes.

How Often and How Long to Practice

Try to practice *Hong Sau* at least once a day for fifteen minutes. As you come to enjoy it more, you can increase your time to thirty minutes, then to an hour or more—always leaving time at the end of your practice of *Hong Sau* to enjoy the peaceful and harmonious results. It is good to meditate twice a day, in the morning and at night. Find a schedule that works for you. It is good to stretch your time meditating, but don't strain. Doing a longer meditation once a week, about one and a half times to twice as long, will help you to increase the length and depth of your regular meditation.

What You Might Experience while Doing the *Hong-Sau* Technique

Difficulty Staying Focused on the Breath

It is quite common to experience difficulty keeping your attention focused on the breath and on mentally repeating *hong* and *sau* in rhythm with the breath. Don't think yourself not capable or not "cut out" for meditation. It is a skill to learn just like any other. When you recognize that you are no longer watching the breath, simply bring your attention back to it again. You may lose focus many times. Be patient with yourself. Your concentration will improve.

Difficulty Not Controlling the Breath

It is also quite common to have difficulty allowing the breath to come in and go out naturally. You may find yourself deliberately breathing in and out more deeply, or holding the breath in or out longer, than if the breath were flowing naturally. If this problem occurs every time you meditate, try doing more rounds of the preparatory breathing exercises before you begin your *Hong-Sau* practice—tense and relax six or twelve times instead of three; do the balancing breath exercise six or twelve times as well. If you still find yourself deliberately controlling the breath after you have begun your *Hong-Sau* practice, you can stop your practice long enough to repeat either or both of the preparatory breathing exercises before continuing the technique itself.

Other solutions: try mentally dissociating yourself from the body by imagining that you are sitting slightly behind yourself and watching another body breathe. You can also consciously relax the area around the solar plexus: Trust that the body will breathe just as it should on its own.

Difficulty Sitting Still

Nearly everyone who is learning to meditate has difficulty sitting still. After you've completed the preparatory breathing exercises, at the very beginning of your meditation, resist the impulse to make little adjustments to your position. If you successfully resist the impulse for even five minutes you will find that the body becomes more still. If you have time, as a further aid to releasing restlessness, you may also want to do yoga postures, or other gentle stretches, before you begin the preparatory breathing exercises. Also trust that sitting still will become more and more supported by rapidly forming neural meditation-habit circuits.

Your Breath May Become Deeper or More Shallow

As you watch your breath you may find that your breath keeps the same rhythm but becomes more shallow. Or you may find that the rhythm of your breath slows and that both inhalation and exhalation become much deeper. Either is good.

Natural Pauses between Breaths Become Longer

You may notice that the natural pause between inhalation and exhalation or exhalation and inhalation becomes longer. This extended pause is normal and positive. Normal because in physical stillness your cells' lessened need to take in oxygen and expel carbon dioxide causes the breath to slow naturally. Positive because you will soon find these natural pauses between breaths to be calming, relaxing, and peaceful. Enjoy these moments particularly, but with no attempt to hold the breath. Forcibly holding the breath, in or out, will disrupt the calm, natural rhythm of your breathing.

Breath Rate Becomes Profoundly Slow

As you become more adept at *Hong Sau* you may find that you are breathing so shallowly or so slowly that it is difficult to be aware of the breath. This experience brings a wonderful feeling. It is very rare, but possible, that your breathing stops altogether; more usually breathlessness comes only after many years of practice. If you experience the cessation of the breath for tens of seconds to minutes, you won't need me to reassure you that this is OK, because it will feel *utterly* wonderful. Nor should you be concerned that the breath will not resume—the slightest physical movement will trigger the breath to begin again.

Heart Rate Becomes Profoundly Slow

Although your focus while practicing *Hong Sau* should not be on your heart rate, slowing of the breath rate will be accompanied by a corresponding slowing of the heart rate and for the same reason. In physical stillness the heart does not need to pump as much oxygenated blood to the cells nor take away as much carbon waste product. If your heart rate slows profoundly, you won't need me to reassure you that this is OK, because it will feel *beyond* wonderful. People who have mastered *Hong Sau* can go for extended periods of time with no heartbeat at all.

If the idea of your heart slowing down or even stopping is scary, I want to assure you that there is zero chance that, while practicing the *Hong Sau*, your heart could stop permanently or be damaged in any way. Your heart will have slowed or stopped because your cells' natural demand for oxygen is reduced or has stopped. As soon as you move or inhale, your cells will call for oxygen, and your heart rate will increase or resume just as naturally as it slowed or stopped. The heart stopping is even more rare than the breath stopping; the experience comes for the most part only to the most advanced practitioners.

Your Concentration Deepens

If you haven't already practiced *Hong Sau*, or a similar meditation technique, it may be difficult to imagine how concentration can become deeper and deeper. With practice you'll find that as the body becomes still, and the breath slows, the mind will slow as well. As the usual flow of thoughts slows, emotional tensions will be released, the body will fade from your awareness, and your concentration will become more and more one-pointed.

You Will Likely See Light

Even early on in your practice of *Hong Sau*, you may see various colors of light in the darkness behind your closed eyes. The light may be perceived at or around the point between the eyebrows. You may see white, blue, or golden light, or a combination of all three. The light may form into a circle at the point between the eyebrows: a deep azure blue field surrounded by golden light, with a tiny white star in the center. This phenomenon, usually referred to as the spiritual eye, is mentioned in many experiential spiritual traditions, perhaps most familiarly to westerners in the New Testament: "if therefore thine eye be single, thy whole body shall be full of light." (Matthew 6:22)

You Will Likely Experience Emotional Release

Hong Sau enables you to relax on deep levels: physical, mental, and emotional. Emotional relaxation is generally first experienced as a sense of peace and well-being. The heart center in your subtle energy body may be closed against situations and conditions in your life that you do not want to experience. Deep emotional relaxation can feel as if a fist in your heart has relaxed or as if warmth is spreading outward from your heart.

You Will Likely Become Inwardly Absorbed in Superconscious Experience

When you have superconscious experience you will have no doubts about its reality. There may be a sense of well-being wholly unrelated to anything happening in your life. There may be a thrill of energy rising in the center of your body that makes you feel energized, positive, and enthusiastic. There may be a feeling of sacred joy or of the "peace that passeth all understanding." Once experienced you'll know, as millions before you have come to know, that there is another world within you and that you are experiencing your superconscious Self in God.

Your Brain Will Rewire to Support Physical, Mental, and Emotional Health

Not only does meditation rewire the brain to support deeper meditation and superconscious awareness, over time the neural habit circuits that support meditation will expand and connect to other circuits in the brain and even alter the structure of brain regions.[1] Our neural meditation-habit circuit can fire to stimulate positive harmonizing emotions;[2] by reducing stress it can activate healthy physiological processes such as detoxification, elimination, digestion, and healing;[3] and can even activate genes that affect our physical, mental, and emotional health.[4][5] Our neural meditation-habit circuit becomes, in time, the most significant positive influence on our health and well-being—it can even positively affect those around us.[6] In times of stress, or during emotional or mental challenges, our neural meditation-supporting, positive emotion–supporting, health-promoting circuits will also influence us to be less emotionally and negatively reactive. While the neural habit circuits that support negative emotions remain in the brain, our meditation-formed neural habit circuit will inhibit or dampen their firing.

Your Life Will Be Changed

The more we practice concentration in meditation the more concentrated we become in life. Concentration brings us intuitive insights we can use in all aspects of our lives. Problem-solving becomes easier and our solutions more creative. We become more focused and less easily distracted. Learning becomes accelerated. We become more efficient. Performance, in everything from sports to playing music, flows more naturally and with less tension. We become more present in the moment.

The more we practice meditation the more our life improves. Minor health issues may fade away. We may find ourselves more open, considerate, lovingly compassionate, and more spontaneously helpful toward others. We may find ourselves more centered and less reactive in our emotions.

We may find that we flow through our day with less resistance. We simply become happier.

Meditate. Meditate regularly. Meditate as deeply and for as long as you can. If you embrace nothing else from this book, if you embrace nothing else from this book, meditate. It will change your life.

CHAPTER 11

Relaxation

A hallmark of saints and sages is their effortless relaxation—physical, mental, and emotional—expressed as serenity, tranquility, peace, and poise.

> With mindfulness and concentration . . . you can find your true
> home in the full relaxation of your mind and body in the present
> moment.
> —Thích Nhất Hạnh, Buddhist monk[1]

> Peace is the simplicity of heart, serenity of mind, tranquility of
> soul. . . .
> —Padre Pio of Pietrelcina, Christian mystic[2]

> Resurrection means relaxation, to relax your awareness from
> your body and mind in meditation. Then you become free. . . .
> —Paramahansa Yogananda, yoga master[3]

While few of us have yet to experience such depth of relaxation, most of us *have* experienced that we feel better when we are relaxed. The more relaxed we are the better we feel. Perfect relaxation accompanies perfect joy and perfect joy accompanies perfect relaxation—they are both an inextricable part of superconscious experience.

Meditation is by far the most effective way to relax. One of the most common experiences people have when they are first learning to meditate is the gratifying release of physical tension. The determination to be physically still in meditation will make you aware of your patterns of tension; the more you meditate, the more you will feel those tensions melting away.

Deeper practice of meditation will bring a deeper experience of relaxation. Practice of *Hong Sau* can cause the breath and heart rate to fall below even the rates experienced in sleep, and in consequence a release of deeper physical and emotional tensions you may not have known you had.

The deepest relaxation in meditation comes in superconscious experience—moments of bliss, exhilarating waves of energy rising from the core of the body to the brain, heart-opening love. Such experiences are wonderful in themselves but also rewire the brain the most broadly, effectively, and rapidly.

As a general rule, the more deeply we meditate, the more able we are to release tension; conversely, the more tense we are, the more difficult it is to meditate. Tension makes the body restless, foiling our attempts to become still; physical restlessness makes the mind restless, foiling our attempts to achieve one-pointed concentration.

If you find yourself having ongoing difficulty meditating because of physical and mental restlessness caused by chronic tension—especially tension caused by emotional stress—you may need to supplement your meditation efforts with other practices.

As with all our habitual physical behaviors, chronic tension is caused by neural circuits in the brain. Most neural habit circuits consist of an interconnected mixture of neurons that stimulate thoughts, memories, and emotions, and neurons that trigger patterns of muscular contraction and relaxation. One result of such mixed circuits is that negative thoughts, memories, or emotions occur simultaneously with the contraction of our muscles into patterns of uncomfortable tension; if our negative thoughts and memories, and particularly our negative emotions, are chronic, then our physical tension patterns will be chronic as well.

To become free of the tension automatically caused by such a circuit when it fires we need to do two things: first, to recognize and avoid the triggers that cause the circuit to fire; second, for a permanent solution, to create new neural habit circuits with an oppositely positive effect—circuits that stimulate positive thoughts, memories, and emotions, and so trigger muscular patterns of relaxation.

There are several approaches and practices that help us do this—but they all begin with *introspection.*

Introspection

Introspection is a methodical process of self-examination that can be used to understand our "autopilot" mode—the "fast-thinking," automatically firing circuits in the brain that determine so much of behavior and experience. Used well, introspection can not only identify that a particular automatic circuit exists, but can also make us aware of the triggers that cause the circuit to fire—and of the thoughts, memories, and emotions awakened by the circuits firing. Introspection can also identify other circuits affected by and affecting the particular circuit we have identified. Finally, introspection helps us appreciate the particular circuit's strength and positive or negative impact on our ability to relax, meditate, or access superconscious awareness.

Introspection is an all-purpose practice. In the chapters ahead we will explore how introspection can be used to help you overcome other limiting behaviors that keep you from accessing the superconscious. In this chapter, we will explore how to use introspection specifically to help you overcome chronic physical tension that is keeping you from the deep stillness in meditation necessary to access the superconscious.

Most Tension Is the Result of Negative Emotions

Negative emotion is the main cause of chronic tension. There are schools of thought that suggest there is no such thing as negative emotion, that all emotion has a positive purpose and a benefit. You will hear people say, for example, that they needed their anger to get through a certain situation, or that fear made them wise. I think there is practical truth in that way of thinking—but I think it is no longer practical truth when such emotions become chronic.

Chronic emotions such as worry, anxiety, anger, guilt, envy, jealousy, hatred, fear of loss, and fear of our responsibilities are what cause the body to stay unnaturally long, even indefinitely, in a fight-or-flight mode. When these emotions are chronic their effect is clearly negative because they leave us unhealthily tense, unhappy, and unable to deliberately relax, meditate, or open to the superconscious. Chronic negative emotions are negative because they are destroyers of present happiness and because they block our potential for even greater future happiness.

All chronic negatively emotional habit circuits automatically affect the body as well as the emotions by sending nerve signals that result in patterns of chronic tension—and which often lead to ill health. Anger and fear make the muscles around the navel tighten up, forcing the torso to lean forward and impairing digestion. Feeling victimized or unsafe makes our shoulders hunch forward and the chest muscles constrict, as if protecting our heart, both of which impair our breathing. Feeling unworthy makes us slump, creating poor posture, which impairs the free flow of life force in the body. Fearful reactions to deadlines, responsibilities, and self-imposed expectations make the backs of the legs tighten up so that we are stiff and uncomfortable. Fear of losing valued possessions, position, or loved ones makes us tighten up and lose flexibility in the lower spine and hips.

Any one of these patterns of chronic tension can make sitting with relaxed stillness in meditation difficult to impossible.

Introspection Gives Us Perspective

Introspection and neuroscience can give us a much-needed impersonal perspective on our personally confusing tangle of chronic negative emotions and resulting patterns of tension. As a starting point, it is helpful to consider that such a confusing tangle is the result of neurons firing in the brain; it does *not* emerge from deep in your character.

One's current brain circuitry is not an expression of destiny; negative emotions are not indicators of who we "really are." The initial choices we have made to react emotionally in negative ways are more likely the result of childhood conditioning, trauma, or the influence of those around us than of a well-considered and deliberate choice. Whatever their source, the negative emotional neural habit circuits we have formed in our life have begun as only temporary experiments in experience—like a child working out how to build a tower of blocks, we were working out how to be happy. Our temporary experiments in such negative emotions as anger and fear have become habitual, alas, not because we really want to keep on experiencing them, not because they come from some inner formless essence of who we really are, but because brain circuits have quickly formed to make them automatic and the more the automatic experience was triggered the stronger it became.

Our habitual negative emotions are not *us*. We are not our neural circuits any more than we are our liver or our left foot.

All Situations Are Neutral

Another basic principle to guide our introspection is that all situations are neutral. Situations have no actual power to *make* us react to them either positively or negatively.

> No person, no place, and no thing has any power over us, for "we" are the only thinkers in our mind.
> —Louise L. Hay, author of *You Can Heal Your Life*[4]

We don't *have to* react negatively to *anything*. Our negative emotional neural habit circuits, however, rather sneakily make us think otherwise. Negative emotional neural habit circuits are self-reinforcing—when triggered, not only does the negative emotion itself emerge, but along with it come familiar mental justifications and emotion-tinged memories to support it. Because of our self-reinforcing mental justifications we often become *convinced* that our reactions are perfectly appropriate, *that the situation is the problem*, and that we have *no choice* but to react to it.

Don't believe everything you think.

We don't have to react negatively to life's difficult situations. In fact, introspection should focus on the intricacies of our neural emotional habit circuit—the triggers, justifications, and core emotional needs that convince us we should react—rather than on the situation that triggered the circuit to fire. The situation itself is always neutral.

How to Introspect

When to Introspect

Introspection is best done in the natural pauses between the times you are engaged in your life's activities. You can introspect at any time in your day. Practicing introspection after meditation is recommended. Your meditation-calmed mind and emotions make it easier to introspect clearly. Once you establish the habit of introspection you will find yourself introspecting often, especially when alone and between activities. I recommend that you take time to deliberately introspect once a day, a couple times a week, or at the very least, once a week.

Ask Yourself a Question

It can be very helpful to focus your introspection by asking yourself a question. It is all too easy to meander mentally through your experiences without gaining any significant insight. A question will give focus to your introspection. I will be sharing several questions you could ask yourself in this and upcoming chapters; you can come up with your own questions as you become comfortable with the process. For the purpose of becoming more able to relax deeply, I suggest you ask yourself this question:

"What made me tense today?"

Journaling

You may want to write down introspective thoughts and insights in a journal. Clarifying thoughts well enough to write them down can lend a clearer focus to the process of introspection. It also allows us to look back in time by rereading the journal to see how our thoughts and insights have evolved. Journaling will give you a strong start to establishing a habit of introspection. Once you have established a strong practice of introspection, however, you may no longer need or want to journal and can successfully introspect in a purely mental fashion.

Look for Three Insights

Ideally, introspection on what makes us tense should give us three types of insight:
- What triggers our emotionally negative neural habit circuits
- Flaws in our justifications for embracing our negative emotions
- The underlying emotional need that causes us to react

Here is a hypothetical example to show how those insights might emerge from introspection.

Mr. X tends to be tense and anxious. Today, his neural anxiety habit circuit fires when he hears a rumor that there will be layoffs at his workplace. Without making a conscious choice to do so, he begins to worry not only about whether he will be laid off, but also about what he will do to make rent payments and car payments, whether he will have to cancel his planned vacation, and whether any other company will want to hire him, and wonders what to do about his out-of-date resume. Simultaneously his body has gone into fight-or-flight mode. His body becomes tense and his concentration diminishes. He remains worried all day, his mind churns through what ifs, he barely eats lunch, and he gets very little accomplished at work.

Work over, Mr. X is back home, and before dinner he decides to introspect. He asks himself the question: What made me tense today? Identifying the trigger of his anxiety is easy: it is the possibility that he may be laid off. Looking for a pattern, he remembers other times when he's felt like this and sees that the triggers were, in those cases, political and economic news that suggested to him that the country was declining and the economy collapsing. Those triggers have set him thinking that politicians these days are interested only in reelection, not about making his world better for him, and worrying about whether his financial situation can withstand a recession.

Mr. X wisely realizes that trying to recognize the flaws in his justifications for anxiety would be difficult because he is still feeling anxious and stressed. He decides to take a break and introspect again later. His evening passes; he begins to relax; he eats dinner with enjoyment. The tension of fight-or-flight mode is replaced by the relaxation of the rest-and-digest mode. Later that evening he begins anew his process of introspection by thinking about his justifications for today's anxiety.

The first thing that he recognizes is that he has been worrying about something that probably won't happen. Next he recognizes that should he, in fact, be laid off, it could be an opportunity to get a better job elsewhere. Loss of his job doesn't automatically mean that he is on the road to financial ruin. He also recognizes, with more than usual insight, that it was not the actual facts of the *situation* but rather his *emotion* of anxiety that convinced him that he needed to worry.

Having made it to this degree of insight he asks himself another question: What unmet emotional need do I have that makes me worry? He examines the times when he has been catapulted into the same negative emotion as today's and he begins to see a pattern. Every trigger—potential loss of job, potential political failure to provide basic services, potential economic recession—has to do with feeling *unsafe*. He realizes that on a deep level he simply doesn't ever feel truly safe. The world has long appeared to him to be a precarious place in which all manner of things can and will go wrong and snatch away his well-being and security.

Although such a realization could at other times have pitched him back into more anxiety, tonight he asks himself a deeper question: why do I always think that I am unsafe? He has a key realization: the *emotion* that he is unsafe and the *thought* that he is unsafe are two parts of the same experience, two aspects of the same neural circuit firing in response to triggers. He realizes that no matter how well his life may go in future he will still tend to *feel* that he is unsafe and he will therefore still *think* he is unsafe whenever that neural circuit fires. He is left, finally, with the most important question: what can I do to *feel* safe regardless of what is going on around me? With that question he is on his way to finding lasting solutions.

Mr. X has gained three types of insight.

1. He has identified a common theme to the triggers of his anxiety: potential loss of his job, unwelcome political events, concerns about the economy—all threats to his current settled world.
2. He has seen how his thoughts justify his anxiety: if he is laid off, no other company will hire him, he'll have no income, he won't be able to pay the rent, he won't get a vacation. . . . He has realized that it is not that those justifications make him anxious, rather that it is his anxiety that makes him come up with those justifications.
3. Most importantly, he has recognized that the core emotion that gives rise to his anxiety is that *he does not feel safe*: he has long had a strong conviction that the world is not a safe place, and that circumstances can at any time change in a way that can destroy his well-being.

Not all of our efforts at introspection will be as neat, tidy, and pat as my example above, nor will they be filled with insights that come so easily and clearly. Most insights only come when we are ready to let go of our justifications, when we are ready to accept that, if we want to release our tensions and be happy, we need to change ourselves rather than our circumstances. And even when we have accepted our need to change ourselves, we tend to gain insights only gradually, much like peeling away the layers of the proverbial onion.

We may also need help. The negative neural habit circuits that cause our unwanted automatic emotions, thoughts, patterns of tension, and behaviors may have formed in childhood or as the result of confusing adult emotional traumas. In either case identifying our core feelings may be difficult. A wise friend that you trust with your feelings may be able to act as a sounding board and to offer insights you can't come to on your own. Spiritual counselors may be able to give you insights born of a different perspective. Professional therapists can employ various methods for helping you to recall hidden emotional experience in a safe way.

If you do go into therapy with a professional, I urge you to make sure your therapist actively embraces experiential spirituality and personally meditates. I offer this caveat because there is a strong bias running through mainstream psychology that all the superconscious experiences I have described and quoted since the beginning of this book are not only not possible, but they are in fact delusional. I also urge you, if you go into therapy or are already in therapy, to maintain your own perspective. If the advice you are receiving, or the insights offered, do not feel right to you, don't assume that your therapist is right and you are wrong. Add the contributions of your therapist to your own practice of introspection to arrive at your own genuine insights. Do not become dependent on your therapist. No one can know you as well as you know yourself.

What to Do with Insights from Introspection

Keep in mind that you need to deal directly with your negative emotions only if they are keeping you from accessing the superconscious in meditation. If you *can* successfully go deeper and deeper into meditation, then make that the focus your efforts. If you *are* able to go deeper and deeper in meditation, your negative emotions will be indirectly transformed by the magnetic influence of the superconscious; your positive emotions and qualities will arise naturally.

If, on the other hand, a particularly strong neural circuit supporting chronic negative emotion and tension is often making meditation difficult—not to mention making you unhappy and unhealthy—and if you are prepared to make a major change in your life, then you may well want to establish methodically and deliberately an oppositely positive neural habit circuit to offset the neural circuit that is supporting your chronic negative emotion.

I want to be very clear that I am not suggesting that you try to *suppress* your negative emotions in order to avoid unwelcome chronic tensions. If anything, we need to develop *more* feeling, not less, to offset the tendency of chronic tension to deaden us to our own and others' feelings. More importantly, superconscious experience is accompanied by profound feeling. If we suppress our negative feelings, we cut ourselves off from all feeling—including the highest feeling of superconscious joy.

Suppressing feeling is not the way to happiness. What I *am* suggesting is that you can free yourself of an automatic negative emotional response by methodically and sensitively *rechanneling your life force* in the form of emotional energy into more positive expression.

In an earlier chapter I described emotion as a movement of life force in the energy body—and what one feels when life force moves in the energy body is what is called an emotion. An emotional experience is not an entity in itself; it is life force moving in a certain way—expanding or contracting, rising or falling—in the energy body. Life force rising and expanding is a wonderful emotional experience—inspiring, joyful. Life force falling and contracting is an unpleasant emotional experience—depressing, sad.

Life force is neutral. It can give life equally to a negative or to a positive emotional experience. Rechanneling life force does not suppress the expression of a negative emotion; it simply rechannels the life force into more positive expression.

How to Rechannel Your Life Force into a More Positive Emotional Expression

Set a Goal

If you feel that you need to deliberately rechannel your life force into a new, positive expression to offset a negative emotion that is keeping you from meditating, carefully select an oppositely positive emotion you want to foster. Mr. X, for example, would be wise to develop a neural habit circuit that supports *feeling safe*—founded on the thought that he is profoundly safe in the superconscious, that nothing and no one can take away the *feeling* of absolute emotional safety he will have in ever-new superconscious joy.

Anxiety and worry can be offset by feeling safe in joy. Jealousy, by feeling loved by the Divine. Envy, by feeling complete in the Self. Fear of loss, by feeling part of Infinite Abundance. Anger, by trusting in a Higher purpose.

You can find help in selecting the positive emotion you want to foster to offset a negative emotion by studying the science of positive affirmation. Think of positive affirmations as antidotes to negative emotions. More on this coming up.

Make a Plan

Come up with a plan—use the methodical process I shared in chapter 9 as a template—a plan that supports your effort to establish a new neural habit circuit. Practices you will find below—affirmations, yoga postures with affirmations, and a deep relaxation exercise—can be used in your plan to deliberately create a new positive neural habit circuit.

Avoid Triggering the Negative Emotion You Are Trying to Offset

Avoiding the triggers that set off the troublesome negative emotional circuit can be a helpful rear-guard tactic while we form an oppositely positive neural habit circuit to fully offset the negative one. We are unlikely to be able to avoid *all* external triggers—unless we live in a cave—and even in a cave we would have brought our own internal mental and emotional triggers with us. Some triggers, however, *can* be avoided. Mr. X could avoid one trigger by simply cutting down on the amount of news he reads.

Affirmations

Affirmations are a powerful support to any effort you make to rewire your brain. They go right to the heart of the new positive emotion you want to experience.

One way to understand the power of affirmations is to realize that your mental justifications for being in a *negative* emotional state are *unintentional* affirmations. Mr. X might say, with great conviction, "How can anyone feel safe in a world where there could be nuclear war at any minute? Or when some idiot tries to kill you on the freeway? Or when you could lose your job and all your money tomorrow?" Unintentionally, in all these thoughts he would be strongly affirming, "I. Don't. Feel. Safe." Such affirmations are very effective. The more strongly he believed them the less safe he would feel. The longer he believed them the stronger the supporting neural habit circuits would become.

You can use the power of affirmations intentionally and positively. Find a wholly positive statement that encapsulates what you want to feel, then deliberately say it and think it until you believe it with conviction. This conviction, born of methodical and concentrated repetition of the chosen affirmation, will form the central circuit of your new positive neural habit circuit. You can, for example, offset chronically feeling unsafe with affirmations such as the following:

> I remain ever safe within the impregnable walls of my inner peace.[5]

> I live in the fortress of God's inner presence. Nothing and no one can break through these walls.[6]

I accept with calm impartiality whatever comes my way. Free in
my heart, I am not conditioned by any outward circumstance.
Whatever comes of itself, let it come.[7]

Once you choose an affirmation, repeat it several times during your
day, especially in meditation. Practice methodically: If you are alone, say it
loudly to get your own attention, then more softly a few times, whisper it a
few more times, and then finally say it mentally with deep concentration.
In the last stage of mental repetition feel it as much as you say it, believe it
as much as you feel it, and, as much as you can, feel that the superconscious
superpowers of the Self, and the blessings of God, are giving your affirmation transformative power.

Affirmations, through methodical and focused repetition, and above all
by supercharged superconscious repetition, can form a new neural habit
circuit to support a new positive emotion, attitude, or conviction in weeks
to months.

For more on the power and use of affirmations, as well as many specific affirmations for various purposes, I recommend two books: *Scientific
Healing Affirmations* by Paramahansa Yogananda and *Affirmations for
Self-Healing* by Swami Kriyananda. As with all my recommendations, I
make these not because I have tried every source of affirmations and know
these to be the best, but because I have used these personally with great
success. If you have other sources of affirmations that you already use and
find helpful, by all means continue to use them.

You can also carefully craft your own affirmation. If you do, be sure to be
wholly positive. The mind hears, "I am no longer unsafe," as "I *am* unsafe."
I also recommend including in your affirmative thought the recognition of
the higher superconscious powers of Self and the powerful support of God:
Rather than just "I am safe, I am sound," add a deeper dimension such as
"in the deep peace of my own Self and God."

Above all, whether you use an affirmation written by another or you
craft your own, use an affirmation that you can *believe*—not necessarily
something you think is already true of yourself—but something you believe

can *become* true of yourself. Sincere belief, and especially sincere belief that includes superconscious potential, will form a new neural habit circuit the most rapidly and effectively.

Yoga Postures with Affirmations

Think of a yoga posture as a positive *physical* affirmation.

If you suffer from not feeling safe, the neural habit circuit that supports that feeling also sends signals to the muscles in your chest. The muscles contract as if protecting the heart from emotional attack and thereby restrict the breathing and pull the shoulders and neck forward. If you chronically do not feel safe, then your posture will become chronically hunched and you will habitually breathe shallowly.

A yoga posture that expands your chest, gently arches your upper back, and in which you breathe fully and deeply is a physical affirmation of feeling relaxed and open to life—the opposite of feeling unsafe—because when you *are* relaxed and open to life, your chest is naturally relaxed, your breathing is full, your head is up, and your shoulders relaxed. When you perform such a yoga posture (or any kind of stretching movements that affect your body in the same way, such as Pilates or tai chi), you are not simply stretching out a particular set of muscles, you are forming circuits in the brain that support the feeling of being open and safe.

The system of yoga postures that I practice—*Yoga Postures for Self-Awareness*, developed by Swami Kriyananda—adds a mental affirmation to the posture. The affirmation reinforces the physical affirmation of the posture itself and thus doubly strengthens the circuits that you are forming to support a new positive emotion (such as being open and safe).

The simple sun pose is a good example of posture and affirmation working together: While standing, extend one leg out before the other, knee of the extended leg bent slightly, both feet flat on the floor. Keep the weight centered between the feet. Bring the arms up from your sides placing the palms together above the head. Gently arch the back, bringing the head and arms slightly back as well, breathe deeply, and while holding the pose, mentally affirm, "I am free; I am free." Then repeat, extending the opposite leg.

Yoga postures done with affirmations are a powerful mental and emotional tonic and can give greater benefits than when practiced purely as a physical exercise. Developed specifically to enable sitting still, yoga postures are especially invaluable as a preparation for meditation.

For specific purposes, such as the development of a new positive emotion, focus on postures whose affirmations support your effort. If you are wiring a new neural habit circuit to support the feeling of being safe, choose a specific set of postures to do every day that expand the chest, arch the upper back, and deepen the breathing and that are accompanied by affirmations that awaken feelings of safety and expansiveness.

Deep Relaxation Exercise

The deep relaxation exercise brings a meditative focus to the physical release of tension. To practice, lie on the floor, legs straight, arms along the sides. Turn up the palms of the hands. Head, neck, trunk, and legs should be in a straight line. Do not use a pillow in this position; the flow of blood should be equal to all parts of the body.

Do the tense-and-relax breathing technique followed by the balancing breath (as taught in the chapter on the *Hong-Sau* technique of meditation). After you finish doing these breathing exercises do not move your body or try to control the breath in any way.

Remaining motionless, visualize the body surrounded by space—space in all directions, spreading out to infinity. Now think of your feet; visualize the surrounding space gradually seeping through the pores of the skin into the feet, until the feet themselves become space. After a pause, visualize space gradually filling the calves. After another pause visualize space gradually entering the thighs. Continue in this manner through hips, abdomen and stomach, hands, forearms, upper arms, shoulders, chest, back of the neck, sides of the neck, throat, face, and brain until the entire body has become space.

When your attention reaches the brain, release from the mind all regrets about the past, all worries about the future. Rest in the infinite ocean of the eternal Present. Be right here and right now.

This deep relaxation exercise is especially effective after yoga postures or after meditation, but you can practice whenever you like. Feel free to remain in the state of deep relaxation that comes after practice for as long as you like. Avoid falling asleep. The deepest benefits, the rewiring of your brain, come only with wakeful attention.

Stay with Your Plan

These practices—affirmations, yoga postures with affirmations, and the deep relaxation exercise, along with as much meditation as you can manage—will rapidly form a new neural circuit to actively support your desired positive emotion. Stick with it for weeks to months until you know without a doubt that changes have occurred: the new positive relaxation-creating emotion arises naturally; you feel the power of your life force flowing in a new channel; the negative emotion you set out to offset is triggered less easily and occurs less and less often.

Focus on Meditation

Our long digression into introspection, affirmations, yoga postures with affirmations, and the deep relaxation exercise was for the purpose of giving you practices to overcome chronic negative emotion and associated tension that have been keeping you from meditating deeply. Don't let the process make you lose sight of the goal—meditating ever more deeply by becoming ever more still.

Meditation is by far the most effective practice to help you relax on all levels—physical, mental, and emotional—and relaxation is one of the keys that unlocks the door to superconscious awareness.

CHAPTER 12

Limitless Energy

We have access to unlimited energy, unlimited life force.

> The body lives in an omnipresent sea of . . . vibratory power. This energy sustains life and recharges the vitality of the body as it becomes depleted by physical and mental activity. The life of the body depends primarily upon the cosmic energy that flows in automatically . . . or is consciously drawn in by the tuning power of the human will.
>
> —Paramahansa Yogananda, yoga master[1]

> There is no limit to the degree of the will and therefore to the measure of energy, that one can summon in any undertaking, simply because a strong will is not limited by the energy potential of the body. It draws directly from the energy of the universe. The greater the will, the greater the flow of energy. Remember it. Repeat it to yourself several times a day. This single truth can revolutionize your life.
>
> —Swami Kriyananda, yoga master[2]

The "crazy strength" of Charlotte Heffelmire, demonstrated when she lifted the front end of a pickup truck off her father trapped beneath, is beyond the physical strength of nearly everyone, including bodybuilders. The astonishing feats of the Mighty Atom, repeatedly demonstrated by his bending horseshoes and steel bars, went far beyond what the strength of physical muscles alone can explain. Add to these feats the abilities of extreme distance runners and advanced martial artists, and the truth emerges that we can access a superconscious source of energy beyond food and oxygen.

Superconscious Energy Brings Superconscious Awareness

While few of us have yet to experience such high energy, most of us *have* experienced that we feel better when we have more energy; the more energy we have the better we feel. Energy and joy go hand in hand; unlimited energy goes hand in hand with unlimited joy; both are inextricable parts of superconscious experience.

Superconscious energy brings with it a shift from conscious to superconscious awareness.

At about the forty-mile mark of a 135-mile endurance race, extreme runner Marshall Ulrich felt himself leave his body and hover above it as he ran. Suddenly the effort of running was gone:

> It was like watching myself on a movie screen. I lost all sense of time. It could have been only ten minutes that had passed, but then I realized that dawn was coming, the sun was about to rise. I knew it was time to go back into my body.
> —Marshall Ulrich, extreme runner[3]

The Mighty Atom was not just a showman. The quest for mastery of life force and the demonstration of its power was Joe Greenstein's life work—his personal "spiritual endeavor."

> This spirituality which he sought was pragmatic, for the higher his understanding, the greater the result in his physical performance. For him, the bending of metal became a spiritual endeavor. An indescribable impulse, a wave of energy, would

sweep over him, as if it were no longer himself but something much greater.

—Ed Spielman, author of *The Spiritual Journey of
Joseph L. Greenstein: The Mighty Atom* [4]

The sudden superconscious transformation of Mei Mei Xiang, who eventually became an extraordinary energy healer, began with an unexpected upsurge in energy. For some months she felt compelled to move, to run, to dance. Only then did her gift for healing begin to manifest.

Mei ran and skipped down the crowded sidewalk without bumping into anyone, feeling weightless, guided with unerring precision by the powerful force. [W]aves of energy flooded through her in cycles, building to an almost unbearable intensity, at which point she was compelled to release it through vigorous movements and dancing.

—Dan Millman, author of *Divine Interventions* [5]

Spiritual teacher Sri Chinmoy often demonstrated superconscious levels of energy. He began lifting weights when he was fifty-four years old and still set records in his seventies. He lifted increasingly large amounts of weight, often in unconventional ways, including over 2400 pounds in a single lift.

From my concentration, prayer and meditation I am able to bring forward inner strength, inner power, and use that power to increase my outer strength.

—Sri Chinmoy [6]

There is a false stereotype that saints and sages are passive, that they meekly accept whatever comes their way and retreat from challenge and adversity into an inner state of peace. The saints and sages don't need to *retreat* to an inner state of peace, they are in that state always. Nor do they meekly accept whatever comes their way. Many saints and sages have been dynamic and expansive builders of organizations, encountering and breaking through many obstacles, and reached thousands with their teachings.

> Do you know why people fail? It is because they give up. If you make up your mind and go like a flame, everything will be burned up in your path. The man of realization walks where bullets fly, with the Divine Will behind him.
>
> —Paramahansa Yogananda, yoga master[7]

Superconscious joy and energy go hand in hand. Superconscious experience courses through the will and provides limitless energy.

> Remember, your mind is part of the Infinite Mind. The more you unite your awareness to the divine consciousness, the more effective your power will be. You alone can't do it all. The power of the will backed by Cosmic Will may be compared to a violin string backed by the violin's sounding board. If the string is stretched between two points in space and the bow is then drawn across it, the sound produced will be very thin. But when the string is positioned on a violin, that same bow stroke can fill a concert hall with sound.
>
> —Swami Kriyananda, yoga master[8]

We can develop the ability to draw on this unlimited source of energy. We can rewire the brain to support bringing nonlocal, superconscious life force into local physical expression—not necessarily to perform physical feats—but for health and vitality, for the effortless stamina to accomplish our goals day after day, for creativity, for our own dynamic emotional well-being, for mental strength and focus—and most importantly, to experience the superconscious.

The Key to Unlimited Energy Is Willingness

One mark of successful people—in business, humanitarian service, creative expression, artistic excellence, athletic prowess, or meditation—is the ability to maintain a strong and *relaxed* flow of energy by remaining free of internal mental or emotional resistance and by being enthusiastically willing to do whatever needs to be done.

> My general attitude to life is to enjoy every minute of every day. I never do anything with a feeling of, "Oh, God, I've got to do this today."
> —Richard Branson, billionaire founder
> of the Virgin Group[9]

> To be successful, you have to have your heart in your business, and your business in your heart.
> —Thomas Watson Sr., founder of IBM[10]

> Nothing great was ever achieved without enthusiasm.
> —Ralph Waldo Emerson, poet, philosopher, and mystic[11]

You might think, "Well, that is all very well for them. They had something they loved to do." Successful people, however, enthusiastically do whatever needs to be done. They learn how to be willing to do anything, even the hard things, with optimism, focus, and complete attention—and without mental or emotional resistance.

> Of all the virtues we can learn no trait is more useful, more essential for survival, and more likely to improve the quality of life than the ability to transform adversity into an enjoyable challenge.
> —Mihaly Csíkszentmihályi, author of
> *Flow: The Psychology of Optimal Experience*[12]

Helen Keller was born deaf and blind. She went on to become the first deaf-blind person in America to get a BA degree. She was an influential author, lecturer, and powerful political activist. To her home came the good and the great including Alexander Graham Bell, Charlie Chaplin, and Mark Twain. She met every US president from Grover Cleveland to Lyndon B. Johnson. She was, in her day, as famous as one can be—and a woman of great stamina and energy.

[Y]ou will find a joy in overcoming obstacles—a delight in climbing rugged paths.

—Helen Keller[13]

Walter Russell was an impressionist painter, sculptor, musician, author, motivational speaker, and exponent of superconscious spirituality. His creative output was varied and prodigious. From the 1930s to the 1950s he was well known for his sculpted busts of Thomas Edison, Mark Twain, General MacArthur, John Philip Sousa, Charles Goodyear, and George Gershwin. His biographer, Glen Clark, wrote:

He ... believes that every man should be master of anything he does, do it in a masterly manner and love it, no matter what it is, whether hard physical work, menial or boring work, or inspirational work.[14]

How to Rewire Your Brain to Draw Limitless Energy

There are two ways to rewire the brain for drawing on limitless energy.

The first is to establish new neural habit circuits of willingness and enthusiasm to offset negative habits of resistance. To this end, you can use introspection and affirmation.

The second is to become more and more directly aware of superconscious energy. To this end, you can practice pranayama (breathing exercises), the Energization Exercises, which enable you to draw energy from your energy body into your physical body, and Kriya Yoga, which will bring profound awareness of life force in meditation.

Introspection

You may not realize it, but if you habitually resist the tasks that life places before you, you are cutting off the flow of life force into your brain and body. Such a habit can bring ill-health, boredom, listlessness, and unhappiness and, above all, can cut you off from superconscious awareness.

Habitual resistance is caused by a well-established neural habit circuit that supports the attitude. To develop a new and positive attitude of willingness and enthusiasm, learn to understand your habit of resistance through introspection. Regularly ask yourself, "What task did I resist today and why did I resist it?"

While trying to answer this question you are likely to discover one or more of many automatic justifications: you *didn't like* that task; you thought you *weren't the right person* to do it; the task would be *too hard*; it was *unfair* that you were asked to do that task; you *weren't in the mood* for it; you *didn't have enough energy* or you *didn't have enough time* to do it. Embracing any of these justifications would have caused an automatic reduction in the flow of life force—like turning down a spigot—with a resulting feeling of *fatigue*.

Without introspective insight we are likely to conclude that we were already fatigued *before* we were presented with the task. What actually happened is that the firing of the neural habit circuit that supported our resistance to a task cut off the flow of energy and so *left* us feeling fatigued. If, instead, a different neural habit circuit that supports a *positive* attitude had been triggered to fire so that we embraced the task at hand, our flow of energy would have increased. Neural habit circuits that support positive attitudes, such as enthusiasm, positivity, and optimism, which stimulate and increase the flow of life force, are beyond price.

We have access to all the energy we can possibly need to accomplish what we set out to do; what we don't have is all the willingness we need. To open the door to unlimited energy we need to rewire the brain to say *yes* to whatever tasks come our way. Saying *yes* is will-ingness-power. Saying *yes* is the heart of willpower because it puts your heart into it. Saying yes, developing enthusiasm, remaining positive when challenged, all these infuse our tasks with a feeling of joyful freedom.

Affirmation

Just as chronic tension-producing negative *emotions* can be offset by methodically wiring positive emotional neural habit circuits, chronic energy-draining negative *attitudes* can be offset by wiring neural habit circuits for positive attitudes that open us to limitless energy. And, just as I suggested for offsetting chronic negative emotions, we can make use of affirmations that express the core attitude we want to wire into our brain in order to offset the negative attitudes that reduce our flow of energy.

Here are some examples:

In everything I do, my enthusiasm soars to embrace infinity![15]

My body cells obey my will: They dance with divine vitality! I am well! I am strong! I am a flowing river of boundless power and energy![16]

Within me lies the energy to accomplish all that I will to do. Behind my every act is God's infinite power.[17]

Once you choose an affirmation, repeat it several times during the day, especially in meditation. Practice methodically. If you are alone, affirm loudly to get your own attention, then more softly a few times, whisper a few more times, and then finally say it mentally with deep concentration. In the last stage of mental repetition feel it as much as you say it, believe it as much as you feel it, and, as much as you can, feel that the superconscious superpowers of the Self, and the blessings of God, are giving your affirmation transformative power.

Affirmations, through methodical and focused repetition, and above all by supercharged superconscious repetition, can form a new neural habit circuit to support a new positive emotion, attitude, or conviction in weeks to months.

For more on the power and use of affirmations, as well as many specific affirmations for various purposes, I again recommend two books: *Scientific Healing Affirmations* by Paramahansa Yogananda and *Affirmations for Self-Healing* by Swami Kriyananda. As with all my recommendations, I make these not because I have tried every source of affirmations and know these to be the best, but because I have used these personally with great success. If you have other sources of affirmations that you already use and find helpful, by all means continue to use them.

As explored previously, you can also carefully craft your own affirmation. If you do, be sure to be wholly positive. The mind hears, "I am no longer resistant," as "I *am* resistant." I also recommend including in your affirmative thought the recognition of the higher superconscious powers of Self and the powerful support of God: Rather than just "I have unlimited energy," add a deeper dimension such as "from God's infinite reservoir of power."

Above all, whether you use an affirmation written by another or you craft your own, use an affirmation that you can *believe*—not necessarily something you think is already true of yourself—but something you believe can *become* true of yourself. Sincere belief, and especially sincere belief that includes superconscious potential, will the most rapidly and effectively form a new neural habit circuit.

Experience Life Force Directly

Life force control, or *pranayama*, goes to the heart of how to increase our energy flow. It gives us direct experience of life force. Pranayama means control of prana, control of life force, or in scientific terms, as explored in previous chapters, control of the subtle, nonlocal intelligent energy that manifests and animates the physical body and nervous system. Regular practice of pranayama techniques will rewire the brain to directly perceive, increase, influence, and, ultimately, control life force.

Many pranayama techniques use the breath as a way of increasing the flow of life force and use concentration to direct that increased life force to the brain. Pranayama techniques are often called breathing exercises because they often use variations of patterns of inhalation and exhalation to stimulate life force.

The simplest pranayama technique of all is simply to take slow deep breaths for a quick lift of energy. There are many pranayama techniques, each with a particular benefit. The following technique increases awareness of life force and directs it to the brain.

Kapalabhati Pranayama

Kapalabhati is a simple but highly effective pranayama technique. To practice, assume a seated, kneeling, or cross-legged position, just as you would to meditate.

Draw the diaphragm inward sharply, letting your breath flow freely out through the nostrils. After the quick thrust of the exhale, let the inhalation take place naturally and fully. That is one repetition. Follow the end of the exhalation with a sharp inhalation to begin the next repetition.

Begin with six to twelve repetitions. Do not overdo this technique. If you feel light-headed, stop immediately. Light-headedness likely indicates that you are doing Kapalabhati too rapidly and/or not allowing your inhalation to be relaxed and full. Slow down. Be sure to inhale fully before you do the next strong exhalation. Lower the number of repetitions until you no longer have any feeling of light-headedness.

When you are finished with the practice of Kapalabhati, pay particular attention to the sensation of life force rising into the brain. Concentrate at the point between the eyebrows. Try to become aware of a continuous flow of energy rising through the core of your body and into the brain.

You can do Kapalabhati at any time but I recommend practice just before you meditate. Kapalabhati can take the place of the two breathing exercises I described in the chapter on the *Hong-Sau* technique—tense-and-relax and the balancing breath.

Regular practice of Kapalabhati pranayama gives two main benefits: one, by bringing life force to the brain, to a focus at the point between the eyebrows, we speed the formation of new neural circuits that help us access superconscious awareness; two, we stimulate and *feel* an increased flow of subtle energy in the energy body. Once life force becomes real to our perception we can more deliberately use and direct it.

Energization Exercises

The Energization Exercises were developed by Paramahansa Yogananda, author of *Autobiography of a Yogi* and widely considered to be the father of yoga and meditation in the West. The full set of exercises takes between twelve and fifteen minutes to do.

The Energization Exercises are a variation on pranayama. They are a means of using will to draw life force into the physical body from the energy body. While doing the exercises one consciously sends energy to specific muscles and muscle groups by tensing and relaxing them—often in combination with a deliberate pattern of breathing. The more one learns to use willpower to direct that energy, the more one is able to feel and increase the flow of energy into the body.

For a better idea of how the exercises work, close your eyes and concentrate in the area of the medulla oblongata, at the base of the brain—the doorway, so to speak, for energy from the energy body to enter the physical body. Now tense the right hand and forearm, visualizing or feeling that you are sending energy from the medulla to the hand and forearm. Continue tensing harder and harder for two or three seconds until the hand and forearm are vibrating. Now relax the muscles and feel the energy in the area you have just tensed.

Regular practice of the Energization Exercises has many benefits: one, you will have more energy to get you through your day; two, you will experientially understand how to draw energy from the energy body into the physical body; three, you will gradually be more continuously aware of yourself as a being of energy rather than of matter; and four, the resulting higher energy will bring increased superconscious awareness and joy.

If you wish to learn the Energization Exercises, I recommend the *The Energization Exercises DVD*. You can find it through Crystal Clarity Publishers: *crystalclarity.com*.

Kriya Yoga

In time, during your practice of the *Hong-Sau* technique you are likely to experience the life force rising through the core of the body. Concentration at the point between the eyebrows naturally draws life force into the brain. It is a wonderful feeling. Soothing, relaxing, pleasant, on the way to being blissful.

Pranayama breathing exercises, such as Kapalabhati described above, enhance awareness of life force. They also help deepen your concentration: the body becomes more still, breathing slows, and the usual physical distractions lessen, all working together to draw life force strongly into the brain.

There is another pranayama technique that I would like to recommend—Kriya Yoga. Kriya Yoga is an ancient and supremely effective method for stimulating the life force and directing it to the point between the eyebrows. Kriya Yoga supercharges your meditation by allowing you to more easily become still and inwardly aware. The deep states of meditation achievable through Kriya Yoga most effectively rewire the brain to support not only higher energy but also superconscious experience.

Gentler forms of meditation and prayer lower stress and anxiety, but they rarely have the power to dramatically alter our
consciousness in the way that intense practices . . . involving
deeper breathing with repetitive movements and sounds, can
break down the neurological circuits that keep old beliefs firmly
rooted in place and transform the ways we think and behave.

—Andrew Newberg, MD, author of
How God Changes Your Brain[18]

One must learn Kriya Yoga directly from a qualified teacher rather than
from the pages of a book. To learn more, I invite you to go to: *ananda.org/*.
Search within the site for Kriya Yoga.

Energize Yourself to Access the Superconscious

You can draw unlimited energy by rewiring your brain to be willing, positive, energetic, and enthusiastic. Experience for yourself that joy and energy
go hand in hand. You can also directly increase your energy awareness
through pranayama. Pranayama will bring increased depth and focus
to your meditation. Increased depth and focus in meditation will bring
increased superconscious experience accompanied by limitless energy and
expanding joy.

CHAPTER 13

Relaxed Concentration

Sustained and relaxed concentration is the key to success in any endeavor—from the material to the mystical.

Successful people have taken their innate ability to concentrate and developed it into a superpower. Those who have developed concentration into a superpower are not simply *better* at concentrating than most people; they have wired their brains to support relaxed and deep concentration as an everyday habit, as a moment-by-moment state of being and way of behaving.

The scientific genius of Einstein, the athletic mastery of Baryshnikov, the artistic distinction of Monet, the business brilliance of Warren Buffet, the extraordinary service of Mother Teresa, or the unity of St. Francis with Christ—were all achieved with the aid of deep and extended states of relaxed concentration.

Benefits of Relaxed Concentration

- Intuition
- Success
- Flow
- Superconscious Awareness

Intuition

Intuition is simply *knowing* without reason or factual support. Reason and factual support can be, and usually are, *involved* in the process of intuition, but intuition draws *directly* on superconscious intelligence. Men and women of genius, those who have world-changing insights or create things never before imagined, are the most likely to attribute their insights or creativity to intuition.

> There comes a leap in consciousness, call it intuition or what you will, and the solution comes to you and you do not know how or why. All great discoveries are made in this way.
> —Albert Einstein, Nobel Prize-winner[1]

A 1974 landmark study, *Executive ESP*, by Douglas Dean and John Mihalasky, explored whether the performance of CEOs revealed any correlation between their intuitive ability and their ability to correctly make the myriad decisions needed to make their companies profitable. Each of 385 CEOs was asked to predict the next number in a sequence of one hundred randomly generated numbers. CEOs who correctly predicted the most numbers in a one-hundred-number sequence were, in fact, also the most successful at making their companies profitable, thus establishing a remarkably strong correlation between intuitive ability and business profitability.

Scientists, businesspeople, and artists alike are known to rely on intuition.

> [It] is always with excitement that I wake up in the morning wondering what my intuition will toss up to me, like gifts from the sea. I work with it, and rely upon it. It's my partner.
> —Dr. Jonas Salk, virologist[2]

> Intuition is a very powerful thing, more powerful than intellect, in my opinion. That's had a big impact on my work.
> —Steve Jobs, founder of Apple Inc.[3]

> I am often, in my writing, great leaps ahead of where I am in my thinking, and my thinking has to work its way slowly up to what the "superconscious" has already shown me in a story or poem.
> —Madeleine L'Engle, author of *A Wrinkle in Time*[4]

Intuition is also the faculty that allows us to know and experience realities beyond our sensory awareness, to realize our superconscious identity and our relationship with God.

> The sixth sense [intuition] . . . is the medium of contact between the finite mind of man and Infinite Intelligence, and for this reason, it is a mixture of both the mental and the spiritual. It is believed to be the point at which the mind of man contacts the Universal Mind.
> —Napoleon Hill, author of *Think and Grow Rich*[5]

> Inspiration and intuition is the language of Light through which men and God "intercommunicate."
> —Walter Russell, sculptor, musician, author, philosopher, and mystic[6]

> Without the power of intuition, you cannot know Truth. Intuition can give you knowledge about things that your senses and understanding can never give.
> —Paramahansa Yogananda, yoga master[7]

Success

A relaxed and concentrated mind is the common denominator among those who are successful in everything from growing a business to expressing an art, from physical ability to scientific achievement, from acquiring money to acquiring skills, from raising children to raising consciousness.

> Concentration is the secret of success in every undertaking. Without concentration, thoughts, energy, inspiration,

purpose—all one's inner forces—become scattered. Concentration is the calm focus of one's full attention on the purpose at hand. Concentration means more than mental effort: It means channeling your heart's feelings, your faith, and your deep aspirations into whatever you are doing.

—Swami Kriyananda, yoga master[8]

The thinking of creative and successful men is never exerted in any direction other than that intended. That is why great men produce a prodigious amount of work, seemingly without effort and without fatigue.

—Walter Russell, sculptor, musician, author, philosopher, and mystic[9]

All men and women of success have devoted much time to deep concentration. . . . [They] could dive deeply into their problems and come out with the pearls of right solutions. If you learn how to withdraw your attention from all objects of distraction and place it upon one object of concentration, then you will know how to attract at will what you need.

—Paramahansa Yogananda, yoga master[10]

Flow and Peak Experience

A relaxed and concentrated mind can engross one in mental processes, creative work, or physical activity. Someone who is engrossed has clearer thoughts, is more inspired and creative, and reaches new heights in physical ability. We become so dynamically focused that the body poses no limitations; we are in the moment, unaware of the passage of time; we feel an effortless supply of energy, and our feelings are deeper, calmer, and more satisfying. These experiences may last for only a few minutes, sometimes a few hours, even a few days, but whatever their length, they are often the highest and most memorable experiences of our lives.

One does not consciously have to plan how to act; instead, one lets the appropriate responses happen of themselves . . . swifter, subtler, deeper, more accurate, more in touch with reality than command by conscious mind.

—Michael Murphy, author of *In the Zone*[11]

I'd liken it to a sense of reverie—not a dreamlike state but the somehow insulated state that a great musician achieves in a great performance. He's aware of where he is and what he's doing, but his mind is on the playing of his instrument with an internal sense of rightness—it is not merely mechanical, it is not only spiritual; it is something of both, on a different plane and a more remote one.

—Arnold Palmer, renowned golf professional[12]

Flow does not come without a foundation of discipline. Only musicians who can play their instruments without thinking can play in a superconscious flow. Only scientists who have gone deeply into their subjects can have the deep intuitive insights of genius in their fields. Only programmers who know their programming language inside and out can enter periods where the coding seems to be coming effortlessly by itself. Only athletes who have trained their bodies to respond to any impulse from the brain can achieve physical feats of greatness.

Flow does not come in passivity; it comes when we are concentratedly and dynamically involved in whatever we are doing.

Contrary to what we usually believe, moments like these, the best moments in our lives, are not the passive, receptive, relaxing times—although such experiences can also be enjoyable, if we have worked hard to attain them. The best moments usually occur when a person's body or mind is stretched to its limits in a voluntary effort to accomplish something difficult and worthwhile. Optimal experience is thus something that we make happen. For a child, it could be placing with trembling fingers the last block on a tower she has built, higher than any she has built so far; for a swimmer, it could be trying to beat his own record; for a violinist, mastering an intricate musical passage.

—Mihaly Csíkszentmihályi, author of
Flow: The Psychology of Optimal Experience[13]

The concentration of a small child at play is analogous to the concentration of the artist of any discipline. In real play, which is real concentration, the child is not only outside time, he is outside *himself*. He has thrown himself completely into whatever it is he is doing. A child playing a game, building a sand castle, painting a picture, is completely *in* what he is doing. His *self*-consciousness is gone; his consciousness is wholly focused outside himself.

—Madeleine L'Engle, author of *A Wrinkle in Time*[14]

Concert pianists, through years of practice, reach a level of skill where something else takes over in the brain—where concentration is replaced by intuition, improvisation, and finally inspiration. At that moment, they alter the normal functioning in their frontal lobe, shifting from the everyday consciousness . . . to . . . a more creative form of expression. When that occurs—when old habits and intentional decision making is interrupted, the music transforms itself from excellence to euphoria. . . .

—Andrew Newberg, MD, author of
How God Changes Your Brain[15]

Flow is brought on by concentrated awareness in the present moment.

There exists only the present instant . . . a Now which always and without end is itself new.

—Meister Eckhart, Christian mystic[16]

Superconscious Awareness

Concentration is required to get past the distractions that deflect us from superconscious awareness. During meditation, especially, we become aware of the barrage of thoughts and sensory stimuli that cause us to lose focus. We can reduce the volume of thoughts and sensory stimuli by becoming as still as possible, and within that stillness achieve a state of inward absorption.

Concentration outside of meditation can also result in superconscious awareness. Flow and peak experiences can take one beyond a state of exceptional productivity and skill, beyond heightened enjoyment of life, into the realm of the sacred.

> Suddenly, everything was flowing. I was both in and out of time. There and not there. It was just pure being . . . I was very close to God at that point.
> —Reverend Neil Elliot, describing experiences he had while snowboarding[17]

> The reason why some people love to engage in dangerous activities such as mountain climbing is that it forces them into the Now—that intensely alive state that is free of time, free of problems, free of thinking, free of the burden of the personality.
> —Eckhart Tolle, author of *The Power of Now*[18]

Superconscious awareness comes with deep concentration. What is most important is not *what* you are doing but whether you are doing it with relaxed and one-pointed concentration.

How to Rewire the Brain to Support Relaxed Concentration

Whatever our aims in life, any level of increased ability to concentrate is of great benefit. Even if we now find ourselves far from genius or mastery, the experience of a relaxed and concentrated mind is a peaceful respite from our usual restlessness. Concentration, even for a short time, gives us the focus we need to improve any facet of our being.

The depth of concentration required for intuition, success, and flow isn't a state that can be casually summoned at will. It is true that a not particularly concentrated individual can become deeply concentrated in an unexpected experience of extreme danger. So, too, in an extreme sport such as free-climbing, during which the climber deliberately courts extreme danger, the individual can achieve deep concentration. These are the exceptions, not the rule—and I can't recommend courting such danger deliberately. There are, fortunately, safer ways, more methodical ways, that the brain, particularly the prefrontal cortex, can be wired to support a habit of deep concentration.

Do One Thing at a Time and Do It Well

We live in an age when distraction is the norm. You may find yourself frequently moving from one screen to the next, one conversation to the next, trying to accomplish several things at the same time in order to be ready for the next thing you need to do. Doing one thing at a time, let alone doing it well, may seem impossible. We tend to *think* that it is impossible, however, simply because we have wired our brains to live at that pace and in that scattered manner.

Think back to times when you went on vacation. During the first few days, perhaps even for your entire vacation, you may have continued to restlessly bounce back and forth between screens, conversations, and activities—even though you were no longer under any time pressure and had no responsibilities. Even during the longed-for and long-imagined time on the beach, we continue to behave restlessly because we have wired our brains to be restless.

To begin wiring a habit of relaxed concentration to offset such habits of restlessness, make an effort to arrange your schedule to give you times when you can focus on one task and one task only. Even if only for fifteen minutes, you will be surprised how deep you can go into a task. Carve out of your day as many of these periods as you can for as long as you can.

It is not unusual to find our minds restlessly and repeatedly thinking about all the things that we currently need to do. To counterbalance that restless neural habit circuit pick any one task then do it. Train yourself to let go of the feeling of having too many things to do, and too little time to do them, by simply doing one thing at a time. In my experience, if I concentrate on one thing at a time, before I know it, all the things I need to do are done. What's more, I have done them with more pleasure, creativity, and success than had I been constantly distracted by thinking about everything else I needed to do.

Your life is unlikely to become less busy, but you *can* become more calm, centered, and concentrated in the midst of busyness by doing one thing at a time and doing it well. You will become more and more able to do one thing at a time, and do it well, because every effort strengthens the developing neural habit circuits that automatically support relaxed concentration.

Cultivate the Habit of Intuition

Give intuition a chance to reveal itself by giving it the mental and emotional space to arise. Intuition doesn't usually announce itself with great fanfare—poet Ruth Stone having been chased across the landscape by a poem not withstanding. Intuition is more likely to reveal itself quietly. You might miss it unless you are also aware of the calm feeling of certainty or inspiration that comes with it.

Intuitive insights often reveal themselves during the process of reasoning, of thinking deeply, as you "feel your way" toward an idea or solution.

Intuition will be clearest when the mind is clearest. The mind is clearest when one is concentrated and emotionally calm. The best time to seek intuitive insight, guidance, and inspiration, therefore, is at the end of your meditation or when you can sit quietly and uninterruptedly to consider your thoughts and feelings—as when you practice introspection. Introspection may be thought of as a methodical process of arriving at intuitive insight.

Test your intuition. When you first begin to cultivate intuition, even if you have a strong feeling of certainty or inspiration about something, it is a good idea to not act on it. Keep it in the back of your mind and watch to see if your intuition proves true. Only if you find your intuitions often proving true should you begin to act on future intuitions.

Build confidence in your intuition by acting first on less impactful intuitions to test their validity. Beware of acting immediately on intuitions that suggest the need for major change in your life—especially if that change will impact others. Consider such an intuition carefully, often in meditation, over days to weeks to see if it still feels right. Break your intuitive idea down into parts and consider each separately. Don't be impatient to act. If your intuition is genuine, it will remain true no matter how long you take to consider.

Be wary of insights you may think you are receiving when you have a strong emotional stake in a situation. What seems like a strong intuition but is accompanied by strong desires is often wrong and is certainly suspect. It is best not to assume that you are being intuitive unless you can be self-honestly neutral about the outcome.

If you hope to persuade other people to embrace your intuition, better not to announce it as an intuition. If your intuition is genuine, then sweet reason and patience will be sufficient to persuade others to your intuition-born idea. If you claim some level of intuitive guidance about your idea, others involved are blocked from using their reason, from offering their insights; you are presenting them with only two options: agree with me or don't.

Intuition can manifest as a calm flow in your dealings with other people. You will find that when your mind is calm and concentrated your intuition will be very clear; and your thoughts and feelings toward others will be effortlessly harmonious, positive, and creative. You may form loving insights into others that will help you interact with them from your highest best—and draw out of them their highest best in return.

Intuition is particularly helpful when it provides personal inner guidance: insights into yourself that help in your own development of superconscious awareness, that deepen your awareness of Self and God.

Introspection

Understanding why the mind isn't concentrated is as important as understanding why one isn't relaxed or energized. It is essential to recognize the habits and attitudes that most keep us from enjoying a relaxed and concentrated mind. Only when we understand those habits can we most effectively choose the appropriate new oppositely positive neural habit circuits with which to offset them.

Regularly ask and answer this question:

Did I remain concentrated today? If not, what did I allow to distract me and why?

There are many reasons we fail to concentrate: emotional entanglements with another matter pull the mind away from the task at hand; lack of energy and enthusiasm; resistance to the task at hand; and, of course, allowing distraction after distraction to carry our mind away.

Be particularly wary of thinking that distractions in your environment are a valid justification for being unable to concentrate. It is not our environment but the interconnected nature of our neural habit circuits that is the root problem. One neural habit circuit can be like a firecracker that sets off a chain reaction of other neural-circuit firecrackers to create a continuous mental and emotional fireworks show. We may think the fireworks show we experience is caused by outer distractions—*but the entire show takes place inside the mind.* Another person, surrounded by the same potentially distracting inputs as you are, may be completely focused on one thing and one thing only.

By developing neural habit circuits that support concentration, one can maintain a relaxed and concentrated mind even in the midst of activity. One of my favorite author stories is about Charles Dickens. He was a prolific writer, producing fifteen novels, five novellas, and hundreds of short stories and nonfiction articles. He was also a prolific father, producing ten children. For years he and his wife lived in London in a very small home with no private space in which to write. Nonetheless, even while the activities of his wife and numerous children swirled around him, he diligently wrote many of his greatest works in a corner of his home's main living area. Now that's concentration.

If you *can* change the circumstances that keep you from concentrating by all means do make these changes. More importantly, however, you'll want to methodically develop the attitudes that support concentration as a habit—calmness, relaxed determination, confidence, positivity, and enthusiasm—so that ultimately you can be concentrated in any situation.

Affirmation

Affirmations can help you develop the neural habit circuits that support concentration. After you have spent time in introspection—gaining insight into what keeps you from being concentrated and what helps you to be concentrated—use affirmation in the methodical and focused way described previously in order to develop the attitudes most needed for deepened concentration.

Apropos to our subject, this is a good time to remind you that the more concentrated you are when doing your affirmation, the more effective you will be at creating new neural habit circuits that support the attitudes or qualities you want to develop.

Here are a few affirmations to choose from or from which you can get inspiration to develop your own. If you do create your own, remember to make it wholly positive.

> Whatever I do in life, I give it my full attention. Like a laser beam, I burn from before me all problems, all obstructions![19]

> I leave behind me both my failures and accomplishments. What I do today will create a new and better future, filled with inner joy.[20]

> I am awake! energetic! enthusiastic! I give my full, alert attention to everything I do, knowing that in absolute consciousness I shall find God.[21]

Meditation

The most effective thing we can do to rewire the brain to support deep and relaxed concentration is to learn to get beyond the usual free-associating thought process we experience while in meditation.

In *The Untethered Soul*, Michael Alan Singer amusingly compares our mind's tendency to produce a constant stream of associated thoughts with having a roommate who won't ever shut up. One minute the roommate is talking about foods he wants to eat, the next he is talking about a project he's working on, the next minute he's talking about someone he knows, the next minute he's talking about something that happened to him in the past, the next minute after that he's planning what he wants to do in the future.

We notice the roommate that won't shut up especially when we are in meditation. One moment we are beginning to watch the breath, the next moment our mental roommate is talking about an article he read on the internet. Our roommate is largely silent when we are in conversation, reading or watching something that captures our attention, engaging in attention-demanding physical activities, or deliberately concentrating on a task, but the moment we stop, the roommate starts talking again. Our mental roommate is, of course, a part of ourselves. His free-associating mental chatter is the ongoing result of the chain reaction of firecracker circuits set off by sensory input—sounds, tastes, smells, sights—and by physical movement, emotions, and thoughts.

While our roommate's free association is most obvious in meditation, meditation itself gives us the best opportunity to overcome the tendency. In meditation we can learn to become so still in heart, mind, and body that our neural habit circuits are no longer being mentally, emotionally, or sensorily stimulated. When the neural habit circuits are no longer stimulated, the mind stills—like waves subsiding on a pond—and we become free of the annoying roommate. When the mind stills, when the continuous chatter of the roommate subsides, we experience meditation at a new level: effortlessly and profoundly aware of intuitive inspiration and superconscious feelings such as peace, love, and joy.

Attaining such stillness of mind rapidly produces new neural habit circuits in the brain, especially in the prefrontal cortex, to support and deepen our ability to concentrate. These habit circuits not only make our meditations more powerfully effective, they also make us more concentrated even when in the midst of activity. The concentration habit circuit may be born in meditation but it fires at any time that we need or want to focus. It also makes us more in the Now because our mental roommate is not restlessly carrying our attention away to the past or future.

The *Hong-Sau* technique of meditation is especially effective for developing a calm and concentrated mind. While practicing the technique, make a particular effort to keep focused on the recitation of *hong* and *sau* in synchrony with your breath. Feel that you are bringing your whole being—attention, feeling, life force—to the point between the eyebrows. If you work at it, you will eventually break through into superconscious awareness.

The experience of going beyond one's thoughts is so deeply satisfying that one becomes profoundly content to remain in the moment. The needs, ideas, and responsibilities that seemed previously so compellingly interesting or important simply no longer enter the mind. One does not strain to maintain this experience; it feels effortless.

Such a concentrated state might last only moments or minutes before a restless movement triggers a thought, which leads to another thought—and the roommate is back. With faithful practice, however, the concentrated state can be maintained for longer and longer periods. Even in a few minutes of that concentrated state you can experience a level of superconscious feeling and awareness that will move and inspire you for days; long-held emotional tensions can drop away; you can feel bathed in such joy that the heart remains happy for a very long time; old unwanted neural habit circuits can weaken and positive circuits grow stronger.

Become Concentrated

Being concentrated is a different way of living. You become more emotionally centered, more in the Now, more productive, more dynamic, more intelligent, more creative, happier, and healthier. Being concentrated draws the life force out of the continuous fireworks show of neural habit circuits, which are reacting to neural habit circuits, and channels it wherever you decide to use it. Being concentrated makes you effortlessly superconscious; it unites you with Self and God.

CHAPTER 14

Creativity

Creativity, rightly approached, awakens superconscious awareness. Creativity, rightly approached, gives expression to unique superconscious qualities and abilities that emerge from our unique Self. Creativity, rightly approached, is an experience of God.

> Our creative dreams and yearnings come from a divine source. As we move toward our dreams, we move toward our divinity.
> —Julia Cameron, author of *The Artist's Way: A Spiritual Path to Higher Creativity*[1]

> I realize that the ability to have such ideas register in my consciousness is a Divine gift. It is a mandate from God, a charge entrusted to my keeping, and I feel that my highest duty is to make the most of this gift—to grow and expand. When in my most inspired moods, I have definite compelling visions, involving a higher selfhood. I feel at such moments that I am tapping the source of Infinite and Eternal energy from which you and I and all things proceed. Religion calls it God.
> —Richard Strauss, composer[2]

Originality is not just "being different," or doing what's never been done before. Originality is being true to the core of one's self. Our Originality is a precious gift. It is an authenticity that originates in the unique pattern of each individual soul. Every one of us is unique in all of eternity. To discover and bring forth our intrinsic unique individual expression is our most sacred duty and our sweetest delight. When we follow our deepest soul intuition we arrive to the source of our existence. Here in this territory that is so uniquely our own, in the very essence of our individuality, we find the universal.

—Dana Lynne Andersen,
artist, author, and founder of The Academy
of Art, Creativity and Consciousness[3]

What geniuses, psychics, and saints all share in common is the sense of nonlocal awareness, a connection to a greater whole— God, the Creator, the collective unconscious, Logos, and a host of other terms, all explicitly nonlocal.

—Stephan A. Schwartz, author of *Opening to the Infinite*[4]

The composer while creating any work of lasting value stands face to face with this Eternal Energy from which all life flows, and he draws on that infinite power. In proportion as he grasps this profound truth will he reveal to the visible, audible world the Divinity within him.

—Arthur M. Abell, author of *Talks with Great Composers*[5]

Superconscious Creative Power

Superconscious creative ability emerges from the creative power of the Self—power that we get from God, the Creator of all. Creative power is limitless. The ability of the saints and sages to manifest miracles comes from that creative power. You may think, understandably, that you are a long way from performing miracles. We are, however, even at this moment, miraculously creating our physical bodies—we just don't know it, or if we know it, we are not consciously controlling it.

We can begin to understand how creative power continuously manifests the body by understanding how mental convictions affect it.

In 1976, a randomized, controlled study of a potential chemotherapy treatment for gastric cancer was conducted by the British stomach cancer group. The results of the study were published in the May 1983 *World Journal of Surgery.*[6] Four hundred eleven patients participated in a double-blind study that involved the use of placebos. Neither the patients nor the clinicians knew who received a placebo/saline drip treatment and who received the actual trial-drug drip treatment. Nonetheless, during the course of the study, which lasted for several months, *30 percent of the patients who were given the placebo/saline drip treatment lost all their hair.*

More dramatic examples of mind affecting body can be found in studies of people suffering dissociative identity disorder (DID), more commonly known as multiple-personality disorder (MPD). Sufferers of multiple personalities have been closely studied. These individuals can change from one personality to another in minutes, even in seconds; they may change personalities as many as ten times in a single hour. While multiple-personality disorder is well-known, what is less well-known is that the rapid personality changes are often accompanied by rapid physiological changes.

In his 1988 paper "Psychophysiologic Aspects of Multiple Personality Disorder," Dr. Philip M. Coons reviews over fifty studies that identify physiological changes occurring when an individual with multiple personalities changes from one personality to another. The studies have shown that one personality can be allergic to specific allergens, such as bee-sting toxin, and other personalities within the same individual are not allergic. One personality can be left-handed while other personalities are right-handed. One personality can have moles or scars that another does not. One personality can need glasses while others do not.[7] In a 1985 study conducted by Shepard and Braun, the eyesight of one multiple-personality sufferer was thoroughly measured—refraction, visual acuity, ocular tension, keratometry, color vision, and visual fields—after each of ten personality changes that took place in the course of one hour. *Each* personality's eyes were uniquely different—including, in one case, *the color of the iris.*[8]

One might argue that the placebo effect takes place over time periods sufficiently long to be explained by our thoughts or feelings *triggering* known biochemical processes. In multiple-personality cases, however, no known biochemical processes can explain the *rapidity* of the physiological changes, much less the changes that would normally be considered genetically impossible, such as a change in the color of the iris.

The placebo effect and the much more dramatic cases of physiological change found among multiple personality disorder sufferers demonstrate how creative power manifests whatever we deeply believe—even if we are not consciously aware of what we deeply believe. If we deeply believe that we would lose all our hair while receiving chemotherapy, then, even if we were being given a placebo, our conviction would direct our creative power to make our hair fall out. If one personality of a multiple personality sufferer believes that she has blue eyes, then regardless of the eye color of the other personalities, this personality will direct creative power to make her eyes blue.

> Great saints who have realized this world as an idea in the Divine Mind, can do as they wish with the body, knowing it to be only a manipulatable form of condensed or frozen energy. Though physical scientists now understand that matter is nothing but congealed energy, illumined masters have passed victoriously from theory to practice in the field of matter control.
>
> —Paramahansa Yogananda, yoga master[9]

The mental control and superconscious awareness possessed by the saints and sages that enable them to perform miracles require extraordinary discipline to develop. Although it is ours to develop, this level of discipline and superconscious awareness is not something we are likely to achieve quickly. But the more we access that creative power by exercising our creativity, the more superconscious we become.

> Use constructively the power you already have, and more will come. Tune yourself with Cosmic Power. Then you will possess the creative power of Spirit. You will be in contact with Infinite

Intelligence, which can guide you and solve all problems. Power from the dynamic Source of your being will flow through you so that you will be creative in the world of business, the world of thought, or the world of wisdom.

—Paramahansa Yogananda, yoga master[10]

How to Rewire the Brain to Access Superconscious Creativity
Be Creative in All Things

Creativity is not limited to the traditional paths of the artist. Everything can be done creatively: raising children, keeping your house, relating to your friends and family, staying physically fit, doing your job, acquiring money. All of these present opportunities for creativity.

Approach everything you do with the intention of doing it as well as it can be done. Your intention will arouse your best and most superconscious effort for the task. It is easy to dismiss things as unimportant and therefore put only minimal thought into them. In the vast scheme of things there is no doubt that, if you decide to redecorate your living space, the end result is not of timeless importance to the world. But it is timelessly important to *you* that you exercise your creativity to make your living space positive, harmonious, uplifting, even inspiring, and in a manner that is uniquely considered and accomplished by you, because by so doing you become aligned, however slightly, with the creative force of superconsciousness.

> [W]e ourselves activate superconsciousness by applying its insights to every aspect of our lives. It is not wandering in a barren desert until you accidentally stumble upon an oasis; it is making the desert bloom around you.
>
> —Swami Kriyananda, yoga master[11]

> . . . every man should be master of anything he does, do it in a masterly manner and love it, no matter what it is, whether hard physical work, menial or boring work, or inspirational work.
>
> —Walter Russell, sculptor, musician, author, philosopher, and mystic[12]

Creativity is a way of Being that allows us to open into a broader reality. When we are in the creative flow we are able to perceive a wider field of possibility.

—Dana Lynne Andersen, artist, author, and founder of the Center for the Arts, Creativity, and Consciousness[13]

The more deliberate and focused we are in doing everything creatively the more we draw on the superconscious. The more we draw on the superconscious in creative endeavors the more new neural habit circuits we form to make us automatically choose to be creative.

You are unhappy because you do not visualize strongly enough the great things which you definitely want, nor do you employ your willpower, your creative ability, and your patience to materialize them. Happiness comes with your ability to manifest first your smallest desires, and later your biggest dreams.

—Swami Kriyananda, yoga master[14]

Find Your Dominant Purpose

We most quickly develop creativity by following our dominant purpose. Our dominant purpose is what gives us the most joy; it is the goal toward which we can most fully give heart and mind.

. . . have the courage to follow your heart and your intuition. Somehow they know what you really want to become. Everything else is secondary.

—Steve Jobs, founder of Apple Inc.[15]

The state of mind which enables a man to do work of this kind is akin to that of the religious worshiper or the lover; the daily effort comes . . . straight from the heart.

—Albert Einstein, Nobel Prize-winner[16]

I think many people have difficulty finding their dominant purpose because they expect or hope that it will be dramatic or important in some way. Our dominant purpose may not always be our job or means of financial support, although it can be. Our dominant purpose may go completely unrecognized by others. Our dominant purpose could be creating a garden, tutoring children, attaining mastery over the body, making a common pursuit uncommonly excellent, by living a conventional life in an unconventional way.

It may take time to find your dominant purpose. In the meantime, don't shrink from giving your heart and mind as much as you are able to everything that comes your way, because the things that come your way will often help you discover and grow into your dominant purpose.

Don't measure your success by whether you are being outwardly successful or recognized. Your dominant purpose is successful if *you* are transformed by it, if you grow more aware of your creative power, if you draw more superconscious inspiration, if you become more immersed in joy and share that joy with others.

Welcome Inspiration

When creative inspiration comes, whenever possible, we should welcome it and try to give it life. How we give it life can also be a creative process—knowing when and how to use that inspiration at the right time and in the right way is an art.

> A writer of fantasy, fairy tale, or myth must inevitably discover that he is not writing out of his own knowledge or experience, but out of something both deeper and wider. I think that fantasy must possess the author and simply use him. I know that this is true of *A Wrinkle in Time*. I can't possibly tell you how I came to write it. It was simply a book I had to write. I had no choice. And it was only after it was written that I realized what some of it meant.
>
> —Madeleine L'Engle, author of *A Wrinkle in Time*[17]

"I can't force inspiration. Ideas just come to me when I'm not seeking them—when I'm swimming or running or standing in the shower." "It happens like magic." "I can just see things that other people can't, and I don't know why." "The muse just sits on my shoulder."

—From a landmark study by Nancy Andreasan[18]

Develop Creative Imagination

Whatever the mind can conceive and believe, it can achieve.

—Dr. Napoleon Hill, author of *Think and Grow Rich*[19]

Before we can create anything we must first create it in the mind. Methodically using creative imagination, which is often called visualization, taps into the same power of mind that we unknowingly use to create our physical bodies. The more clearly you imagine what you want to create, and the more deeply you believe you can create it, the more successful your creative efforts will be.

Creative imagination is not limited to *visual* imagination. We can creatively imagine the subjective experience of all five senses: a composer can hear imagined music; a chef can smell and taste an imagined dish; an athlete can feel and see an imagined movement.

Creative imagery is so effective that it can create new neural habit circuits even *before any physical actions are taken.* Creative imagination can even make the body stronger without exercise.[20]

> Known for hitting shots at the buzzer, [Former NBA great Jerry West] acquired the nickname "Mr. Clutch." When asked what accounted for his ability to make the big shots, West explained that he had rehearsed making those same shots countless times in his mind.
>
> —Frank Niles, PhD, social scientist,
> adventure athlete, business strategist[21]

The deliberate process of creative imagination is most effective when the mind is calm, when you are free of outer distractions, and especially after you have meditated. Creative imagination can, however, occur at any time. You will often see someone "staring into space" when working at a computer or reading. They may in fact be staring into *inner* space, imagining the right response to an email, exploring the solution to a problem, putting something together in three dimensions, or conceiving a strategy.

Practice Introspection and Affirmation

You may want to introspect on what negative emotions or attitudes are sabotaging your creativity. Most likely you will discover that chronic tension, fatigue, or lack of mental focus are getting in your way not only in creative efforts but in almost everything you want to do. These problems are best dealt with separately as we have already explored.

If, on the other hand, you are reasonably relaxed, energetic, and concentrated, it is likely that the only thing holding you back from being creative is that you are simply not making the *effort* to be creative. Perhaps you don't think of yourself as a creative person. Perhaps you think creativity lies only in the realm of the arts and you do not consider yourself an artist. Perhaps you have difficulty putting your heart into your work; perhaps you think doing things "well enough" is all that is required, or see tasks as necessary chores rather than opportunities to improve. If these thoughts are your thoughts, affirmations will be a good way to kindle the fire of creativity that leads to superconscious awareness.

Affirmations for creativity:

My outer life is a reflection of my inner thoughts. Filled with the joy of God, I express His joy and harmony in everything I do.[22]

Mine is the power of the universe, channeled for my own awakening and the awakening of other sleeping souls![23]

CHAPTER 15

Openhearted Determination

A highly charged electromagnet generates a powerful magnetic field that can permanently reorient the iron molecules in a solid iron bar. Similarly, superconscious awareness places us in a powerful subtle-energy field that permanently rewires the neural circuits in the physical brain. The deeper and longer our superconscious awareness the more our neural circuits are rewired.

> An Enlightenment experience *radically rearranges* [italics mine] many neuronal connections in a relatively short time. The result is a tremendous benefit to our brain and body as we discover new positive ways of thinking, feeling, and experiencing the world around us.
>
> —Andrew Newberg, MD, author of
> *How God Changes Your Brain*[1]

Attaining deeper and longer superconscious awareness is best achieved not only by utilizing the impersonal science of meditation but by adding to it the more personal art of *openhearted determination*. Meditation gives us the *opportunity* to have superconscious awareness; we can make more of this opportunity when we approach meditation with openhearted determination.

Developing superconscious awareness is an adventure. Give it your all. Put your heart into it. Athletes who have had peak experiences testify that when they flowed into their experience by becoming totally absorbed in what they were attempting to do, everyday thoughts fell away, emotional involvements receded from awareness, actions became intuitive, the body became as though energy itself, time became the Now, and they were carried along on waves of joy. When we put our heart into it, we open ourselves to experience such an engrossing peak experience in meditation.

Openhearted determination is the ultimate aid to experiencing superconscious awareness. Openhearted determination is the driving force, the intention, the resolve, the strong desire that will make you become just that much more still in order to leave behind awareness of the body, to concentrate just that much more one-pointedly that you leave behind random thoughts, and put your heart just that much more fully into attaining superconscious awareness.

Inspire Yourself

If you are thinking that you just don't have the openhearted determination needed for directly achieving superconscious awareness, know that openhearted determination can be developed and that your brain will rewire to support your doing so.

Kindle the fire of determination. Read books, watch videos, or listen to audiobooks that share experiences of the superconscious. Read about near-death experiences. Study the teachings of saints and sages. Spend time with people who share your aspirations. Listen to music that uplifts you. Sing to celebrate the Divine. Saturate your mind and heart with superconscious reminders.

Affirm Your High Potential

Use affirmations to develop the conviction that you are superconscious. The more deeply you believe in your higher nature the more effortlessly you will desire to experience it fully.

I will live in the remembrance of what I am in truth: bliss infinite! eternal love![2]

I am a child of eternity! I am ageless. I am deathless. I am the changeless Spirit at the heart of all mutation![3]

I am infinite. I am spaceless, I am tireless; I am beyond body, thought, and utterance; beyond all matter and mind. I am endless bliss.[4]

Meditate Longer

Give yourself time to linger in the uplifting superconscious awareness that comes after you have practiced your meditation technique. Drink it in. Immerse yourself in it. Let it percolate through mind, heart, and body. Expand with it beyond the narrow confines of the body. Use the time after you have practiced your meditation technique to deliberately open to superconscious experience, to open to the subtle reality that is who you really are.

What You Might Experience

Joy or Bliss

Joy or bliss is the highest experience of the superconscious. Even superconscious experiences of sound, light, wisdom, love, or peace will be *suffused* with joy because the Superconscious *is* ever-existing, ever-conscious, ever-new joy—and, just as truly, ever-existing, ever-conscious, ever-new joy *is* the superconscious.

> The highest experience man can have is to feel that Bliss in which every other aspect of Divinity—love, wisdom, immortality—is fully contained.
>
> —Paramahansa Yogananda, yoga master[5]

Then I simply remember I became more blissful, more rapturous, more ecstatic. I was just filling and filling with this light and love that was in the light. They are so dynamic and so much going on in there of love and joy and knowledge.

—Jayne Smith, near-death experiencer[6]

I felt that same sense of bliss, a joy beyond comprehension . . . a feeling that all ills were healed, everything was all right, always had been, really, and always would be. There was nothing wanting in all of creation; anything less than perfection was impossible.

—Rob Schultheis, extreme climber[7]

Sound

Many people experience heavenly, uplifting, inspiring, all-encompassing sound in the depths of stillness. This inner sound has many names across many traditions. The ancient Greeks called it the music of the spheres. The yogis call it Om or Aum. The Christians call it the Word, the Holy Ghost, the Comforter, or the Amen. It is often experienced by near-death experiencers. The cosmic sound is experienced as much as heard.

And then I heard the MUSIC. It was a tone so sublimely perfect that remembering it still brings me to tears. . . . I was hearing the symphony of angels, the song of the universe. . . .

—Lynnclaire Dennis, near-death experiencer[8]

Music surrounded me. It came from all directions. Its harmonic beauty unlike earthly vocal or instrumental. . . .

—Dr. Richard Eby, near-death experiencer[9]

You can deliberately try to hear and feel the celestial sound by listening for it once you have become still and inwardly absorbed in meditation. When you hear and feel it, stay focused on it; try to become immersed in it. To most effectively tune into this wondrous experience I practice a specific technique called, unsurprisingly, the Om or Aum Technique. If you would like to learn more about this practice I invite you to go to: *ananda.org.* Once at the site search for "Aum Technique."

Light

Being filled with or surrounded by light is perhaps the most common way superconscious experience is described and depicted. We are said to be enlightened or illumined when filled with the superconscious. Saints are often pictured enhaloed with light. Many people have movingly described becoming immersed in the Light.

> And then I was in the light. Like a nuclear explosion, the light pierced me. Every particle of me was shot through with blinding, brilliant light, and I had a feeling of transparency. I floated in this light, bathed in it, and the love that surrounded me and filled me was sweeter and finer than anything I had ever felt. I was changed by it, refined, rarified, made pure. I basked in its sweetness, and the traumas of the past were far behind me, forgotten and transformed by peace.
>
>   —RaNelle Wallace, near-death experiencer[10]

> All of a sudden I felt more uplifted than ever before—I knew timelessness, spacelessness, and lightness—I did not seem to be walking on the earth. Every bush, every tree seemed to wear a halo . . . a light emanation around everything and flecks of gold fell like slanted rain through the air. The most important part was not the phenomena . . . it was the realization of the unity of all creation.
>
>   —Mildred Norman, the Peace Pilgrim[11]

Relaxed concentration at the point between the eyebrows will often reveal light. Continued concentration can expand the light or resolve the light into the spiritual eye—an opalescent blue field, surrounded by a golden halo, with a tiny five-pointed white star in the center. Continued concentration can not only immerse you in the light but profoundly uplift and inspire you.

Develop a Personal Experience of Superconscious Love

Superconscious experience can be both impersonal and personal. Sound, light, energy, peace, and joy can be experienced impersonally in the superconscious Self. They are the natural attributes of our godlike essence. They are what we are. The experience of love, by contrast, is more personal.

I have often described the superconscious as infinite intelligent consciousness. This description may strike you as being completely impersonal—a reality far too vast, far too involved in maintaining creation, to allow a personal relationship. Infinite intelligence, however, is not only *infinitely* aware but also *infinitesimally* aware: aware of every atom of creation; minutely aware of every living creature; fully aware of the thoughts, feelings, needs, and desires of each one of us. Thus can we approach the superconscious as a knowing, loving being—what is usually thought of as "God"—and superconscious God may respond to us in the language of love, joy, blessings, guidance, or even, rarely, directly heard words.

> [This radiant being] loved me in a way that I had never known that love could possibly be. He was a concentrated field of energy, radiant in splendor indescribable, except to say goodness and love. This was more loving than one can imagine . . . it was loving me with overwhelming power.
>
> —Howard Storm, near-death experiencer[12]

> . . . you can actually obtain God perception. In that way you can see, hear and play with God. Perhaps this may sound weird, but God is really there next to you.
>
> —George Harrison, Beatle[13]

God is Eternal Bliss. His being is love, wisdom, and joy. He is both impersonal and personal, and manifests Himself in whatever way He pleases. He appears before His saints in the form

each of them holds dear: a Christian sees Christ, a Hindu be-
holds Krishna or the Divine Mother. . . .

        —Paramahansa Yogananda, yoga master[14]

Because we are all used to having personal relationships, a personal relationship with God may feel the most natural to you. You may approach God
as the Heavenly Father, Divine Mother, Beloved Lord, Beloved Friend, or
as a savior such as Christ or Krishna, or as a saint or sage you hold dear.
The way in which we approach God is the way in which God will respond.

Prayer and Devotion

Prayer is often thought of as reciting a formula, such as the Lord's Prayer,
and most often done without any thought that there will be an actual response. Effective prayer is heartfelt and spontaneous, more feeling than
words, and the Divine response is more often in feeling, like a wordless
moment between lovers, than in words.

> I had a feeling of being lifted out of an immensity of dark space
> into spaciousness of warm and brilliant sunlight. . . . I knew;
> God with His boundless and matchlessly patient love was there
> to help me.
>
>   —J. C. Penney, founder of the J. C. Penney department
>   stores[15]

To many westerners spiritual devotion is a foreign and sometimes unsettling concept. It conjures up images of will-less cyphers blindly worship-
ping in mindless thrall. Real devotion is far from will-less or blind. Real
devotion is the lovingly openhearted, focused, and willful determination to
give and share love with God, or a particular personal expression of God,
in order to become one with God.

Devotion to God can be perhaps best understood by comparing it to any
attempt to succeed at a high level. Musicians, athletes, scientists, inventors,
entrepreneurs, or artists—anyone attempting to succeed at a high level—
have to love what they are doing, have to be passionate about it, in order to

succeed. Determination is the driving force of devotion; love is the quality through which that determination is channeled.

Make Openhearted Determination a Habit

Most of us have busy, full lives juggling relationships, careers, family, responsibilities, health, finances—you name it. It is quite easy and common to be so distracted by it all that we lose touch with any resolution we may have made to experience the superconscious. The best defense against losing touch with the goal of becoming more superconsciously aware is to develop openhearted determination.

Openhearted determination is also the greatest aid to achieving superconscious awareness. While meditation is the anchor habit for developing superconscious awareness, we need also to develop the neural circuit-supported habit of deliberately, intensely, and with openhearted determination immersing ourselves in the superconscious experience our meditation enables us to have.

CHAPTER 16

We Are So Much More than We Know

We are so much more than we know—but the brain keeps us from knowing it.

The brain has been wired to automatically and continuously support sensory perception—wiring that keeps us always distracted from perceiving the ever-present subtle reality that surrounds us.

Our brain's focus on sensory and bodily perception, our one foot on earth, makes us feel small and limited, fearfully subject to illness, injury, and death—unaware of our one foot in heaven and of our immortal superconscious Self.

Our brain's millions of mental and emotional neural habit circuits—which fire in a mesmerizing and continuous fireworks show—compel us to be involved in the physical world, and keep our interest focused away from subtle reality, finding what fulfillment and happiness we can in relationships, accomplishments, and possessions.

The saints, sages, and near-death experiencers tell us that when we die, when the brain ceases to function, we will quickly and automatically perceive a vast luminous reality, as if we've awakened from a dark dream.

When we die, when the brain ceases to function, we experience a profound freedom from the hundreds of worldly concerns that are currently the focus of our life.

When we die, when the brain ceases to function, we have perfect health, limitless energy, and vast intuitive knowledge.

When we die, when the brain ceases to function, we feel profound fulfillment, belonging, peace, love, and joy—ours to experience without striving because they are part of who we are in our deathless essence, in our Self.

Why wait until we die?

The saints and sages have learned to rewire their brains to experience freedom, health, limitless energy, intuitive knowledge, fulfillment, belonging, love, and joy while also using their brains to function in this physical world.

We can, too.

Rewire your brain to support meditation. Open your heart and focus your mind. Stillness and inward absorption will take you beyond the body, beyond the brain, and into superconscious awareness—into the ever-new-joy of God.

Rewire your brain to draw superconscious qualities into your daily life so that you may regularly experience more superconscious awareness. Develop positive neural habit circuits that support being relaxed, energized, concentrated, and creative. With these qualities you can do amazing things: athletic feats, unique creative expression, success in any endeavor, acts of great love and service. Nothing is beyond your superconscious abilities.

Rewire your brain to connect directly to the superconscious. Immerse yourself with openhearted determination in your blissful Self. Establish a relationship with God. Let the superconscious transform you by magnetically rewiring your brain.

In all these ways we can rewire our brains to function with one foot on earth and one foot in heaven, with both conscious and superconscious perception, with joy in the here and *now*—not only in the hereafter.

> God is the Fountain of health, prosperity, wisdom, and eternal joy. Give your attention to the Almighty Power that is giving you life and strength and wisdom. Pray that unceasing truth flow into your mind, unceasing strength flow into your body, and unceasing joy flow into your soul. Right behind the darkness of

closed eyes are the wondrous forces of the universe, and all the great saints; and the endlessness of the Infinite. Meditate, and you will realize the omnipresent Absolute Truth and see Its mysterious workings in your life and in all the glories of creation.

—Paramahansa Yogananda, yoga master[1]

NOTES

CHAPTER 1

1. Fox, "Teen Girl Uses 'Crazy Strength' To Lift Burning Car off Dad."
2. Maxwell, *Seeing the Invisible: Modern Religious and Other Transcendent Experiences*, 56.
3. Gilbert, "Your Elusive Creative Genius."
4. Mitchell, *The Way of the Explorer*, 16.
5. Lindberghh, *The Spirit of St. Louis*, 389–90.
6. Bucke, *Cosmic Consciousness: A Study in the Evolution of the Human Mind*, loc. 518, Kindle.
7. Spielman, *The Spiritual Journey of Joseph L. Greenstein: The Mighty Atom: World's Strongest Man*, 100–102.
8. Yogananda, "Love Human and Divine."
9. Abell, *Talks with Great Composers*, loc. 280–286, Kindle.
10. Aurobindo, *The Life Divine*, 97–99.
11. Yogananda, *Autobiography of a Yogi*, loc. 93, Kindle.
12. Tennyson, *The Major Works*, 520.
13. Neal, *Sport and Identity*, 166–167.
14. Whitt, *Road Signs for Success*, 61.
15. Chang, *Wisdom for the Soul: Five Millennia of Prescriptions for Spiritual Healing*, 26.

CHAPTER 2

1. Adams, "Rupert Sheldrake: The 'Heretic' at Odds with Scientific Dogma."
2. Eccles, *The Wonder of Being Human*, 36.
3. Anthony, "Human Consciousness Is Simply a State of Matter, Like Solid or Liquid—but *Quantum*."

4. Dossey, "Brains and Beyond: The Unfolding Vision of Health and Healing."

5. Fancher, *Pioneers of Psychology*, 117.

6. Kliemann, "Intrinsic Functional Connectivity of the Brain in Adults with a Single Cerebral Hemisphere."

7. Lorber, "Is Your Brain Really Necessary?" 1232–1234.

8. Forsdyke, "Wittgenstein's Certainty Is Uncertain: Brain Scans of Cured Hydrocephalics Challenge Cherished Assumptions," 336–342.

9. Chow, "Why Your DNA May Not Be Your Destiny."

10. Baltimore, "Our Genome Unveiled," 814–816.

11. Lipton, *The Biology of Belief*, 33–34.

12. McCaffrey, "There Will Always Be Limits to How Creative a Computer Can Be."

13. Kassan, "A.I. Gone Awry: The Futile Quest for Artificial Intelligence."

14. Chalmers, "Facing Up to the Problem of Consciousness," 200–201.

15. Dennett, *Consciousness Explained*.

16. Carruthers, *Consciousness: Essays from a Higher-Order Perspective*, 32.

17. Searle, "'The Mystery of Consciousness': An Exchange."

18. Dossey, "Consciousness: Why Materialism Fails."

19. Herbert, *Quantum Reality: Beyond the New Physics*, 15.

20. Hoffman, "Conscious Realism and the Mind-Body Problem," 90.

21. Horgan, "String Theorist Edward Witten Says Consciousness 'Will Remain a Mystery.'"

22. Mumford, "An Evaluation of Remote Viewing: Research and Applications."

23. Grinberg-Zylberbaum, "The Einstein-Podolsky-Rosen Paradox in the Brain: The Transferred Potential."

24. Thaheld, "An Interdisciplinary Approach to Certain Fundamental Issues in the Fields of Physics and Biology: Towards a Unified Theory."

25. Wackerman, "Correlations between Brain Electrical Activities of Two Spatially Separated Human Subjects."

26. Thompson, "Scientific Evidence for a Connecting Matrix: An Introduction to Biofield Science, Part 2."

27. Penman, "Could there Be Proof to the Theory that We're ALL Psychic?"

28. Heisenberg, *Physics and Philosophy*, 154.

29. Goswami, *The Self-Aware Universe*, 10.

30. Haisch, *God Theory: Universes, Zero-Point Fields, and What's Behind It All*, 3.

31. Linde, "Universe, Life, Consciousness."

32. Schrödinger, as quoted in in *Psychic Research*, 91.

CHAPTER 3

1. Einstein, *The World as I See It*, 28–29.

2. Connolly, "World Renown Scientist Says He Has Found Proof of God! We May Be Living the 'Matrix.'"

3. Braden, *The Spontaneous Healing of Belief*, 212.

4. Jeans, *The Mysterious Universe*, 137.

5. Maxwell, *Seeing the Invisible: Modern Religious and Other Transcendent Experiences*, 47.

6. Bevan, "Mountain Mavericks: Patrick Vallençant."

7. Maxwell, *Seeing the Invisible: Modern Religious and Other Transcendent Experiences*, 52.

8. Coffey, *Explorers of the Infinite: The Secret Spiritual Lives of Extreme Athletes—and What They Reveal about Near-Death Experiences, Psychic Communication, and Touching the Beyond*, 57.

9. Maslow, *Motivation and Personality*, 234.

10. Ibid. 93.

11. Maslow, *Religions, Values, and Peak Experiences*, ix.

12. Wikipedia, "Peak Experience."

13. Csíkszentmihályi, *Flow: The Psychology of Optimal Experience*, 27.

14. Murphy, *In the Zone: Transcendent Experience in Sports*, 28.

15. Assagioli, *Psychosynthesis*, 7.

16. Grof, *The Adventure of Self-Discovery: Dimensions of Consciousness and New Perspectives in Psychotherapy and Inner Exploration*, 1.

17. Wilber, *Integral Psychology: Consciousness, Spirit, Psychology, Therapy*, loc. 121, Kindle.

18. Russell, *Universal Law, Natural Science and Philosophy*, Prelude.

19. Wallace, *The Burning Within*, 99.

20. Smith, "Moment of Truth: A Window on Life after Death."

21. Rumi, *Hush, Don't Say Anything to God: Passionate Poems of Rumi*.

22. Martin, *Searching for Home: A Personal Journey of Transformation and Healing after a Near-Death Experience*, 27.

23. Williams, "Christian Andréason's Near-Death Experience."

24. St. Teresa, *The Life of St. Teresa of Jesus*, Ch. XXIX, 16–17.

25. Wallace, *The Burning Within*, 95.

26. Besant, *Introduction to Yoga*, Synopsis.

27. Vivekananda, *Complete Works of Swami Vivekananda*, Vol. I, Ch. VII: Dhyana and Samadhi, 184.

28. Yogananda, "Benefits of Kriya Yoga."

29. Coffey, *Explorers of the Infinite: The Secret Spiritual Lives of Extreme Athletes—and What They Reveal about Near-Death Experiences, Psychic Communication, and Touching the Beyond,* 49.

30. Csíkszentmihályi, "Flow: The Secret to Happiness." TED Talk. 5:50. 2008.

31. Coffey, *Explorers of the Infinite: The Secret Spiritual Lives of Extreme Athletes—and What They Reveal about Near-Death Experiences, Psychic Communication, and Touching the Beyond,* 52.

32. Clark, *The Man Who Tapped the Secrets of the Universe,* loc. 516–520, Kindle.

33. Aurobindo, *Letters on Himself and the Ashram,* 257.

34. Rumi, *The Essential Rumi,* 22.

35. Yogananda, *The Essence of Self-Realization: The Wisdom of Paramahansa Yogananda,* Chapter 10, 9.

36. Lao Tzu, *Tao Te Ching,* Chapter 16.

37. Huang Po, *The Zen Teaching of Huang Po on the Transmission of Mind; Being the Teaching of the Zen Master Huang Po as Recorded by the Scholar P'Ei Hsiu of the T'Ang Dynasty,* 79.

38. Sivananda, "How to Find Peace of Mind."

39. Yogananda, *How to Awaken Your True Potential,* 109.

40. Newberg, *Why God Won't Go Away: Brain Science and the Biology of Belief.*

41. Newberg, *How Enlightenment Changes Your Brain: The New Science of Transformation,* 156.

42. Alexander, *Proof of Heaven: A Neurosurgeon's Journey into the Afterlife,* 130.

43. Greyson, "Consciousness without Brain Activity: Near Death Experiences."

44. Gillihan, "Dr. Eben Alexander—Exploring Consciousness, Heaven, and Unconditional Love."

45. Gillihan, "Dr. Eben Alexander—Exploring Consciousness, Heaven, and Unconditional Love."

46. Kriyananda, *Awaken to Superconsciousness,* opening of chapter 2.

47. Harvard Gazette, "Eight Weeks to a Better Brain."

48. Thorpe, "Experts Reveal What Happens in Your Brain When You Meditate."

49. Ibid.

50. Gotink, "Meditation and Yoga Practice Are Associated with Smaller Right Amygdala Volume: The Rotterdam Study," Vol. 12, pages 1631–1639 (2018).

51. Holzel, "Mindfulness Practice Leads to Increases in Regional Brain Gray Matter Density."

52. Joss, "Effects of a Mindfulness-Based Intervention on Self-Compassion and Psychological Health among Young Adults with a History of Childhood Maltreatment."

53. Sevinc, "How Does Mindfulness Training Improve Moral Cognition: A Theoretical and Experimental Framework for the Study of Embodied Ethics."

54. Vivekananda, *Complete Works of Swami Vivekananda*. Vol. I, Ch. VII: Dhyana and Samadhi. 184.

CHAPTER 4

1. St. Maarten, *Divine Living: The Essential Guide to Your True Destiny*, 49.

2. Yogananda, *How to Have Courage, Calmness, and Confidence*, 39.

3. Williams, "Josiane Antonette's Near-Death Experience."

4. Atwater, *Beyond the Light: What Isn't Being Said about Near-Death Experience*, 142.

5. Williams, "Mellen-Thomas Benedict's Near-Death Experience."

6. Besant, *The Nature and Practice of Yoga*, 12.

7. Steiner, *How to Know Higher Worlds: A Modern Path of Initiation*, 36.

8. Williams, "Mellen-Thomas Benedict's Near-Death Experience."

9. Yogananda, *How to Awaken Your True Potential*, 143.

10. Hawkins, *Power vs. Force: The Hidden Determinants of Human Behavior*, 22.

11. Yogananda. *Autobiography of a Yogi*, loc. 97, Kindle.

12. Bucke, *Cosmic Consciousness: A Study in the Evolution of the Human Mind*, loc. 419–423, Kindle.

13. Sivananda, "Cosmic Consciousness."

14. Eckhart, *Meister Eckhart*, 153.

15. Sasaki, *The Zen Eye: A Collection of Zen Talks by Sokei-an*, 41.

16. Rumi, *Hush, Don't Say Anything to God: Passionate Poems of Rumi*.

CHAPTER 5

1. Carrel, *Man the Unknown*.

2. Ho, "Quantum Coherence and Conscious Experience."

3. Enz, *Wolfgang Pauli: Writings on Physics and Philosophy*, 259.

4. Swedenborg, *Heaven and Hell*, 57.

5. Eadie, *Embraced by the Light*, 47–48.

6. Williams, "Christian Andréason's Near-Death Experience."

7. Williams, "Nora Spurgin's Near-Death Experience."

8. Livio, "Description of Heaven."

9. Yogananda, *The Second Coming of Christ: The Resurrection of the Christ Within You: A Revelatory Commentary on the Original Teachings of Jesus*, Vol. 1, Discourse 10.

10. Yogananda, *The Essence of Self-Realization: The Wisdom of Paramahansa Yogananda*, Chapters 9, 10.

11. Yogananda, *Autobiography of a Yogi*, loc. 261–262, Kindle.

12. Ho, "Bioenergetics and Biocommunication."

13. Swedenborg, *Heaven and Hell*, 456.

14. Chow, "Why Your DNA May Not Be Your Destiny."

15. Yogananda, *Autobiography of a Yogi*, loc. 76, Kindle.

16. Dennis, *The Pattern*, 29.

17. Atwater, *Beyond the Light: What Isn't Being Said about Near-Death Experience*, 182.

18. Dürr, Television Interview.

CHAPTER 6

1. Yogananda, *How to Be Happy All the Time*, 18.

2. Barrett, "Are Emotions Natural Kinds?"

3. Barrett, "The Conceptual Act Theory: A Précis," 6, 292–297.

4. Bohm, *The Undivided Universe*, 389.

5. Fowler, "Dynamic Spread of Happiness in a Large Social Network: Longitudinal Analysis over 20 Years in the Framingham Heart Study."

6. Belluck, "Strangers May Cheer You up, Study Says."

7. Stein, "Happiness Can Spread among People Like a Contagion, Study Indicates."

8. Dossey, "Brains and Beyond: The Unfolding Vision of Health and Healing."

9. Baldwin, *Edison: Inventing the Century*, 376.

10. Henson, *It's Not Easy Being Green: And Other Things to Consider*, Section: Listen to Your Heart.

11. Yogananda, *Autobiography of a Yogi*, loc. 2346, Kindle.

12. Brunton, quoted in: Network Newsletter, 33: 18.

13. Forsdyke, "Wittgenstein's Certainty Is Uncertain: Brain Scans of Cured Hydrocephalics Challenge Cherished Assumptions," 336–342.

14. Borsellino, "Holographic Aspects of Temporal Memory and Optomotor Responses." 10 (1): 58–60. doi:10.1007/bf00288785.

15. Baev, "Solution of the Problem of Central Pattern Generators and a New Concept of Brain Functions," 4: 414–432.

16. Heine, "Resting State Networks and Consciousness. Alterations of Multiple Resting State Network Connectivity in Physiological, Pharmacological and Pathological Consciousness States." doi:10.3389/fpsyg.2012.00295. 3: 295.

17. Pribram, "The Neurophysiology of Remembering."

18. DiCarlo, Exploring the Human Energy System."

19. Besant, *Karma*, Sec. 13.

20. Clark, *The Man Who Tapped the Secrets of the Universe*, loc 91-93, Kindle.

21. Jung, *Psychology and Religion: West and East*, 12.

CHAPTER 7

1. Kriyananda, *Awaken to Superconsciousness*, opening of chapter 2.

2. Ibid.

3. Ibid.

4. Johns Hopkins Medicine, "Experiences of 'Ultimate Reality' or 'God' Confer Lasting Benefits to Mental Health."

5. Taylor, "An Awakening."

6. Dennis, *The Pattern*, 40.

7. Maxwell, *Seeing the Invisible: Modern Religious and Other Transcendent Experiences*, 49.

8. Wallace, *The Burning Within*, 95.

9. Newberg, *How Enlightenment Changes Your Brain: The New Science of Transformation*, 153.

CHAPTER 8

1. Rumi, *The Essential Rumi*, Ch. 11: Union.

CHAPTER 9

1. Yogananda, *How to Awaken Your True Potential*, 67.

CHAPTER 10

1. Fox, "Is Meditation Associated with Altered Brain Structure? A Systematic Review and Meta-Analysis of Morphometric Neuroimaging in Meditation Practitioners."

2. Weng, "Compassion Training Alters Altruism and Neural Responses to Suffering."

3. Sharkey, "How Transcendental Meditation Alters the Brain."

4. Coventry University, "Meditation and Yoga Can 'Reverse' DNA Reactions which Cause Stress, New Study Suggests."

5. Bhasin, "Specific Transcriptome Changes Associated with Blood Pressure Reduction in Hypertensive Patients after Relaxation Response Training." doi: 10.1089/acm.2017.0053.

6. May, "Mindfulness Meditation Is Associated with Decreases in Partner Negative Affect in Daily Life."

CHAPTER 11

1. Hanh, "Returning Home."

2. Treece, *The Joyful Spirit of Padre Pio: Stories, Letters, and Prayers*, 47.

3. Yogananda, *Karma and Reincarnation*, 85.

4. Hay, *You Can Heal Your Life*, 1.

5. Kriyananda, *Affirmations for Self-Healing*, 30, Non-Injury.

6. Ibid. 7, Security.

7. Ibid. 44, Acceptance.

CHAPTER 12

1. Yogananda, *The Second Coming of Christ: The Resurrection of the Christ Within You: A Revelatory Commentary on the Original Teachings of Jesus*, 418.

2. Kriyananda, *The Art and Science of Raja Yoga*, 258.

3. Coffey, *Explorers of the Infinite: The Secret Spiritual Lives of Extreme Athletes—and What They Reveal about Near-Death Experiences, Psychic Communication, and Touching the Beyond*, 249–250.

4. Spielman, *The Spiritual Journey of Joseph L. Greenstein: The Mighty Atom: World's Strongest Man*, 100–102.

5. Millman, *Divine Interventions: True Stories of Mystery and Miracles That Change Lives*, 121.

6. Chinmoy, "Weightlifting."

7. Yogananda, *How to Be a Success*, 78.

8. Kriyananda, *Awaken to Superconsciousness*, opening of chapter 11.

9. Aitkenhead, "Buy Gatwick? Why Not?"

10. Belden, *The Lengthening Shadow: The Life of Thomas J. Watson*, 127.

11. Emerson, *Emerson: The Ultimate Collection*, 213.

12. Csíkszentmihályi, *Flow: The Psychology of Optimal Experience*, 200.

13. Keller, "Address to American Association to Promote the Teaching of Speech to the Deaf," 222–224.

14. Clark, *The Man Who Tapped the Secrets of the Universe*, loc. 227–231, Kindle.

15. Kriyananda, *Affirmations for Self-Healing*, 15, Enthusiasm.

16. Ibid. 14, Good Health.

17. Ibid. 4, Energy.

18. Newberg, *How Enlightenment Changes Your Brain: The New Science of Transformation*, 152.

CHAPTER 13

1. Miller, *Old Man's Advice to Youth: "Never Lose a Holy Curiosity,"* 62–64.

2. Rowan, "Those Business Hunches Are More than Blind Faith," 110-114.

3. Isaacson, *Steve Jobs*, 48.

4. L'Engle, *Circle of Quiet*, 40.

5. Hill, *Think and Grow Rich*, 137.

6. Clark, *The Man Who Tapped the Secrets of the Universe*, loc. 431–432, Kindle.

7. Yogananda, *How to Have Courage, Calmness, and Confidence*, 116.

8. Kriyananda, *Affirmations for Self-Healing*, 31, Concentration.

9. Clark, *The Man Who Tapped the Secrets of the Universe*, loc. 73–74, Kindle.

10. Yogananda, *How to Be a Success*, 17.

11. Murphy, *In the Zone: Transcendent Experience in Sports*, 25–26.

12. Ibid. 23.

13. Csíkszentmihályi, *Flow: The Psychology of Optimal Experience*, 3.

14. L'Engle, *Circle of Quiet*, Chapter 1, 3.

15. Newberg, *How Enlightenment Changes Your Brain: The New Science of Transformation*, 121–122.

16. Coffey, *Explorers of the Infinite: The Secret Spiritual Lives of Extreme Athletes—and What They Reveal about Near-Death Experiences, Psychic Communication, and Touching the Beyond*, 52–53.

17. Ibid. 10.

18. Ibid. 63.

19. Kriyananda, *Affirmations for Self-Healing*, 31, Concentration.

20. Ibid. 1, Success.

21. Ibid. 34, Alertness.

CHAPTER 14

1. Cameron, *The Artist's Way: A Spiritual Path to Higher Creativity*, 3.

2. Abell, *Talks with Great Composers,* loc. 1722–1725, Kindle.

3. Anderson, Unpublished Work.

4. Schwartz, "Nonlocality and Exceptional Experiences: A Study of Genius, Religious Epiphany, and the Psychic," 227–236.

5. Abell, *Talks with Great Composers,* loc. 2379–2390, Kindle.

6. Fielding, "An Interim Report of a Prospective, Randomized, Controlled Study of Adjuvant Chemotherapy in Operable Gastric Cancer: British Stomach Cancer Group," 390–399.

7. Coons, "Psychophysiologic Aspects of Multiple Personality Disorder: A Review. Dissociation," 47–53.

8. Shepard, "Visual Changes in Multiple Personality," 85.

9. Yogananda, *Autobiography of a Yogi,* loc. 4208-4209, Kindle.

10. Yogananda, *How to Be Happy All the Time,* 76.

11. Asha, *Swami Kriyananda: Lightbearer: The Life and Legacy of a Disciple of Paramahansa Yogananda,* 244.

12. Clark, *The Man Who Tapped the Secrets of the Universe,* loc. 227–231, Kindle.

13. Anderson, Unpublished Work.

14. Yogananda, *How to Be Happy All the Time,* 99.

15. Jobs, "You've Got To Find What You Love, Jobs Says."

16. Einstein, "Address at the Physical Society, Berlin, for Max Planck's sixtieth birthday."

17. L'Engle, *A Wrinkle in Time: 50th Anniversary Commemorative Edition,* 235.

18. Bergland, "The Neuroscience of Imagination."

19. Hill, *The Science of Success: Napoleon Hill's Proven Program for Prosperity and Happiness,* 17.

20. Slimani, "Effects of Mental Imagery on Muscular Strength in Healthy and Patient Participants: A Systematic Review."

21. Niles, "How to Use Visualization to Achieve Your Goals."

22. Kriyananda, *Affirmations for Self-Healing,* 41, Positive Thinking.

23. Ibid. 36, Power.

CHAPTER 15

1. Newberg, *How Enlightenment Changes Your Brain: The New Science of Transformation,* 153.

2. Kriyananda, *Affirmations for Self-Healing,* 51, God Remembrance.

3. Ibid. 49, Immortality.

4. Yogananda, *Metaphysical Meditations,* 41.

5. Yogananda, "Knowing God."

6. Smith, "Moment of Truth: A Window on Life after Death."

7. Murphy, *In the Zone: Transcendent Experience in Sports*, 124.

8. Williams, "Lynnclaire Dennis' Near-Death Experience."

9. Ibid.

10. Wallace, *The Burning Within*, 95.

11. Millman, *Divine Interventions: True Stories of Mystery and Miracles That Change Lives*, 108.

12. Williams, "Howard Storm's Near-Death Experience."

13. Bhaktivedanta, *Kṛṣṇa: The Supreme Personality of Godhead*, Introduction.

14. Yogananda, "Knowing God."

15. Full Gospel Businessmen's Training, "J. C. Penney Story."

CHAPTER 16

1. Yogananda, *Journey to Self-Realization*, 113.

BIBLIOGRAPHY

Abell, Arthur M. *Talks with Great Composers*. San Francisco: Pickle Partners Publishing, 2016, Kindle Edition.

Adams, Tim. "Rupert Sheldrake: The 'Heretic' at Odds with Scientific Dogma." *The Guardian*. February 4, 2012. *theguardian.com*.

Aitkenhead, Decca. "Buy Gatwick? Why Not?" *The Guardian*, September 19, 2008. *theguardian.com*.

Alexander, Eben. *Proof of Heaven: A Neurosurgeon's Journey into the Afterlife*. New York: Simon & Schuster, 2012.

Andersen, Dana. Unpublished Work. Center for the Arts, Creativity, and Consciousness.

Anthony, Sebastian. "Human Consciousness Is Simply a State of Matter, Like Solid or Liquid—But *Quantum*," ExtremeTech, April 24, 2014, *extremetech.com*.

Asha. *Swami Kriyananda: Lightbearer: The Life and Legacy of a Disciple of Paramahansa Yogananda*. Palo Alto, CA: Chela Publications, 2019.

Assagioli, Roberto. *Psychosynthesis*. New York: Penguin. 1977.

Atwater, P. M. H. *Beyond the Light: What Isn't Being Said about Near-Death Experience*. New York: Carol Pub. Group, 1994.

Aurobindo. "Letters on Himself and the Ashram." PDF, 2011, *sriaurobindo ashram.org*.

———. *The Life Divine*. New York: Dutton, 1951.

Baev, K.V. "Solution of the Problem of Central Pattern Generators and a New Concept of Brain Functions." *Neurophysiology*, 2012.

Baldwin, N. *Edison: Inventing the Century*. New York: Hyperion, 1995.

Baltimore, David. "Our Genome Unveiled." *Nature* 409, no. 6822 (2001): 814–816.

Barrett, L. F. "Are Emotions Natural Kinds?" *Perspectives on Psychological Science*, March 1, 2006, *journals.sagepub.com*.

———. "The conceptual act theory: A précis." *Emotion Review*, 2014, *journals .sagepub.com*.

Belden, Thomas Graham, and Marva Belden. *The Lengthening Shadow: The Life of Thomas J. Watson.* Boston: Little, Brown, 1962.

Belluck, P. "Strangers May Cheer You Up, Study Says." *New York Times,* December 4, 2008, *nytimes.com.*

Bergland, Christopher. "The Neuroscience of Imagination." *Psychology Today,* February 8, 2012, *psychologytoday.com.*

Besant, Annie Wood. *An Introduction to Yoga.* CreateSpace, 2018.

———. *Karma.* Krotona, Hollywood, Los Angeles, CA: Theosophical Pub. House, 1918.

———. *The Nature and Practice of Yoga.* BookRix GmbH & Co., KG80331, Munich, 2018.

Bevan, William. "Mountain Mavericks: Patrick Vallençant." *Snow News,* 2003.

Bhaktivedanta. *Kṛṣṇa: The Supreme Personality of Godhead.* Bhativedanta Book Trust, 1972.

Bhasin, M. K., et al. "Specific Transcriptome Changes Associated with Blood Pressure Reduction in Hypertensive Patients after Relaxation Response Training." *Journal of Alternative and Complementary Medicine,* May 2018, *doi.org/10.1089/acm.2017.0053.*

Bohm, David, and B. J. Hiley. *The Undivided Universe.* Reprint edition, London: Routledge, 1995.

Borsellino, A., and T. Poggio. "Holographic Aspects of Temporal Memory and Optomotor Responses." *Kybernetik,* 1972, 10 (1): 58–60, *doi.org/10.1007/bf00288785.*

Braden, Gregg. *The Spontaneous Healing of Belief.* Carlsbad, CA: Hay House, 2009.

Brunton, Paul. Quoted in Network Newsletter: Scientific and Medical Network, UK, April 1987.

Bucke, Richard Maurice. *Cosmic Consciousness: A Study in the Evolution of the Human Mind.* Dover Publications, 2009, Kindle Edition.

Cameron, Julia. *The Artist's Way: A Spiritual Path to Higher Creativity.* New York: TarcherPerigee, 2002.

Carrel, Alexis. *Man the Unknown.* London: Hamish Hamilton, 1942.

Carruthers, Peter. *Consciousness: Essays from a Higher-Order Perspective.* New York: Oxford University Press, 2005.

Chalmers, David. "Facing Up to the Problem of Consciousness." Journal of Consciousness Studies, 2(3):200-19, 1995.

Chang, Larry. *Wisdom for the Soul: Five Millennia of Prescriptions for Spiritual Healing.* Washington, DC: Gnosophia Publishers. 2006.

Chinmoy. "Weightlifting." Sri Chinmoy's Official Site, *srichinmoy.org.*

Chow, Denise. "Why Your DNA May Not Be Your Destiny." *LiveScience*, June 4, 2015, accessed November 10, 2015. *livescience.com*

Clark, Glen. *The Man Who Tapped the Secrets of the Universe*. Unknown, 2014, Kindle Edition.

Coffey, Maria. *Explorers of the Infinite: The Secret Spiritual Lives of Extreme Athletes—and What They Reveal about Near-Death Experiences, Psychic Communication, and Touching the Beyond*. New York: Penguin Publishing Group, 2008, Kindle Edition.

Connolly, Marshall. "World Renown Scientist Says He Has Found Proof of God! We May Be Living the 'Matrix'." *Catholic Online*, June 8, 2016, accessed July 10, 2016, *catholic.org*.

Coons, Philip M. "Psychophysiologic Aspects of Multiple Personality Disorder: A Review." Dissociation, Ridgeview Institute and the International Society for the Study of Multiple Personality & Dissociation, Vol. 1, No. 1 (1988).

Coventry University. "Meditation and Yoga Can 'Reverse' DNA Reactions which Cause Stress, New Study Suggests." Science Daily: Science News, June 15, 2017, *sciencedaily.com*

Csíkszentmihályi, Mihaly. *Flow: The Psychology of Optimal Experience*. New York: Harper Perennial Modern Classics, 1990.

———. Mihaly. "Flow: The Secret to Happiness." TED Talk, 2008, *youtube.com*

Dennett, D. C., and Paul Weiner. *Consciousness Explained*. New York: Little, Brown and Company, 2017.

Dennis, Lynnclaire. *The Pattern*. Lower Lake, CA: Integral Pub. in association with Entagram Productions, 1997.

DiCarlo, Russell. "Exploring the Human Energy System." HealthyNet. *healthy .net*.

Dossey, Larry, MD. "Brains and Beyond: The Unfolding Vision of Health and Healing." Science Direct, Volume 12, Issue 5, September–October 2016, 314–324, *doi.org/10.1016/j.explore.2016.06.011*.

———. "Consciousness: Why Materialism Fails." Open Sciences, Open Sciences Blog, May 30, 2015.

Dürr, Hans-Peter. Television Interview. *PM Magazine*, May 2007.

Eadie, Betty J, and Curtis Taylor. *Embraced by the Light*. Placerville, CA: Gold Leaf Press, 1992.

Eccles, J., and D. N. Robinson. *The Wonder of Being Human*. Boston: Shambhala, 1985.

Eckhart, Meister, C. de B. Evans, and Franz Pfeiffer. *Meister Eckhart*. London: John M. Watkins, 1952.

Einstein, Albert. "Address at the Physical Society, Berlin, for Max Planck's six-tieth birthday." Principles of Research, 1918, *site.uottawa.ca.*

———. *The World As I See It.* New York: Philosophical Library. 1949.

Emerson, Ralph Waldo. *Emerson: The Ultimate Collection.* Titan Read, 2015.

Enz, Charles P., and Karl von Meyenn. *Wolfgang Pauli: Writings on Physics and Philosophy.* Heidelberg: Springer-Verlag, 1994.

Fancher, R. E., and A. Rutherford. *Pioneers of Psychology.* New York: W. W. Norton & Company, 2012.

Fielding, J. W. et al. "An Interim Report of a Prospective, Randomized, Controlled Study of Adjuvant Chemotherapy in Operable Gastric Cancer: British Stomach Cancer Group." *World Journal of Surgery* 7 (3), 1983.

Forsdyke, Donald R. "Wittgenstein's Certainty Is Uncertain: Brain Scans of Cured Hydrocephalics Challenge Cherished Assumptions." *Biological Theory* 10, July 24, 2015. *doi.org/10.1007/s13752-015-0219-x.*

Fowler, J. H., and N. A. Christakis. "Dynamic Spread of Happiness in a Large Social Network: Longitudinal Analysis over 20 Years in the Framingham Heart Study." *BMJ*, December 4, 2008, *doi.org/10.1136/bmj.a2338.*

Fox, K.C., et al. "Is Meditation Associated with Altered Brain Structure? A Systematic Review and Meta-Analysis of Morphometric Neuroimaging In Meditation Practitioners." Neuroscience and Biobehavioral Reviews, June 2014, *doi.org/10.1016/j.neubiorev.2014.03.016.*

Fox, Peggy. "Teen Girl Uses 'Crazy Strength' To Lift Burning Car off Dad." WUSA-TV, Washington, January 2016, *usatoday.com.*

Full Gospel Businessmen's Training. "J. C. Penney Story." FGBT. *fgbt.org.*

Gilbert, Elizabeth. "Your Elusive Creative Genius." TED Talk, February 2009, *ted.com*

Gillihan, Seth. "Ep. 54: Dr. Eben Alexander—Exploring Consciousness, Heaven, and Unconditional Love." *Think Act Be*, interview, *sethgillihan.com.*

Goswami, Amit. *The Self-Aware Universe.* New York: Putnam's Sons, 1993.

Gotink, R., et al. "Meditation and Yoga Practice Are Associated with Smaller Right Amygdala Volume: The Rotterdam Study." Brain Imaging and Behavior, February 7, 2018, *link.springer.com*

Greyson, Bruce. "Consciousness without Brain Activity: Near Death Experiences." YouTube, 2011, *youtube.com*

Grinberg-Zylberbaum, J., et al. "The Einstein-Podolsky-Rosen Paradox in the Brain: The Transferred Potential." *Physics Essays*, Volume 7, number 4. 1994, *physicsessays.org.*

Grof, Stanislav. *The Adventure of Self-Discovery: Dimensions of Consciousness and New Perspectives in Psychotherapy and Inner Exploration.* Albany, NY: SUNY Press, 1988.

Haisch, Bernard. *The God Theory: Universes, Zero-Point Fields, and What's Behind It All.* Weiser Books. 2009.

Hạnh, Thích Nhất. "Returning Home." *Shambala Sun*, March 2006.

Harvard Gazette. "Eight Weeks to a Better Brain." *Harvard Gazette*, January 21, 2011, *news.harvard.edu.*

Hawkins, David R. *Power vs. Force: The Hidden Determinants of Human Behavior.* Veritas, 1995.

Hay, Louise. *You Can Heal Your Life.* Carlsbad, CA: Hay House, 2017.

Heine, Lizette, et al. "Resting State Networks and Consciousness. Alterations of Multiple Resting State Network Connectivity in Physiological, Pharmacological And Pathological Consciousness States." *Frontiers in Psychology*, 2012.

Heisenberg, Werner. *Physics and Philosophy: The Revolution in Modern Science.* New York: Harper, 1958.

Henson, Jim. *It's Not Easy Being Green: And Other Things to Consider.* Kingswell, 2011, Kindle Edition.

Herbert, Nick. *Quantum Reality: Beyond the New Physics.* Garden City, NY: Anchor Press/Doubleday, 1985.

Hill, Napoleon. *The Science of Success: Napoleon Hill's Proven Program for Prosperity and Happiness.* New York: TarcherPerigee, 2014.

———. *Think and Grow Rich.* White Dog Publishing, 2009, Kindle Edition.

Hoffman, Donald D. "Conscious Realism and the Mind-Body Problem." Mind and Matter 6(1), 2008.

Ho, Mae-Wan. "Bioenergetics and Biocommunication." 1996, accessed November 2015. *ratical.org*

———. "Quantum Coherence and Conscious Experience." Institute of Science in Society, 1997, *ratical.org.*

Holzel, Britta, et al. "Mindfulness Practice Leads to Increases in Regional Brain Gray Matter Density." Psychiatry Research, November 10, 2010, *ncbi.nlm.nih.gov.*

Horgan, John. "String Theorist Edward Witten Says Consciousness 'Will Remain a Mystery.'" *Scientific American*, August 18, 2016, *blogs.scientific american.com.*

Huang Po, and Xiu Pei. *The Zen Teaching of Huang Po on the Transmission of Mind; Being the Teaching of the Zen Master Huang Po as Recorded by the Scholar P'Ei Hsiu of the T'Ang Dynasty.* New York: Grove Press, 1959.

Isaacson, Walter. *Steve Jobs.* New York: Simon & Schuster, 2015.

Jeans, James. *The Mysterious Universe.* New York: The Macmillan Company, 1932.

Jobs, Steve. "You've Got To Find What You Love, Jobs Says." *Stanford News,* June, 14, 2005.

Johns Hopkins Medicine. "Experiences of 'Ultimate Reality' or 'God' Confer Lasting Benefits to Mental Health." Johns Hopkins Medicine: Newsroom, April 23, 2019, *hopkinsmedicine.org.*

Joss, D., et al. "Effects of a Mindfulness-Based Intervention on Self-Compassion and Psychological Health among Young Adults with a History of Childhood Maltreatment." *Frontiers in Psychology,* October 23, 2019, *doi.org/10.3389 /fpsyg.2019.02373.*

Jung, C. G. *Psychology and Religion: West and East.* Volume 11 of *The Collected Works of C. G. Jung.* Second edition. Princeton, NJ: Princeton University Press, 1975.

Kassan, Peter. "A.I. Gone Awry: The Futile Quest for Artificial Intelligence." Skeptic, Vol 12:2 *skeptic.com*

Keller, Helen. "Address to American Association to Promote the Teaching of Speech to the Deaf." *American Annals of the Deaf,* Vol. 36, No. 3, June 1891.

Kliemann, et al. "Intrinsic Functional Connectivity of the Brain in Adults with a Single Cerebral Hemisphere." *Cell Reports, doi.org/10.1016/j .celrep.2019.10.067.*

Kriyananda. *Affirmations for Self-Healing.* Nevada City, CA: Crystal Clarity Publishers, 2005.

———. *The Art and Science of Raja Yoga.* Nevada City, CA: Ananda Sangha, 2010.

———. *Awaken to Superconsciousness.* Nevada City, CA: Crystal Clarity Publishers, 2008.

Lao Tzu. *Tao Te Ching. terebess.hu*

L'Engle, Madeline. *Circle of Quiet.* San Francisco: HarperOne, 1984.

———. *A Wrinkle in Time: 50th Anniversary Commemorative Edition.* Square Fish, 2012.

Lindberghh, Charles A. *The Spirit of St. Louis.* New York: Scribner, 2003.

Linde, Andrei. "Universe, Life, Consciousness." PDF, *andrei-linde.com.*

Lipton, Bruce H. *The Biology of Belief.* Carlsbad, CA: Hay House, 2008. Kindle Edition.

Livio, Fr. "Description of Heaven." *medjugorje.com.*

Lorber, John. "Is Your Brain Really Necessary?" *Science,* Vol. 210, Issue 4475. December 12, 1980.

Martin, Laurelynn G. *Searching for Home: A Personal Journey of Transformation and Healing after a Near-Death Experience.* St. Joseph, MI. Cosmic Concepts, 1996.

Maslow, Abraham. *Motivation and Personality.* TBS, 1987.

——. *Religions, Values, and Peak Experiences.* London: Penguin Books Limited, 1964.

Maxwell, Meg, and Verena Tschudin. *Seeing the Invisible: Modern Religious and Other Transcendent Experiences.* Lampeter: Religious Experience Research Centre, 2005.

May, C. J., et al. "Mindfulness Meditation Is Associated with Decreases in Partner Negative Affect in Daily Life." *European Journal of Social Psychology,* May 16, 2019, *doi.org/10.1002/ejsp.2599.*

McCaffrey, Tony. "There Will Always Be Limits to How Creative a Computer Can Be." *Harvard Business Review,* April 24, 2017, *hbr.org.*

Miller, W. *Old Man's Advice to Youth: "Never Lose a Holy Curiosity."* New York: Time Inc., 1955.

Millman, Dan. *Divine Interventions: True Stories of Mystery and Miracles That Change Lives.* Emmaus, PA: Daybreak/Rodale, 2000.

Mitchell, Edgar, with Dwight Williams. *The Way of the Explorer.* New York: G. P. Putnam's Sons, 1996.

Mumford, Michael D., et al. "An Evaluation of Remote Viewing: Research and Applications." Palo Alto, CA: American Institutes for Research, 1995.

Murphy, Michael. *In the Zone: Transcendent Experience in Sports.* New York: Open Road Media, 2011, Kindle Edition.

Neal, Patsy. *Sport and Identity.* Philadelphia: Dorrance, 1972.

Newberg, Andrew B., and Mark R. Waldman. *How Enlightenment Changes Your Brain: The New Science of Transformation.* New York: Penguin Publishing Group, Kindle Edition.

Newberg, Andrew B., Eugene G. d'Aquili, and Vince Rause. *Why God Won't Go Away: Brain Science and the Biology of Belief.* New York: Ballantine Books, 2001.

Niles, Frank. "How to Use Visualization to Achieve Your Goals." HuffPost, August 17, 2011, *huffpost.com.*

Penman, Danny. "Could there Be Proof to the Theory that We're ALL Psychic?" *Daily Mail,* January 2008, *dailymail.co.uk.*

Pribram, Karl. "The Neurophysiology of Remembering." *Scientific American,* Vol. 220, Issue 1, January 1, 1969.

Rowan, R. "Those Business Hunches Are More Than Blind Faith." *Fortune,* April 23, 1979.

Rumi and Coleman Barks. *The Essential Rumi.* San Francisco: Harper, 1995.

Rumi and Shahram Shiva. *Hush, Don't Say Anything to God: Passionate Poems of Rumi.* Fremont, CA: Jain Pub, 2000.

Russell, Walter, and Lao Russell. *Universal Law, Natural Science and Living Philosophy.* Waynesboro, VA: The Walter Russell Foundation, 1950.

Sasaki, Shigetsu, and Mary Farkas. *The Zen Eye: A Collection of Zen Talks by Sokei-an.* Tokyo: Weatherhill, 1993.

Schrödinger, Erwin. As quoted in *Psychic Research.* Psychic Research. Vol. 25, 1931.

Schwartz, Stephan. "Nonlocality and Exceptional Experiences: A Study of Genius, Religious Epiphany, and the Psychic." Elsevier, Vol. 6, Issue 4, July–August 2010.

Searle, John. "The Mystery of 'Consciousness': An Exchange." *The New York Review,* December 21, 1995, *nybooks.com*

Sevinc, G., and S. W. Lazar. "How Does Mindfulness Training Improve Moral Cognition: A Theoretical and Experimental Framework for the Study of Embodied Ethics." *Current Opinion in Psychology,* Feb. 22, 2019, *doi.org /10.1016/j.copsyc.2019.02.006.*

Sharkey, Lauren. "How Transcendental Meditation Alters the Brain." Medical News Today, March 5, 2020, *medicalnewstoday.com.*

Shepard, K. R., and B. G. Braun. "Visual Changes in Multiple Personality." Proceedings of the Second International Conference on Multiple Personality/Dissociative States. Chicago: Rush-Presbyterian-St Luke's Medical Center, 1985.

Sivananda. "Cosmic Consciousness." Accessed October 7, 2015, *sivananda online.org.*

———. "How to Find Peace of Mind." Accessed October 7, 2015. *sivananda online.org*

Slimani, Maamer, et al. "Effects of Mental Imagery on Muscular Strength in Healthy and Patient Participants: A Systematic Review." *Journal of Sports Science and Medicine,* August 5, 2016, *pubmed.ncbi.nlm.nih.gov.*

Smith, Jayne. "Moment of Truth: A Window on Life after Death." Video transcript, Starpath Productions, 1987.

Spielman, Ed. *The Spiritual Journey of Joseph L. Greenstein: The Mighty Atom: World's Strongest Man.* Cobb, CA: First Glance Books, 1998.

Stein, R. "Happiness Can Spread Among People Like a Contagion, Study Indicates." *Washington Post,* December 5, 2009, *washingtonpost.com*

Steiner, Rudolf, and Christopher Bamford. *How to Know Higher Worlds: A Modern Path of Initiation.* Hudson, NY: Anthroposophic Press, 1994.

St. Maarten, Anthon. *Divine Living: The Essential Guide to Your True Destiny.* Indigo House, 2012.

St. Teresa of Avila with David Lewis. *The Life of St. Teresa of Jesus.* Project Gutenberg, 2005, *gutenberg.org.*

Swedenborg, Emanuel, and George F. Dole. *Heaven and Hell.* New York: Swedenborg Foundation, 1984.

Taylor, Steve. "An Awakening." *The Psychologist,* September 2018, *thepsychologist .bps.org.uk.*

Tennyson, Alfred, and Adam Roberts. *The Major Works.* Oxford: Oxford University Press, 2009.

Thaheld, Fred H. "An Interdisciplinary Approach to Certain Fundamental Issues in the Fields of Physics and Biology: Towards a Unified Theory." 99 Cable Circle, #20, Folsom, CA 95630, US.

Thompson, Eric. "Scientific Evidence for a Connecting Matrix: An Introduction to Biofield Science, Part 2." Iawake, *iawaketechnologies.com.*

Thorpe, J. "Experts Reveal What Happens in Your Brain When You Meditate." Bustle, August 11, 2019, *bustle.com*

Treece, Patricia. *The Joyful Spirit of Padre Pio: Stories, Letters, and Prayers.* Servant Books, 2014.

Vivekananda. *Complete Works of Swami Vivekananda.* Advaita Ashrama, 1947.

Wackerman, J., et al. "Correlations between Brain Electrical Activities of Two Spatially Separated Human Subjects." *Neuroscience Letters,* 336, 2003.

Wallace, RaNelle, and Curtis Taylor. *The Burning Within.* Carson City, NV: Gold Leaf Press, 1994.

Weng, H. Y., et al. "Compassion Training Alters Altruism and Neural Responses to Suffering." *Psychological Science,* May 21, 2013, *doi.org/10.1177 /0956797612469537.*

Whitt, Jim. *Road Signs for Success,* Lariat Press. 1993.

Wikipedia. "Peak Experience." *en.wikipedia.org.*

Wilber, Ken. *Integral Psychology: Consciousness, Spirit, Psychology, Therapy.* Shambhala, 2000, Kindle Edition.

Williams, Kevin. "Christian Andréason's Near-Death Experience." September 18, 2019, *near-death.com.*

———. "Howard Storm's Near-Death Experience." September 18, 2019, *near -death.com.*

———. "Josiane Antonette's Near-Death Experience." September 18, 2019, *near-death.com.*

———. "Lynnclaire Dennis' Near-Death Experience." September 18, 2019, *near-death.com.*

———. "Mellen-Thomas Benedict's Near-Death Experience." September 18, 2019, *near-death.com.*

———. "Nora Spurgin's Near-Death Experience." September 18, 2019, *near -death.com.*

Yogananda. *Autobiography of a Yogi.* Nevada City, CA: Crystal Clarity Publishers, Reprint of The Philosophical Library 1946 First Edition, Kindle Edition.

———. "Benefits of Kriya Yoga." Self-Realization Fellowship, *yogananda.org.*

———. *How to Awaken Your True Potential.* Nevada City, CA: Crystal Clarity Publishers, 2016.

———. *How to Be a Success.* Nevada City, CA: Crystal Clarity Publishers, 2008.

———. *How to Be Happy All the Time.* Nevada City, CA: Crystal Clarity Publishers, 2006.

———. *How to Have Courage, Calmness, and Confidence.* Nevada City, CA: Crystal Clarity Publishers, 2010.

———. *Journey to Self-Realization.* Los Angeles, CA: Self-Realization Fellowship, 2000.

———. *Karma and Reincarnation.* Nevada City, CA: Crystal Clarity Publishers, 2007.

———. "Love Human and Divine." Self-Realization Fellowship, *yogananda.org.*

———. "Knowing God." Self-Realization Fellowship, *yogananda.org.*

———. *Metaphysical Meditations.* Los Angeles, CA: Self-Realization Fellowship, 1967.

———. *The Second Coming of Christ: The Resurrection of the Christ Within You: A Revelatory Commentary on the Original Teachings of Jesus.* Los Angeles, CA: Self-Realization Fellowship, 2004.

Yogananda, and J. Donald Walters. *The Essence of Self-Realization: The Wisdom of Paramahansa Yogananda.* Nevada City, CA: Crystal Clarity Publishers, 1990.

ACKNOWLEDGMENTS

I would like to thank Michael Pye and the Red Wheel/Weiser team for having faith in this book; my agent John White for his wise advice and the understanding of a fellow author; my editor, Prakash Van Cleave, for always making me appear to write better than I do; and my wife and first reader, Lakshmi, who always insightfully and helpfully improves my thinking and presentation.

INDEX

ABOUT THE AUTHOR

Joseph Selbie makes the complex and obscure simple and clear. A dedicated meditator for nearly fifty years, he has taught yoga, meditation, and universal experiential spirituality throughout the US and Europe. He has also been an avid follower of the unfolding new paradigm of post-materialistic science—with groaning bookshelves to show for it—and he is known for creating bridges of understanding between the modern evidenced-based discoveries of science and the ancient experience-based discoveries of the mystics.

Selbie has also authored *The Physics of God*, a unification of science and religion, and *The Yugas*, a factual look at India's tradition of cyclical history.

Selbie is a founding member of Ananda—a meditation-based community and spiritual movement inspired by Paramahansa Yogananda. He lives with his wife at Ananda Village near Nevada City, California.

You can visit his website at *josephselbie.com*.